Know Your Legal Rights

Protect Yourself From
Common Legal Problems
That Can *Really* Cost You

Know Your
Legal
Rights

By the Editors of
KIPLINGER'S PERSONAL FINANCE

Dearborn™
Trade Publishing
A **Kaplan Professional** Company

Published by Dearborn Trade Publishing, a Kaplan Professional Company

First edition. Printed in the United States of America.

9 8 7 6 5 4 3

Cover design by Heather Waugh

Library of Congress Cataloging-in-Publication Data

Know your legal rights : protect yourself from common legal problems that can really cost you / by the editors of Kiplinger's personal finance.
    p.   cm.
    Originally published: 1st ed. Washington, D.C. : Kiplinger Books, ©2001.
    Includes index.
    ISBN 1-4195-0519-X (pbk.)
    1. Law—United States—Popular works. I. Kiplinger Washington Editors, inc.
  II. Kiplinger's personal finance magazine.

KF387 .K573 2005
349.73—dc22

2005007824

Contents

Contents

Contents

Contents

Introduction

Years ago, most people went through life without any great likelihood of involvement in our legal system. They fulfilled the obligations of citizenship—voting, serving on jury duty and paying taxes, incurred the occasional traffic violation or maybe served as executor of an estate.

Now, our society is more complex—and perhaps because of that—more litigious. There are more of us, we live closer together, and though we have differing needs and expectations, we share a common concern for getting a fair shake and the recurring fear we might not.

For these reasons and more, people resort more readily to legal procedures to settle disputes that were once resolved more informally. And governments of all types, seen and unseen, set more and more rules governing our civil lives. That's why it's so important for all citizens to know the legal risks of their everyday behavior—and know their legal rights and obligations in anticipation of finding themselves on either side of a dispute, with their neighbor or with their government.

We at Kiplinger have dedicated our professional lives to helping people earn, manage and invest their money carefully, and increasingly, the protection of assets requires a knowledge of legal risks, rights and obligations. Consider:

- **As a home seller,** you could be sued for not fully disclosing problems with the house you sell.
- **You could be denied needed credit** because of a mistake in your credit record that is no fault of your own. Despite your credit-record rights, the burden of seeing that the mistake is eliminated will be on you.

- **You could be liable for the injury** of almost anyone who enters your property, even those who are uninvited. And, depending on the accident and your assets, your homeowners policy might not be sufficient protection.
- **You might have thought** you were just getting some help with cleaning your house or caring for your kids, and instead, you find you are an employer with tax and other legal obligations.
- **You marry and choose to share** your resources and responsibilities. If you part company, how will you divide your property? To what degree should one partner be responsible for the other's continued welfare? If you've spent the better portion of your marriage contributing to your spouse's success, what portion of his or her retirement funds will you be entitled to?
- **Or, you remarry** and want to ensure that, in the event of your death, your children from your previous marriage, as well as your new spouse, are provided for in your will.

The possibilities for dispute are as numerous as the many relationships in your life. There are few decisions you'll make in your life, from those that create a family to those that take effect after your death, that aren't bounded by law and don't entail legal liability with direct consequences on your pocketbook.

This book addresses many of them. But it isn't a replacement for good legal counsel. It's a handy introduction to some everyday legal issues and situations to help you identify possible trouble spots, figure out whether you might need professional advice, find it, and prepare you for using that advice wisely. It will help you protect what you've worked so hard to build up.

Knight Kiplinger

Editor in Chief
Kiplinger's Personal Finance

Living With the Law

You probably don't think about it much, but the law affects you every single day of your life, in every area of your life. Consider your many roles—citizen, consumer, home or property owner, newlywed or aggrieved spouse, parent or adult child with dependent parents, employee or employer, patient, retiree, surviving spouse and more. Each role has corresponding rights and obligations defined by the law. In turn, each brings assorted legal hazards and hassles, many of which can be prevented if you just know how.

In fact, in an increasingly complicated world, we rely more and more on the law to impose order on the disorder of our affairs, and we turn to the principles of rights, fairness and equity to protect us from the self-interest of others, and others from our own self-interest.

Not surprisingly, many legal disputes have to do with money—earning it, spending it, investing it, keeping it, passing it to your heirs—because where there's money, there's likely to be conflict between people. If we know the law and work within its limits, we can protect ourselves, our loved ones and our resources and property. This book will show you how.

This is not a book for those who are interested in exploiting the legal system for their own gain. It is for reasonable people who want to mind their own business, to live up to their promises and have others do the same, to avoid legal problems in their personal and financial lives, and to reasonably redress them when they occur.

Are you at a turning point in your life and making a major life decision, such as marrying, having a child, buying a house or divorcing?

This book is written for the layman, in plain language, with legal terms included and defined where necessary.

But make no mistake: This book is no substitute for a lawyer's advice and work. Like a household medical guide, it will help you identify your problem by its symptoms (circumstances), evaluate your options, and educate you should you decide to handle the situation yourself or seek expert advice.

Unfortunately for authors and book publishers, the law isn't static; it changes all the time. Congress and state governments pass new legislation. State and federal agencies impose new regulations. And there are always new trends in local ordinances. This book reflects the most current law on the books at the time of publishing.

Because state law may well vary among the 50 states, *Know Your Legal Rights* doesn't try to present a state-by-state survey. Instead, it typically tries to summarize where the majority of states stand on various legal questions and what the minority's view is, and to note the rare exceptions by name. And, wherever possible, it will tell you what federal, state or consumer agency or other legal advocacy organization can give you more information on the topic at hand.

How Do I Know That I Have a Legal Problem?

Even if you don't know the law, there are some questions you might ask yourself that would cause you to seek legal advice and information, either from this book or from a lawyer.

■ **Are you at a turning point in your life** and making a major life decision, such as marrying, having a child, buying a house or divorcing?

■ **Do you think you've been treated unfairly** or that your rights may have been violated?

■ **Does someone think you've treated them unfairly** or that you've violated their rights?

■ **Are you going to have to sign your name** to a written

A CIVIL LAW PRIMER

Civil law is the whole body of legal principles and procedures that define and govern the rights, duties and obligations of individuals, corporations, governments and other associations in their relationships with each other. Unlike criminal law, which governs crimes against society (or the people) that are usually punishable by imprisonment, civil offenses are likely to result in financial penalties.

Of course, this body is the sum of its parts—numerous categories of the law developed by the courts and legislatures. Many are discussed in *Know Your Legal Rights,* including: bankruptcy, civil rights, consumer law, divorce, domestic relations, employment, estate planning, wills, family law, guardianship and adoptions, health, housing, insurance, labor, landlord-tenant relations, motor vehicles, power of attorney, probate, property law, tax law and zoning. And you could hardly write a book about your legal rights without delving into contract law, the set of legal principles that gives contracts their power in agreements between people.

Civil disputes usually arise when one party—the plaintiff or petitioner—believes he has been unfavorably affected by the actions of another—the defendant or respondent—and so seeks "judicial relief"

(that is, a court judgment that will correct the situation). Court judgments usually take one of two forms: The defendant must either pay money (damages) or, in a form of judgment called "injunctive relief," perform some duty or refrain from some activity.

Once the court has made its judgment, the parties are legally obliged to live up to it. Someone who deliberately ignores or disobeys the court's order can be found in contempt of court, could be fined or sent to jail until he agrees to comply or it's clear that no amount of jail time will coerce him into doing so. His wages could be garnished or he could be forced to sell his possessions in order to make good on the amount he owes.

For more information, or for those who want to do legal research
This brief explanation of civil law is drawn from a more detailed discussion in *Legal Research, How to Find and Understand the Law,* 10th ed,. by Stephen Elias (Nolo Press, $34.99). If you want to read the law for yourself—that is, read the written record of legal principles and procedures—that book can be your guide. It will show you how the law is organized, how to figure out which body of law applies to your question or area of interest, and how to access it.

agreement such as a lease or a contract, especially one that commits you to the exchange of money or property?

■ **Are you in complicated or confusing circumstances** due to an accident, change in financial status or change in family status?

If you know the rules before the game begins, you're more likely to win—or at least avoid losing badly.

- **Do you think that someone** hasn't lived up to his or her part of a bargain?
- **Have you recently been arrested?** If so, you should consult a lawyer immediately because this book focuses on civil, not criminal, law. (For more on what to do if you're arrested, see the Appendix, page 297.)

How Can I Prevent Legal Hassles in My Life?

Probably the best way to prevent trouble is to try to anticipate any problematic situations you might come across and learn about your rights and obligations ahead of time. If you know the rules before the game begins, you're more likely to win—or at least avoid losing badly. For example, if you are going to hire a live-in housekeeper, you need to know what laws affect such an arrangement and what forms you need to fill out to make sure you are in compliance with federal and state regulations. You need to check out the potential worker's immigration status, what taxes you'll be responsible for and what kind of insurance you need. (For more on this topic, see page 250 in Chapter 11, "Parenthood" and page 138 in Chapter 6, "Your Home and the Law.")

This book is full of the legal steps and strategies you can take to prevent conflict and legal confusion in your personal and financial life. In any area of your life, there are three rules to follow that should make things infinitely easier.

Remember the Golden Rule

This is truly the bottom line for preventing legal disputes: Do unto others as you would have them do unto you. Generate goodwill by exercising common sense and communicating clearly—try to be a cooperative neighbor, for example, by keeping your dog under control and warning neighbors that they should be careful approaching your house. If you make such a good-faith effort and something unfortunate does happen, an injured person may be more inclined to be understanding than if you've allowed your dog to terrorize the neighborhood and ignored neighbors' complaints about it.

Choose Your Battles Carefully

If you're the one who has been trespassed against, try to maintain your perspective. Know when it's appropriate to speak your piece yourself and then just walk away if the dispute is not worth ending up in court over or ruining a family or business relationship for.

Get a Good Contract

A contract is an agreement between two or more parties, and it's perhaps the most common legal arrangement. In fact, much of our civil law is based on the theory of contracts. If you join a health club, you sign a contract. Rent an apartment, you sign a contract. Get married, and you may sign a prenuptial contract.

To be legally enforceable—a deal that a court can make you and any other parties live up to—a contract needs three essential elements: an offer, an acceptance, and a consideration—something of value given in return for a promise of performance, such as an exchange of money for goods or services. One example: "I will buy your used car and you agree to sell it to me for $7,000."

An agreement without a consideration is merely a promise without legal obligation. But an agreement usually leads to a contract. A contract must also be made by people who are of legal age and mentally competent to understand what they are doing. It's a good idea for a contract to be in writing and reviewed by lawyers, but even a simple, handwritten agreement or an oral agreement and a handshake can be considered a legally enforceable contract.

And even if you don't have an express (formally written or stated) contract, sometimes situations are governed by implied contracts, agreements that are implied by people's actions. For example, if you pull up at a self-serve gas station and pump the gas your-

Much of our civil law is based on the theory of contracts.

Ideally, a good contract should both ensure you'll get what you want and protect you from losing everything if something goes wrong.

self, it's understood under an implied contract that you will pay for the gas.

Ideally, a good contract should both ensure you'll get what you want and protect you from losing everything if something goes wrong. But since a contract is legally binding—a court can make you live up to the terms you agreed to—be careful to read and understand all the fine print and its implications before signing. Elsewhere in this book, you'll find discussions of the specific provisions a contract should include, depending on the situation—for example, if you're buying and selling a home or negotiating a prenuptial agreement.

Alternatives to Going to Court

I f you find yourself involved in a dispute, there are some increasingly popular ways that allow you to first try to resolve the problem yourself—with a little help—and avoid going to court.

Negotiation

One reason there are so many lawsuits is that people often go out and hire a lawyer at the first sign of a dispute, instead of trying to work out their differences. And it can be worth your while to try to attempt to settle on your own.

Say you're having a dispute with your neighbor over the fact that his dog keeps digging up your garden, resulting in aggravation and the loss of plants that will cost you money to replace. Before you hire legal counsel, you might try this approach:

Discuss the matter reasonably, and keep detailed notes, including dates, of all your conversations, just in case.

Put yourself in your neighbor's position and try to see how the problem can be solved to satisfy you both. Perhaps he can agree to pay for the plants lost so far, then fence in his yard so his dog can run without damaging your flowers.

If no agreement is reached, try writing a letter recapping the details of the problem—what it is, when and where it occurred, and what promise, if any, was broken—and setting a date by which you would like to see the situation fixed. Called a "settle or else" letter, this last stop before hiring a lawyer shows you mean business. It may resolve the whole problem before it gets out of hand—and, if it comes to that, it will also show a court that you made a serious attempt to resolve the problem.

Mediation

An informal, often free, method of voluntary dispute resolution, mediation uses a neutral person to help two parties make peace. A mediator doesn't have to be a lawyer or judge, though training in mediation techniques is helpful. One way to find a mediator is to contact your local bar association (you can find your local bar association by checking the American Bar Association's Web site, www.abanet.org), county clerk, city attorney general's office or neighborhood citizens' dispute-settlement center. Unlike a judge, the mediator doesn't make a decision; she helps the opposing parties come to mutually acceptable terms. Despite the informality of the process, the contract drawn up to finalize the agreement is legally enforceable. For more information about mediation in cases of divorce, see page 225 in Chapter 10, "Ending a Marriage."

Arbitration

If you think you need something more structured than mediation, arbitration may be the choice for you. As in mediation, the process is usually voluntary and the arbiter is a third party but not a judge. Unlike a mediator, the arbiter has authority to rule on the case. Arbitration is usually economically priced and is often used to solve contract or commercial problems. It's a sort of informal court; you needn't follow strict legal rules of procedure and evidence as you present your case. You can ask questions about the case, as can the arbiter. If you and your opposing party can't come to a mutual decision, the arbiter will make one, typically

Unlike a judge, the mediator doesn't make a decision; she helps the opposing parties come to mutually acceptable terms.

Both parties must agree to abide by the arbiter's decision; it's very rare that either party could appeal the arbiter's decision.

within a ten-day period. Before you can take your case to an arbiter, however, both parties must agree to abide by the arbiter's decision; it's very rare that either party could appeal the arbiter's decision. One advantage of arbitration over small-claims court, described beginning on page 9, is that there is no dollar limit on the amounts awarded. (See also the discussion of arbitration in cases of investor grievance, beginning on page 45 in Chapter 3, "The Law and Your Finances.")

HOW DO YOU FIND AN ARBITRATOR? If you have a consumer dispute, contact your local Better Business Bureau and ask about its National Consumer Arbitration Program.

You can also contact the American Arbitration Association (335 Madison Ave., 10th Floor, New York, NY 10017-4605; 800-778-7879; www.adr.org). The AAA charges a flat fee based on the amount of the claim—for example, $500 for claims under $10,000 on up to $8,500 for claims of $1 million or more; incidental fees may be incurred.

If You Must Go to Court

One look at the docket of any U.S. court will show you that almost anyone can be sued over anything. Still, there are exceptions. You generally can't sue the federal government unless there is a law stating that you may do so. For example, the government can't be sued for failing to regulate properly—say, if it doesn't inspect planes carefully and a crash results.

Call it going to court, bringing a lawsuit or an action, suing, or making a claim: If all else fails, you will have no choice but to take your case to court and hope that the judge and, in some cases, the jury rules in your favor. If the problem is fairly straightforward and the amount of damages you're seeking is within your state's limits, small-claims court is a likely option. In that case, you probably won't need to call a lawyer (see the discussion of small claims court, opposite). Otherwise, it may be time to seek legal counsel; Chapter 2, "Your Lawyer," will show you how to find the right attorney.

How do you know which court you'll end up in and whether your decision will be rendered by a judge or a jury? It depends on where you live and the nature of your legal problem. But don't worry: Most cases never end up in any court. To save time and money, the parties agree to settle—that is, compromise and resolve the matter before the case comes before a judge. If you do have to go to court, it will be your attorney's job to bring your lawsuit to the appropriate court and follow the correct civil procedures for filing the necessary papers, meeting deadlines, offering proof in court and appealing unfavorable judgments.

Small-Claims Court

Small-claims court is the place to settle simple disputes—say, the dry cleaner ruins an expensive piece of clothing or someone refuses to pay you for services or goods that you rendered. There needn't necessarily be an amount of money in dispute for a case to go to small-claims court—you might simply want someone to make good on a promise—but you still must assign a dollar value to your claim. The dollar limits of claims that these courts will consider varies from state to state (see the box on page 10). In Kansas, for example, it's $1,800, while in Minnesota, it's $7,500. If the dollar amount of your claim exceeds your state's limit, you'll probably have to engage legal counsel and sue elsewhere in a higher court. Small-claims courts also generally don't hear slander or libel cases.

If you pursue this option, you won't really need a lawyer (some courts don't even allow lawyers) because traditionally strict legal rules of procedure don't apply. There isn't a jury, just a judge. And there's not a lot of paperwork or expense involved. In order to win in small-claims court, however, you must show that you are legally in the right: You must be able to document for the court that you suffered a loss, and you must show that the person you are suing was legally responsible for that loss. To that end, gather documents such

Continued on page 11

Most cases never end up in any court. To save time and money, the parties agree to settle—that is, compromise and resolve the matter.

SMALL-CLAIMS COURT LIMITS

This chart will give you an idea of your state's dollar limits for small-claims court. Be sure to call your local clerk of small-claims court for the most accurate and up-to-date information for your particular need.

(Reprinted with permission from *Everybody's Guide to Small Claims Court*, 9th ed., by Ralph Warner; Nolo Press,$26.99; available in bookstores, online at www.nolo.com, or by calling 800-728-3555)

Alabama	$3,000	**Kansas**	$1,800	**Oklahoma**	$4,500
Alaska	$7,500	**Kentucky**	$1,500	**Oregon**	$5,000
Arizona	$2,500	**Louisiana**	$3,000	**Pennsylvania**	$8,000
Regular justice court	$5,000			Philadelphia municipal	
Arkansas	$5,000	**Maine**	$4,500	court	$10,000
		Maryland	$2,500	**Rhode Island**	$1,500
California	$5,000				
Except that a plaintiff may not		**Massachusetts**	$2,000	**South Carolina**	$7,500
file a claim over $2,500 more					
than twice a year.		**Michigan**	$3,000	**South Dakota**	$8,000
Suits involving a surety company					
or licensed contractor	$4,000	**Minnesota**	$7,500	**Tennessee**	$15,000
				In Shelby and Anderson	
Colorado	$7,500	**Mississippi**	$2,500	counties	$25,000
				No limit set in suits to	
Connecticut	$3,500	**Missouri**	$3,000	recover personal property	
No limit for landlord-tenant cases					
involving security deposit claims		**Montana**	$3,000	**Texas**	$5,000
Delaware	$15,000	**Nebraska**	$2,400	**Utah**	$5,000
District of Columbia	$5,000	**Nevada**	$5,000	**Vermont**	$3,500
Florida	$5,000	**New Hampshire**	$5,000	**Virginia**	$2,000
				General district court	
Georgia	$15,000	**New Jersey**	$3,000	(but no limits on eviction	
		Special civil part,		suits in this court)	$4,500
Hawaii	$3,500	Superior court	$15,000	Circuit court	$15,000
Idaho	$4,000	**New Mexico**	$10,000	**Washington**	$4,000
Illinois	$5,000	**New York**	$3,000	**West Virginia**	$5,000
Cook County "Pro Se"					
branch	$1,500	**North Carolina**	$4,000	**Wisconsin:**	$5,000
				No limit on eviction suits	
Indiana	$3,000	**North Dakota**	$5,000		
Marion and Allen counties	$6,000			**Wyoming**	$3,000
		Ohio	$3,000	County circuit court	$7,000
Iowa	$5,000				

OTHER TYPES OF COURTS

Small-claims courts are one part of a state court system. Each state—and the District of Columbia—has its own system. In different states, courts that hear the same kinds of cases may have different names. Most states have several levels of courts, one of which will include such single-focus courts as divorce and family courts.

Courts of limited jurisdiction

First, lower courts—such as small-claims court, traffic court and justice of the peace or magistrate's court—handle the bulk of cases. Cases involve minor crimes punishable by fines or under a year of jail time and civil cases up to a certain dollar limit.

State courts of general jurisdiction

Next, there are state courts of general jurisdiction that go by names such as county court, circuit court, superior court, district court and the court of common pleas. These courts hear civil or criminal cases with no upper dollar limits and no limits on jail times. Unlike in lower courts, decisions here are often made by juries.

State intermediate appellate courts
(courts of appeal)

Next, about three-fourths of the states have intermediate appellate courts, which hear appeals from those dissatisfied with lower court rulings. They review the case ruling and legal procedures used to arrive at it, but do not entertain new evidence.

State supreme court and U.S. Supreme Court

All states have their own state supreme court, usually the court of last resort that hears final appeals. A very few cases go on from here to the U.S. Supreme Court,.

The federal court system

These courts hear only cases violating federal law or the Constitution. Within this system is the Tax Court. Federal courts are broken into districts; their decisions can be appealed to the U.S. Courts of Appeals and ultimately the Supreme Court.

It's possible that a case might appropriately be heard by both state and federal courts. You and your lawyer may be able to choose to pursue your case in whichever you think will be more advantageous.

as receipts, bills, estimates and warranties that show that the other party is liable and that you have suffered a loss, as well as any record of your attempts to settle, such as notes from conversations about the problem.

Probably the biggest mistake people make in their own defense in small-claims court is trying to act like a lawyer and using legal terms they don't really understand. They either end up looking silly or the judge treats them as if they were lawyers and shifts his or her sympathy to the other party.

To find out how to file a small-claims suit in your state, check with the clerk of your small-claims court. You can find the number in the blue pages of the telephone book under "Courts." Or read *Everybody's Guide to Small Claims Court,* 9th ed., by Ralph Warner (Nolo Press; $26.99; available in bookstores, online at www.nolo.com, or by calling 800-728-3555).

The issues presented in small-claims court are typically pretty simple, so to reduce the case load, some states give you the option of pursuing either mediation or arbitration instead of small-claims court.

Your Lawyer

Chapter 2

Sooner or later you're going to need a lawyer. It will probably be when you're in a situation with high financial or emotional stakes. Maybe you'll need advice about handling a divorce or a tax problem. Or perhaps you'll want to sue someone for injuring you, or you'll need someone to defend you if you are charged with a crime. But how do you select the right one for your problem and get the most for your money? Read on.

What Is a Lawyer?

A lawyer, also known as an attorney-at-law or counselor-at-law, is someone licensed by one or more states to offer you legal advice and represent you in court. Any licensed lawyer has graduated from college and law school, passed a state bar (licensing) exam as well as a character review, and sworn to uphold laws and the state and federal constitutions. While all lawyers have the same basic background, they don't all have the same areas of expertise. Some are generalists, while others focus in one particular area, such as family law, estate planning, immigration, personal injury, real estate, taxation, civil liberties or bankruptcy.

Can I Act as My Own Lawyer?

You are always entitled to act as your own lawyer, that is, to represent yourself in legal situations, even if you are neither trained nor licensed. But, as you can imagine, it's seldom a good idea. As a non-

To get help selecting a lawyer, contact your local or state bar association.

lawyer, you may not fully understand the laws pertaining to your problem or its legal context, and you may lack the background to spot ambiguous language that could lead to possible complications down the road. In high-stakes situations, such as a complex divorce or personal injury case, acting as your own lawyer could be as dangerous as trying to perform an appendectomy without any medical training. Moreover, you'll probably find yourself at a great disadvantage; the other side will most likely have a trained legal expert to represent its interest. So, for most complicated legal transactions, to make sure you're getting the most protection, you're better off seeking professional legal advice.

Locating a Lawyer

For years, lawyers were not permitted to advertise their services, but today you see them advertised on TV and listed in the Yellow Pages. Still, it's hard to judge much from an ad, and the phone book isn't the most effective route to finding competent counsel.

THE NATIONAL CHAINS. Some of the names listed may be familiar, however, especially the national chains of law offices such as Jacoby & Meyers. These chains, whose services are usually less expensive than those of a big, private law firm, have professional lawyers who are licensed to offer legal advice. They are generally considered by the profession as best for basic legal work such as wills, simple divorces or traffic violations. For more complicated or groundbreaking legal problems, you're probably better off seeking a lawyer who is an expert in your particular area of concern.

STATE AND LOCAL BAR ASSOCIATIONS. To get help selecting a lawyer, you can contact your local or state bar association (check www.abanet.org), a professional membership organization in which membership may be mandatory for practicing lawyers. Besides providing professional development for members and engaging in public service, many offer a referral service, which, for a fee of about $35, can provide you with the name of a lawyer. When you call, you'll talk with a "screener," someone who will ask a little about your problem and give you the name of the lawyer in that area of expertise who is next on the list. Still, this is not a guarantee that you'll find your dream lawyer; all it means is that you will be hooked up with a lawyer—usually young and less experienced—who is looking for new clients.

BEWARE THE AMBULANCE CHASERS. There are also private referral services listed in the Yellow Pages under "Lawyers." They typically charge up to $40 per referral and usually are interested only in referring clients involved in personal injury cases or medical malpractice cases that can yield participating lawyers hefty fees.

PREPAID LEGAL PLANS. One way to always have some access to a lawyer is to become a member of a prepaid legal plan, which works like a health maintenance organization (HMO) insurance plan for law. Such plans are usually offered for workers through employers, credit unions or labor unions, but now individuals can buy into them as well, either directly from sales representatives, over the Internet or through offers from credit card companies and mortgage brokers. Be aware that all prepaid legal plans are not the same. They can vary widely both in cost and in services provided; the more services included, the more expensive the plan. Some are offered on a payroll-deduction basis, typically for about $18 a month. Others are paid by the employer. Still others must be paid for by the individual subscriber.

You can't assume that your prepaid legal plan is the answer to all your legal problems. A few comprehensive plans do provide for all your legal needs, but many limited-access ones work on a sliding scale—your monthly dues cover only limited telephone consultations and services such as letter writing and document review, and after that you pay a discounted hourly rate for further legal advice or court proceedings.

> **All prepaid legal plans are not the same. They can vary widely both in cost and in services provided; the more services included, the more expensive the plan.**

Finding a good lawyer is like finding a good doctor: The best place to start is to ask your friends and family for referrals.

Prepaid legal plans are not right for everyone. If you have few legal needs—and don't need the free will typically included in the plan—it may not be worth the money to belong to a prepaid legal plan. On the other hand, a plan can help you avoid legal problems by giving you access to preventive legal advice before a situation becomes a legal problem or the problem gets too severe.

If you want to find out about a prepaid legal plan in your area, contact:

■ **The National Resource Center for Consumers of Legal Services** (6596 Main St., P.O. Box 340, Gloucester, VA 23061; www.nrccls.org), or

■ **The American Prepaid Legal Services Institute** (541 N. Fairbanks Court, Chicago, IL 60611; www.abanet .org/api). It will send you a list of plans and the states they operate in, or you may access this information online.

The Best Way to Find a Good Lawyer

Finding a good lawyer is like finding a good doctor: The best place to start is to ask your friends and family for referrals. Once you've put together a list of about five names, try to get as much background on each lawyer as you can.

For a start, go to your local library and look each prospect up in a law directory such as the multivolume *Martindale-Hubbell Law Directory*, which will tell you the lawyer's education, specialty, law firm and rating by fellow lawyers. The rating, though not ideal given the possibility of bias, is generally respected within the legal community.

An increasing number of lawyers are choosing to be recognized as having special knowledge and experience by becoming certified specialists in certain fields of law. Over 25,000 lawyers have been certified across the U.S. in specialty practice areas, with trial practice specialists—civil and criminal trial advocacy and personal injury—being the most prevalent. A lawyer who is a certified specialist has been recognized by an independent professional certifying organization as having an enhanced level of skill and expertise, as well as substantial involvement in an established legal specialty. These organizations require a lawyer to demonstrate special training, experience and knowledge to insure that the lawyer's recognition as a certified specialist is meaningful and reliable.

Lawyers can be board-certified in certain legal specialties through programs sponsored by legal organizations in certain states and by national organizations of legal specialists. If you need a legal specialist, ask if he or she is board-certified and by whom. A list of available certifying boards and specialty areas is available on the Web at www.abanet.org/specialization/state.html. While certification will show that a lawyer has at least a minimum background in an area of supposed expertise, such as bankruptcy or personal injury, it's no guarantee that your lawyer is the ultimate authority on the topic. Don't discount a lawyer simply because he or she is uncertified; it's a relatively new trend, so not all good lawyers have taken the test yet.

Prescreen by Telephone

Once you have some names, call each lawyer and ask a few questions without going into the details of your case:

■ **Does she offer a free initial consultation?**
■ **Has he practiced long?**
■ **Will she give you references of satisfied customers?**
■ **Does he have experience in handling legal problems like yours?**
■ **Has she won many cases like yours?**

You're looking for the best, fastest and most up-to-date legal advice, and an experienced lawyer who specializes in your problem should be your top choice. You'll be at a disadvantage, for example, if an attorney who deals mostly in commercial law for local businesses and is unfamiliar with your state's domestic relations laws handles your divorce.

If you need a legal specialist, ask if he or she is board-certified and by whom. A list of available certifying boards and specialty areas is available on the Web.

Never hire a lawyer over the phone. If your initial conversation seems promising, set up a meeting to discuss your needs face to face.

Interviewing a Prospect

Never hire a lawyer over the phone. If your initial conversation seems promising, set up a meeting to discuss your needs face to face. To get your business, lawyers will often discuss the preliminaries of your case with you for free or at a reduced rate. Come to this first meeting prepared with background information. Try to be organized; bring all the pertinent papers, addresses and phone numbers with you to the meeting. Get an idea of what the lawyer thinks are the strengths —and weaknesses—of your case.

Be ready to discuss payment plans. If you're concerned about cost, ask how amenable the lawyer would be to your helping and trying to cut costs by photocopying, gathering documents or making trips to the courthouse. To prevent future disputes and for your own protection, ask for a fee agreement in writing. If a lawyer is offended by this, think about getting a different lawyer. Ask whether you will receive periodic itemized bills, so you can see how your money is being spent— and be sure you are not paying a lead attorney's hourly rate to have a secretary photocopy your documents.

Don't be intimidated by the idea of hiring a lawyer. After all, you will be paying him or her. Be sure to get the kind of person you want, with the kind of expertise you need. You'll be working with this person closely, so you'll want someone you feel good about. Trust your judgment. If something bothers you about an attorney, don't hire him or her. You're probably right. If you're on the fence about hiring a lawyer, try asking yourself:

- **Am I more comfortable with a male or female?**
- **Does this person answer my questions clearly and succinctly?**
- **Am I getting the hard sell?**

Steer clear of any lawyer who guarantees that you'll win your case or who'll accept a case that he thinks has no basis except to harass or injure an innocent party.

Just as you can pick who you want to handle your case, so, too, can a lawyer select which cases he or she wants to handle. He might turn you down because he doesn't have the time to pursue your case thoroughly or doesn't think he can win, for example. Once he does take your case, he must maintain confidentiality; he can't divulge anything you tell him to anyone else. Before or after a lawyer takes your case, if she perceives a conflict of interest with someone or something else that she's representing, then she is ethically bound to refer you to another lawyer.

How You'll Pay

There are three ways that lawyers usually charge: by the hour, on contingency (they are paid a percentage of the amount of damages won in a suit) or with a flat fee. While an hourly rate is the most common arrangement, the payment plan may often be determined by the kind of case you have. A complicated real estate transaction would usually be billed by the hour, while a simple will could be done for a flat fee because the work is straightforward and predictable. If you are about to sue your doctor for malpractice, however, you'll probably end up with a contingency arrangement—the lawyer gets paid only if you win and are awarded monetary compensation for damages.

Do some preliminary shopping by phone (see the discussion on the previous page). Talk to two or three lawyers about your case and get some prices. Save the lawyer you think you'll want for last; talking with the lesser prospects first will help you clarify your questions and how you present yourself. Go in to meet him (most lawyers won't bargain over the phone) and once you're sure he's right for you, tell him you'd like to work with him, but Mr. Law is offering a better price. He just might agree to meet it. Bear in mind, however, that price isn't everything. One lawyer might charge more per hour than another, but he may know the field better, handle the case faster and end up costing you less than the lower-priced one.

HOURLY FEES. Hourly fees vary from city to city and state to state; the average lawyer in a medium-size metropolitan area charges between $100 and $200 an

Do some preliminary shopping by phone. Talk to two or three lawyers and get prices. Save the lawyer you think you'll want for last.

hour, and will often ask for a retainer—in effect, a down payment—before taking the case. When you hire a lawyer on an hourly basis, his or her time is your money, so be careful about monopolizing his attention. If you call, make it brief; the clock is always running, even in a casual conversation. Again, ask if there are ways you can help reduce costs and what you can do to make the whole process smoother—and less expensive—such as gathering documents or doing other clerical work. The advantage of an hourly fee arrangement is that you pay only for work that is actually done; the disadvantage is that if your case gets complicated or drags on, your legal bill can approach Schwarzenegger proportions.

> ## IF YOU CAN'T AFFORD A LAWYER
>
> If you can't afford a lawyer, contact your local legal aid society (look in the phone book under "Legal Aid"). Legal aid is supported by government and private funds, and offers free or inexpensive legal advice to people who meet its eligibility criteria. (See also the discussion of court-appointed lawyers under Your Rights When You're Arrested, on page 197 of the Appendix.)

CONTINGENCY FEES. A lawyer paid a contingency fee takes a percentage of the amount of damages that the court awards you, which the defendant (the person you've made a claim against) will pay. Such a fee is usually used only in injury cases or when the suit involves a yet-to-be determined amount of money. Although such fees can range from about 15% to 50% of the award, they're customarily about 33% of the award, and the maximum percentage is often fixed by state statute. In a workman's compensation suit, for example, the contingency fee can range from 10% to 20%. Medical malpractice suits, by contrast, typically have a high contingency fee—up to 50%—because they are expensive to conduct, often come to trial and are very hard to win. So, the good news is that you need to pay your lawyer only if you win. But what if you lose? You're still expected to foot the bill for whatever expenses your lawyer incurs while pursuing the case, including things like photocopying, postage, telephone bills and court-filing fees.

The most important thing to be aware of when negotiating a contingency fee is whether you will be obligated to give him a percentage of the gross award or a percentage of the net award left after you pay whatever legal expenses he's incurred. Many lawyers will insist on being paid from the larger gross award. If your lawyer does, try to save yourself some money by negotiating a lower percentage. No matter what, try to get him to agree that if the case gets settled before coming to trial he'll take a lesser percentage of the award. After all, he won't have to do as much work as originally anticipated.

FLAT FEES. Flat fees are exactly what they sound like: one-time charges for specific legal tasks. Flat fees are used when the legal problem is uncomplicated and the amount of time needed to resolve it is predictable, such as writing a will or setting up a trust. It's easy to check out the marketplace and see whether the flat fee being offered by your attorney is competitive. Be sure to ask if the fee will include court-filing fees, photocopying, phone bills and postage.

If You're not Satisfied With Your Lawyer

Because a lawyer works for you, you can fire him or her whenever you like. Be warned, however, that this can get complicated, and you shouldn't expect to get all your money back. Lawyers will often fight to keep any retainer you've already forked over and might try to collect any other payment they think they deserve. To that end they may hold on to any original documents involved in your case or even go so far as to put liens on your house for nonpayment.

If the outcome of your case isn't what you hoped for, you may be upset with your lawyer. That's understandable, but it doesn't necessarily mean that he's done anything wrong. Still, if you have doubts, get a second opinion from another lawyer or contact your local bar association (see page 14).

If you think your lawyer was unethical or unprofes-

> **Be aware when you negotiate a contingency fee whether you will be obligated to give the lawyer a percentage of the gross award or a percentage of the net award.**

sional, ask how to contact your state or local bar association's disciplinary or grievance committee. Be aware, however, that unless several complaints like yours have already been filed against the lawyer, action—not to mention restitution—is usually unlikely.

If the problem has to do with your bill, you might be better off asking about the local bar association's fee-arbitration service, which settles billing disputes between lawyers and clients.

If your lawyer didn't conduct your case with what would generally be considered a reasonable degree of professional competence under the circumstances—in other words, if he ruined your case and your chances of recovery—he may have violated the standard of care he is expected to uphold as a licensed legal practitioner under the law, and you could sue him for malpractice. Like doctors, most lawyers have malpractice insurance. Finding a lawyer willing to sue another lawyer isn't the easiest thing in the world, however; nor are such cases easy to win. To prove malpractice, you must show that your lawyer is guilty of misconduct and did not put your needs first.

FOR MORE INFORMATION

- *The Legal Resource Directory: Your Guide to Help, Hotlines and Hot Web Sites,* published by HALT, a national non-profit advocacy organization working for legal reform ($20.00).
- *100 Ways to Cut Legal Fees and Manage Your Lawyer,* by Erwin G. Krasnow and Robin S. Conrad (National Chamber Litigation Center, 1615 H St., N.W., Washington, DC 20062; 202-463-5337; $10.95.
- *Using a Lawyer...And What to Do If things Go Wrong: A Step-by-Step Guide,* by Kay Ostberg in association with HALT (Random House; $8.95).
- *If You Want To Sue A Lawyer...A Directory of Legal Malpractice Attorneys,* by Kay Ostberg and Theresa Meehan Rudy in association with HALT (Random House; $10).

The Law and Your Finances

As the song says, money makes the world go round. The law is designed to grease the works, ensuring that the exchange of goods and services proceeds fairly and smoothly. The idea is to make sure that everyone gets what they're entitled to under written, spoken or sometimes even implied agreements within the bounds of fair play. This chapter will show you how the law protects you and your money—when you borrow other people's money and when you give yours to other people to invest for you—and will show you how to remedy various financial wrongs. The section on tax compliance will help make sure you keep up your end of the bargain with Uncle Sam. (For information about how the tax law affects you and your household help, see the discussion beginning on page 138 of Chapter 6, "Your Home and the Law.")

Credit Is an Equal Opportunity

Under the federal Equal Credit Opportunity Act (ECOA), as well as a myriad of states laws, you are entitled to be treated fairly when you apply for credit. In a nutshell, a lender cannot:

- **discourage or prevent you** from applying for credit because of your sex, marital status, age, national origin, or because you receive public assistance income;
- **ask whether you are divorced or widowed;**
- **ask about your plans for having or raising children;**
- **refuse to consider** reliable public-assistance income in the same manner as other income;

Lenders must judge you on the same basis as all their other customers. That doesn't guarantee that they will give you credit.

■ **consider the race of the people** living in a neighborhood where you want to buy or improve a house with borrowed money; or

■ **refuse to consider** consistently received alimony, child support or maintenance payments as income.

Remember, these laws guarantee that lenders must judge your creditworthiness on the same basis as that of all their other customers. They don't guarantee that lenders will give you credit.

HOW DO YOU KNOW YOU ARE BEING DISCRIMINATED AGAINST? It's hard for you to know, because you probably don't know what other people are being offered. Still, there are a few things that should make you think twice:

■ **Are the terms you're being offered different** from the advertised ones?

■ **Have you learned that your lender lends** in your town, but not in your neighborhood (also known as redlining)?

■ **Has the lender made no effort to help you?** For example, you aren't given a chance to explain negative marks on your credit history if other applicants are.

To obtain a copy of the Equal Credit Opportunity Act, write to the Consumer Response Center, Federal Trade Commission, 600 Pennsylvania Ave., N.W., Washington, DC 20580; call toll-free 1-877-382-4357, (TDD 202-326-2502), or check the FTC's Web site (www.ftc.gov).

Equal Credit for Spouses

The law contains a number of provisions that were originally designed to protect women, but apply to both husband and wife in two-income households.

■ **Creditors must permit each spouse** to open and maintain credit accounts in his or her first name and choice of family surname, married surname or combined surname.

- **Creditors can't require someone**—say, your spouse—to co-sign your loan if you meet the creditor's standards.

- **When considering an application for credit,** prospective creditors must consider income derived from a part-time job, or from a pension, an annuity, or retirement-benefits program.

- **If you want them to, creditors must count** as income long-term alimony or child-support payments. They can ask you for proof, and they can check the credit record of your ex-spouse.

- **Creditors cannot ask you for information** about your spouse unless: your spouse is applying with you; your spouse will be allowed to use the account; you rely on your spouse's income, or on alimony or child-support income from a former spouse; or you reside in a community-property state.

- **Husband and wife** must get equal acknowledgment for the credit history of a joint account. That is, creditors must report information about the account in both names. That way, if you split up, neither of you will be without a credit history; you will each have a documented credit record.

- **Whether married or single,** if you have an individual account, you alone are responsible for paying the debt on the account and the account will appear on your credit report. If you and your spouse have a joint account, both of you are responsible for seeing that all debts charged to it are paid. A creditor who reports the credit history of a joint account to credit bureaus must report it in both names (if the account was opened after June 1, 1977).

- **Regardless of whether a woman** is applying separately or jointly, creditors can't ask her about her child-bearing intentions or capability, or her birth-control

Creditors must report information about a joint account in both names. That way, if you split up, neither of you will be without a credit history.

Under the federal Truth in Lending Act, a lender is legally obligated to tell you clearly and accurately everything you need to know about any loan it is offering you.

practices. Though it's more likely that a woman would be questioned about this, it's just as illegal for a lender to ask a man.

■ **Creditors can't close a credit account** just because of a change in marital status. But creditors can require you to update your application or reapply for the credit.

What Lenders Must Tell You

Under the federal Truth in Lending Act, a lender is legally obligated to tell you clearly and accurately everything you need to know about any loan it is offering you, including all the key terms, such as finance charges and amount financed, and the total amount of payments. In particular, it must express the cost of borrowing as the annual percentage rate (APR)—the relative cost of credit on a yearly basis. Lenders can otherwise use a variety of methods to compute interest, making it sound like much less than it really is. With the APR, you can compare apples with apples, one lender's offering with another's. The APR and the finance charge must be disclosed for consumer credit transactions.

If You're Turned Down for Credit

If you suspect you have been denied credit unfairly, ask the lender why it turned you down. By law, it must tell you why it rejected you.

If a credit report influenced the decision against you, you must be told the name and address of the bureau that provided the information so that you can find out whether outdated or mistaken information was to blame.

The lender must also tell you whether a bank regulatory agency or the Federal Trade Commission has jurisdiction over it, in case you want to lodge a complaint. While such agencies may launch general investigations if they get enough complaints, they will not pursue individual legal action on your behalf. For that, you'll have to contact a lawyer; if you believe discrimination was a factor, find counsel well-versed in civil-rights law. Be sure to keep a file of any documents related to your loan request, including copies of your application, your credit report, notes you took in conversations with the prospective lender, and correspondence.

When a Lender Isn't Dealing Straight

What if you think that the lender has deliberately misled or misinformed you about the terms of your deal? Perhaps the interest rate sounds suspiciously low, the loan officer will speak only in terms of "low" monthly payments instead of the APR, or she doesn't seem to want to review the required disclosure forms with you.

■ **If you haven't yet signed on the dotted line:** Demand that the lender review the appropriate disclosure form with you and explain it in language you can understand. If you've caught the lender in a deception or lie, tell the loan officer that you'll be reporting the firm to the appropriate authorities, and move on to a lender you can rely on.

■ **If you have already committed yourself:** You can confront your lender, demanding that you be given a corrected contract or that you be released from your obligations. If the lender fails to correct the situation, you can complain to either the FTC or the proper bank regulatory agency (again, agencies may investigate but won't pursue your individual case legally; see the discussion above), or you can contact a lawyer to handle your case.

For information about discrimination by home sellers and real estate agents, see Chapter 5, "Buying and Selling a Home."

Credit Card Law

The Fair Credit Billing Act exists to prevent foul-ups on your bills and to provide a way to fix them when they occur. Basically, the law obligates credit card issuers and firms that extend revolving-type credit to:

If you believe discrimination was a factor in denying you credit, find counsel well-versed in civil-rights law. Be sure to keep a file of any documents related to your loan request.

- **credit payments to your account** the same day as they are received at the address the company has specified. This prevents you from incurring finance charges after the credit card company has your payment in hand.
- **send you your bill** at least 14 days before payment is due, if your account is the type that gives you time to pay before finance charges accrue.
- **inform you of your rights and remedies** twice a year, or briefly with every bill or at length upon your request.
- **resolve billing errors appropriately,** as described below.

Errors You Might Expect

The law covers these common billing problems:

- **an unauthorized charge,** or one with the wrong amount or date, or that is otherwise incorrectly identified;
- **a charge or debt** for which you want an explanation, clarification or more documentation from the creditor;
- **a charge for goods or services** that weren't delivered to you or weren't accepted by you according to your agreement with the seller;
- **a failure to properly reflect** a payment or credit to your account;
- **a mistake in computation or accounting** (for example, a goof in computing finance or late-payment charges); and
- **an additional finance charge** or minimum payment due because the creditor failed to deliver your bill to your current address. (If you moved, however, you must have notified the creditor of your new address at least ten days before the closing date of the billing cycle involved.)

How to Dispute an Error

Although you may be tempted to just pick up the phone and call your credit card company's toll-free customer-service number, telephoning alone may not preserve your rights under the law. Instead, send a

WHAT IF YOUR CARD IS STOLEN?

As soon as you realize that you are missing a credit card for any reason—whether you believe it's been stolen, you've lost it, or an unauthorized person is going to use it—you should call the credit card company and report it right away.

Assuming that you have reported the card before it has been used, you will have zero liability. If there's already been unauthorized activity in your account, you are liable only up to $50, no matter how much has been charged or how late you report it.

Your report of a missing card need not be in writing; you can simply call the credit card company to notify it verbally. That's why it's a good idea to keep an up-to-date list of all your credit cards, noting your account numbers and the appropriate "800" numbers to call.

notice in writing (certified mail is a good idea; keep the receipt) to your credit card company within 60 days of the postmark on the statement in question; the appropriate address for billing errors should be noted on your bill. Identify the charge involved, its date and dollar amount, and your reason for thinking a billing error exists. Include any other information that will help the company help you more quickly, such as your account number and your address, including zip code.

The company is obligated to acknowledge your letter within 30 days of receiving it and resolve your problem within two billing cycles or 90 days of notification. In the meantime, you are not obligated to pay for the disputed charge—including the affected portions of minimum payments and finance charges—until the dispute is resolved, even though the charge may continue to appear on your bill. Until the problem is solved, the creditor must not hassle you in any way about the disputed charge or your account in general. It can't report the disputed charge to a credit-reporting agency as a delinquent debt. You are, however, responsible for any other charges on your bill.

DEFECTIVE MERCHANDISE

What if you use your credit card to buy a microwave that doesn't work or a sofa with a loose leg? Your first step should be to try and resolve the dispute with the merchant. If that doesn't work, you may withhold payment. But you must have used a store-issued credit card. If you used another card, you're covered only if the sale was for more than $50 and took place in your home state or within miles of your home address.

When you request a credit from a merchant rather than from the card issuer, ask that a copy of the credit be mailed to you right away. If you don't receive it, dispute the claim in writing with the credit card issuer (see the accompanying discussion).

If the company finds in your favor, it must credit your account for the disputed charge and for any finance charges that have accrued on that amount.

If the merchant argues that it was a valid charge, not an error, and you still dispute it, you can ask for supporting documents. Then you go back to the credit card company and make your case again.

If the card issuer decides the deal was valid, you must be told why. Then it will put the charge back on your statement. You then have ten days, or your normal credit-card grace period, to either pay the charge or to protest it again in writing.

If you don't pay, the charge is reported to credit agencies as delinquent. Make sure there's a note on your credit reports explaining that the item is in dispute. That will help lessen the impact of the claim on your ability to get other credit.

Throughout this process, make sure to keep credit card statements and receipts. If you have phone conversations with merchants or the card issuer, write follow-up letters that repeat what you discussed. Keep copies of any related correspondence, receipts and telephone records to prove that you followed the proper procedures.

NOW YOU'RE REALLY MAD. If you've done your best to follow those steps and the problem still isn't resolved, one option is to turn to your state and local consumer laws, which often provide more protection than federal laws. Your state or local consumer-affairs office can tell you whether your state's laws differ from the federal law.

If you think that the Fair Credit Billing Act hasn't been followed in your case, start with the compliance officer at the credit card issuer. It's his job to make sure that the law is properly administered. Present your argument in writing, showing where procedures weren't followed. (For help in writing your response, get a copy of *Fair Credit Billing* by calling the FTC toll-free at 877-382-4357, (TDD 202-326-2502) or logging onto www.ftc.gov.

To complain about a credit-card billing problem, you can write to the Division of Consumer and Community Affairs, Board of Governors of the Federal Reserve System, Washington, DC 20551. Be sure to provide the complete name and address of the bank, a brief description of your complaint, and any documentation that may help them investigate your complaint. Do not send original documents, only copies; remember to sign and date your letter. The Federal Reserve will acknowledge your complaint within 15 business days, letting you know whether a Federal Reserve Bank will investigate your complaint or whether your complaint will be forwarded to another federal agency for attention. The Board of Governors of the Federal Reserve System has an online *Consumer Handbook to Credit Protection Laws* in the Consumer Information section of their Web site; www.federalreserve.gov.

YOUR CREDIT RECORD. A credit report reflects your bill-paying history—who your creditors are and whether you've made your payments to them on time. There's no rule of thumb about how often you should check your credit record, but if you are planning on applying for a loan or other credit, double-check your

If you think that the Fair Credit Billing Act hasn't been followed in your case, start with the compliance officer at the credit card issuer.

If you are planning on applying for a loan or other credit, double-check your credit record beforehand for accuracy.

credit record beforehand for accuracy. Potential lenders will look at it before approving your application. Credit information, kept by private agencies (see the box on the opposite page), is compiled from information supplied by your creditors.

The kinds of errors that could show up and keep you from getting credit? Wrong information about late payments, the merging of your data with someone else's, and the listing of accounts that aren't yours.

Federal law requires that any negative information be dropped from your credit record after seven years; bankruptcies may remain for up to ten years.

To locate and contact the credit agencies that may have information on you, look in your local phone book under "Credit Agencies" or contact the sources listed in the accompanying box.

You can request a copy of your credit record by writing to the credit agency. If you've been turned down for credit in the past 30 days, the agency must send you your report for free.

You should receive the report within about three weeks. After reviewing it, send a letter to the agency telling them about any mistakes. Within a reasonable period after being notified—usually 30 days—the agency must check with your creditor. If the agency finds that you are right, it must adjust your record.

Even if the agency says you are wrong and refuses to change your record, you still have the right to amend your record with a written statement of no more than 100 words, explaining your position. And, if you ask, the agency must send the revised file to all creditors who have seen the previous version in the past six months.

If you believe that such a statement isn't enough to counteract the misinformation, consider writing your state attorney general's office or office of consumer affairs, or even the Federal Trade Commission. If the FTC gets enough complaints from consumers about the credit-reporting company, it may inquire into the company's practices.

Another option open to you is legal action. You

NATIONAL CREDIT-REPORTING AGENCIES

You may request a free copy of your credit report if you have been denied credit, employment or insurance in the past 60 days. Residents of Colorado, Georgia, Massachusetts, Maryland, New Jersey, or Vermont can also receive one free report annually from each credit-reporting agency. Otherwise, there is a small fee of about $9. The credit-reporting agencies are Equifax, Experian (formerly TRW) and Trans Union. Call, log onto the Web or write:

- **Experian National Consumer Assistance Center** (P.O. Box 2104, Allen, TX 75013-2104; 1-888-397-3742; www.experian.com)
- **Equifax** (P.O. Box 740241, Atlanta, GA 30374; 800-997-2493; www.econsumer.equifax.com)
- **Trans Union** (Trans Union LLC, Consumer Disclosure Center, P.O. Box 2000, Chester, PA 19022; 800-888-4213; www.transunion.com)

---

can sue the credit agency or even the creditor who reported false information. Be warned, however, that such action is extreme and such cases are tough to win; bringing suit might be merited if the agency's mistake is clear and you've suffered significant damage to your financial life and standing.

Credit Problems
Calling Off the Bill Collectors

If you fall behind in paying your creditors, you may be contacted by a collection agency, which will pursue payment from you. Though it would be the fair thing to do, your creditor needn't warn you that it's going to turn your account over to a debt-collection agency. The Fair Debt Collection Practices Act protects debtors from being mistreated by professional debt collectors. Its provisions include the following:

- **In general, debt collectors** may not harass, oppress or abuse you. That means they can't threaten or harm you, your property or your reputation, nor can they repeatedly telephone you or use obscene or profane language when speaking with you.

■ **Debt collectors** may not lie when collecting a debt. For example, they can't falsely imply that they are attorneys or government representatives or that you have committed a crime, nor can they misrepresent the amount of your debt. They also can't state that you will be arrested if you don't pay up or that they will seize, attach or sell your property or garnish your wages, unless the collection agency or creditor actually intends to and it's legal for them to do so.

■ **Debt collectors** may not engage in unfair practices in attempting to collect a debt, such as making you accept collect calls or pay for telegrams, or deposit a postdated check prematurely.

Bill collectors will try to scare you or annoy you into paying up any way they think they can within these limits. For example, aside from calling you repeatedly at home, bill collectors may try to rattle you by contacting you at work or calling you long after you've gone to bed. But debt collectors may not contact you at unreasonable times or places, such as before 8 A.M. or after 9 P.M. unless you agree. They also may not contact you at work if the collector knows that your employer disapproves. Under no circumstances are they allowed to tell other people, such as co-workers or family members, about your debt problem, but they may contact other people to find out where you live and work.

You can protect yourself. Whether or not you can pay up, if you tell bill collectors in writing to stop bothering you, by law they must stop—except to notify you that there will be no further contact or that they intend to take some specific action. If you inform them that a lawyer represents you, they can't contact you directly anymore but only through your legal counsel. If they continue to pester you, you could con-

CREDIT REPAIR

When You Don't Want to Do It Yourself

In spite of the numerous ads you may see to the contrary, when it comes to credit repair self-help may be best. There is no easy way to repair your credit, and some of the companies that offer to help you succeed only in helping themselves to your money.

You may sign on with them and find that after paying exorbitant fees they don't do anything for you that you couldn't have done for yourself. Or worse, you discover that your credit is just as bad as it was before, and the credit-repair service has disappeared.

Still, if you feel you can't repair your credit on your own, the Federal Trade Commission warns you to avoid companies that do the following:

- **want you to pay for credit-repair services before any services are provided;**
- **do not tell you your legal rights and what you can do—yourself— for free;**
- **recommend that you not contact a credit bureau directly;**
- **suggest that you try to invent a "new" credit report** by applying for an Employer Identification Number to use instead of your Social Security Number; or
- **advise you to dispute all information in your credit report** or take any action that seems illegal, such as creating a new credit identity. If you follow illegal advice and commit fraud, you may be subject to prosecution.

A credit-repair organization must provide you with a written contract and a copy of *Consumer Credit File Rights Under State and Federal Law*. Read all documents before signing the contract. By law a credit-repair company must not:

- **make false claims about their services;**
- **charge a fee before they complete promised services; or**
- **perform any services until three days after you have signed the contract.**

During these three days, you have the right to cancel the contract without paying any fees.

Your contract must include the following information:

- **the payment terms for services, including their total cost;**
- **a detailed description of the services to be performed;**
- **how long it will take to achieve the results;**
- **any guarantees they offer; and**
- **the company's name and business address.**

If you feel you have been wronged by a credit-repair service, you may file a complaint by contacting the FTC's Consumer Response Center by phone toll-free (877-382-4357); by mail (Consumer Response Center, Federal Trade Commission, 600 Pennsylvania Ave, NW, Washington, DC 20580); or online (www.ftc.gov).

tact the police and attempt to bring charges of harassment, or you could sue, though you may not recover money for the damages even if you win. Of course, your creditor could always bring suit against you for the unpaid bills.

When Wages Are Garnished

Wage garnishing, which is governed by state and federal law, means that your employer must regularly withhold a set amount from your paycheck because a court has ordered you (via a writ of garnishment or writ of attachment of wages) to repay your creditors. Some states don't allow certain workers—usually military or government workers—to have their wages garnished. Even if your wages are garnished, you're allowed to keep 75% of your weekly net wages (after taxes) or 30 times the federal minimum hourly wage, whichever is greater.

FOR MORE INFORMATION

- **National Foundation For Credit Counseling** (801 Roeder Rd., Suite 900, Silver Spring, MD 20910; 301-589-5600; crisis hotline, 800-388-2227; www .debtadvice.org), a national nonprofit organization with counselors who try to help you straighten out debt problems.
- **Federal Trade Commission (Consumer Response Center, Federal Trade Commission)** (600 Pennsylvania Ave., N.W., Room H-130, Washington, DC 20580-0001; 877-382-4357; www.ftc.gov) has consumer information online including "Credit and Your Consumer Rights." You may also obtain pamphlets by mail.
- *The Ultimate Credit Handbook: How to Double Your Credit, Cut Your Debt and*

Have a Lifetime of Great Credit, by Gerri Detweiler (Plume, $14.00)
- *All About Credit: Questions (and Answers) About the Most Common Credit Problems,* by Deborah McNaughton (Dearborn Trade, $15.95)
- *Getting and Keeping Credit: Your Guide to Credit Cards and Credit Records* (American Bar Association, $2.50. Order by phone at 800-285-2221or online at www.abanet.org/publiced/publicpubs.html) This booklet provides practical tips on saving money and protecting yourself in credit transactions. Discusses how to get credit, what credit costs, choosing a credit card, equal-credit laws, and checking your credit record.

Can Creditors Seize My Car?

State laws on these issues vary, but generally, if you pledge a possession such as a car as collateral for a loan and fall behind in your payments, the car can be "peaceably repossessed." That means that an agent of the creditor may remove the item from your possession only if he does it without conflict. Many repossessions take place in the dead of night, when owners are fast asleep in their beds. In some states, cars can't be repossessed when parked on private property, and in others, when parked on public streets. Most states don't allow cars to be taken by breaking into a locked garage.

What About My Home?

In order to repossess a home, the creditor must go through court-ordered foreclosure proceedings. In a foreclosure, the lender forces the sale of your house to get the money you owe in back mortgage or home-equity-payments.

Foreclosure laws vary from state to state, but generally, they begin after the lender has tried and failed for two or three months to get you to pay the money you owe. The lender will then send you a notice of default; you'll have a specified amount of time to stop the foreclosure process by making up the payments and late fees. You can even sell the house yourself during this period to pay back the lender.

If you don't meet the deadline for paying up, the lender goes to court, gets an order to sell your house and publishes a notice of sale in the newspaper for several weeks. Even after the notice is published, your lender may still let you reinstate the loan—pay what you owe and take your house back. If the loan is not reinstated, then the lender can go ahead and sell the house to the highest bidder.

No Need to Default on Government-Guaranteed Student Loans

If you are having difficulty paying on your student loans, either beginning payments or continuing them, contact your loan officer as soon as possible and try to

Continued on page 40

Even if your wages are garnished, you're allowed to keep 75% of your weekly net wages (after taxes) or 30 times the federal minimum hourly wage, whichever is greater.

SOME COMMON CONSUMER PROBLEMS

Mail and Telephone Orders

Q. *I received a book in the mail that I hadn't ordered, and I'll be darned if I want to waste my money paying return postage. What's my obligation?*

A. If a product arrives at your home unsolicited, it is legally considered a gift and you can keep it. Period. If someone tries to make you pay for it or return it, they are violating the law.

Q. *I do a lot of mail-order shopping. What are my rights as a mail-order shopper?*

A. You can prevent problems if, before you place an order, you consider the company's general reputation and any prior experiences that you or your acquaintances have had with it. Also, ask about its refund and return policies.

The merchant must deliver the item within the time stated in its ads or within 30 days of your phone order or its receipt of your order by mail. If the merchant doesn't comply, it must give you a chance to cancel the order.

If the product isn't up to par, contact the merchant and ask for a refund upon return of the merchandise. Reputable mail-order companies will promptly reimburse you, either by refunding your money or crediting the charge on your credit card.

Kids and Mail-Order Clubs

Q. *I recently discovered that my 14-year-old subscribed to a CD club without my permission. She not only collected on the initial offer but ordered another $200 worth of CDs, which she can't pay for. What should we do?*

What is our legal responsibility?

A. Though contract law varies from state to state, in general, minors (usually those under age 18) aren't legally able to enter into a contract. They can't be held to contracts they sign, nor can their parents or legal guardians. In this case, you write to the CD club, explaining that your daughter is not an adult, and return the merchandise. The club will cancel the membership.

How Can I Protect Myself From Stolen Identity?

Q: *I've read a lot of stories about identity theft and am starting to worry about it. What can I do to make sure the wrong people don't get ahold of my social security number?*

A: You're wise to be concerned. With little more information than your name and social security number, identity thieves can apply for credit cards, open bank accounts, rent apartments and withdraw money in your name, leaving you with a big bill or a bad credit record.

It's impossible to keep your social security number entirely private. Employers, brokerage firms, banks and anyone else who pays you money need the number to report your income to the IRS. But many places that ask for your social security number have no good reason for needing it.

Colleges, video stores and libraries have traditionally used social security numbers as an easy way to identify you but usually can't require it. Others may have your name but you should be the only one with your social security number. If you're asked for your number, explain why you don't want to provide the information and see if they'll let you use another identifier.

Many states, for example, will put another number on your license instead of your social security number if you ask for the change. To protect yourself, don't carry your social security card in your wallet (you rarely need to show it except when starting a new job) and don't write it on your checks.

If your bank or brokerage firm uses it as your PIN number to make trades or shift funds, ask to use a different number; otherwise, it's too easy for impostors to access your money.

And be careful with your trash. Identity thieves often find social security numbers, credit-card numbers and other private information in dumpsters. Rip up or shred the papers before throwing them away. To be safe, check your credit report every year or so to make sure it contains no unexplained entries, especially if you've received strange calls from creditors.

Airline Woes

Q. *What are my rights if an airline tries to bump me off a flight because they've over-booked the aircraft?*

A. Airlines usually try to avoid bumping passengers by asking for volunteers. These volunteers are offered cash or vouchers good for travel on the airline as compensation. This procedure is purely airline policy; there is no law regulating how much an airline must offer.

If you have a confirmed reservation on a 60-passenger or larger aircraft that is taking off from the U.S. and you are involuntarily bumped because of overbooking, the airline will try to get you to your destination within an hour of your originally planned time of arrival. If it can't, and you arrive as much as two hours late, federal regulations require the airline to pay you an amount equal to the one-way fare to your final destination, up to $200 maximum. If you arrive more than two hours late, or if the airline does not make any substitute travel arrangements for you, the compensation doubles.

Luggage Grief

Q. *What if an airline loses my luggage?*

A. If an airline loses or damages your luggage in the U.S., or your luggage is stolen, federal regulations say you are entitled to reimbursement of up to $2,500 toward the value of your lost possessions. On international flights, you get $9.07 per pound of luggage, up to a maximum of $635 (the maximum allowed weight of 70 pounds times $9.07).

Don't expect to get the entire amount unless virtually every article in your luggage is brand-new. The airline will often account for depreciation of your items. Check with your insurance company; it might make up the difference. Be warned that airlines can exempt jewelry, electronics and cash.

If your luggage has merely been rerouted or delayed, no federal regulations apply, though many airlines have policies that allow passengers to receive interim expenses to pay for new clothes or whatever they need until their luggage turns up.

SOME COMMON CONSUMER PROBLEMS, continued

My Kid and My Cards

Q. *My son snuck my credit card from my purse and used it without my permission. Does that count as unauthorized use, or am I responsible for the charges he racked up?*

A. Because you didn't lend the card to your son or imply that he had permission to use it, it probably would count as unauthorized use. If you're willing to file a complaint that your card was lost or stolen, you could limit your liability for his charges, but, of course, he could be prosecuted. The same would be true if your son had gained access to your automatic teller machine (ATM) card and personal identification number (PIN) and withdrew cash from your bank account without your knowledge. Our guess is that most parents would decide to handle either situation privately. You could require your son to return the merchandise for a refund or pay you for the amount he charged or withdrew.

---

work out some new terms. You might be able to arrange, for example, an extended repayment plan or one that considers your income.

Depending on your loan agreement, you could become exempted from repayment under certain circumstances, which your loan officer could review with you. For example, your payments might be deferred if you join the military, become a full-time volunteer in a tax-exempt organization like the Peace Corps, return to school or take a parental leave from work. Your loan might be canceled altogether if you become disabled.

Otherwise, as with any loan, it's always better to admit that you're having difficulty with repayment, even if it's embarrassing, than to default on the loan. A government-guaranteed student loan is by definition unsecured; no collateral was required for you to take out the loan, and the lender can't come for your car in the middle of the night. But the lender can sic a collection agency on you, take you to court for the money owed plus interest, and report your failure to pay to a credit bureau. Such negative credit information will remain on your report for as long as seven years and could prevent you from receiving a loan later in life.

If the original lender turned the loan back to a

guaranty agency or the Department of Education to collect, any tax refunds—including your spouse's if you file jointly—could be denied you. The government could also garnish your wages (without a court order) and even put a lien on your property (with a court order), meaning it could place a claim against your property by way of securing your debt. It must notify you of its plan of action in any case.

Note that your student loan may be a "non-dischargeable debt"—that is, declaring bankruptcy may not wipe it out (see below).

When All Else Fails: Declaring Bankruptcy

When you can't possibly pay what you owe and informal arrangements with creditors have failed, it might be time to think about declaring bankruptcy. Remember, bankruptcy is a last-ditch solution, and it's not a do-it-yourself proposition; you'll want to hire an attorney with expertise in bankruptcy to help you make important decisions that will affect the outcome. As this book was going to press, House was once again considering a bankruptcy reform bill, which, if passed by both houses and ultimately signed by President Bush, will likely make declaring bankruptcy more difficult and require increased paperwork, more stringent limitations and financial counseling.

Home and car exemptions will change drastically. Because some wealthy people (residents of Texas and Florida in particular) have been able to declare bankruptcy yet continue to live in multi-million dollar homes, the new law will put stringent limits on how much home equity will be exempt—probably in the range between $100,000 to $250,000 Under the new law, when you declare bankruptcy you will still have to pay off car loans completely if you have owned the car for three years or less. In the past you were required to pay only the car's blue book value.

When you can't possibly pay what you owe and informal arrangements with creditors have failed, it might be time to think about declaring bankruptcy.

WEB-WISE BUYING

Cybervandalism can't help but cause concern about the security of online shopping, even though there's no indication that customer information has been compromised. That's why it pays to be Web-wise when transacting business online:

Use your credit card only through a secure server, where the information is actually safer than it is when you hand your card to a store clerk or give your number over the phone to a catalog order-taker.

Don't disclose your social security number or other information in the "optional" fields on your screen.

Reserve one credit card specifically for Web use. If you have to cancel your card, your off-line transactions won't be disrupted.

Patronize sites that meet the security and privacy requirements for certain industry seals of approval, such as BBB Online and TRUSTe.

WHAT KIND FOR YOU? Many people may think of bankruptcy as the process of "filing Chapter 11," but that's usually a legal out for corporations, not for individuals. Individuals in tough financial straits typically can declare one of two types of bankruptcy: either Chapter 7 or Chapter 13, named for sections of the Bankruptcy Reform Act of 1978.

In Chapter 7, known as straight bankruptcy, you give up your property to the court, which will divide it among your creditors, and ask the court to erase your debts. (The court can't repossess certain exempt property, which the law deems necessary for your survival. That might include, for example, a certain amount of your equity in a residence or a motor vehicle.)

According to the new legislation, in order to qualify for Chapter 7 bankruptcy you must pass a complicated "means test" involving an analysis of your income and expenses. The income limits will vary from state to state, but are expected to be in the $50,000 to $60,000 annual income range for a family of four. If your income exceeds the limit you will not qualify for Chapter 7 and will have to file for Chapter 13 bankruptcy instead.

In Chapter 13, known as the wage-earner plan, you usually keep your property and pay back your creditors in installments during a three- to five-year program controlled and approved by the court.

If you have to declare bankruptcy, which type should you choose? That depends on your individual circumstances, but you should know that Chapter 13 has two important advantages over Chapter 7.

■ **In Chapter 13, anyone who co-signed** a loan for you is initially protected from your creditors, and you must repay the balance of the loan. In Chapter 7, creditors can go after your co-signers almost immediately to help you pay your debt. However, under Chapter 13, if it's been determined that you will not be able to pay back the debt in full, your creditors can try to collect from co-signers (see also the discussion of division of debt and divorce on page 228 of Chapter 10, "Ending a Marriage").

■ **Future creditors may look more favorably** on Chapter 13 bankruptcy because you will have repaid your debt rather than simply discharging it and washing your hands of it altogether.

If you choose Chapter 13, however, it's important to make sure that you and your lawyer have set up a reasonable repayment plan, one that takes into account your current resources and future prospects, so that your actions end up matching your intentions. Otherwise, you may eventually end up in Chapter 7, anyway.

Either way, no one has to extend you further credit, at least until your debts are repaid, and the bankruptcy will appear as a black mark on your credit record for up to ten years.

HOW IT WORKS. To declare bankruptcy you must file the appropriate papers with a bankruptcy court. That

> **To declare bankruptcy you must file appropriate papers with a bankruptcy court. That just begins the process.**

You have the right to appropriate investment advice. You do not, however, have the right to make money.

begins the bankruptcy process, but you'll have to wait for the court to give you a discharge of your debt, after which you can notify your creditors of the court's judgment.

Your creditors in most cases must accept your bankruptcy and whatever arrangements the court decides on. They could contest the court's decision, but unless they can demonstrate that you have substantially abused the process, they won't win. For example, a Chapter 7 bankruptcy might be denied or dismissed if on the eve of bankruptcy you went out and purposely ran up big credit card debts.

The Bankruptcy Reform Act of 1994 imposed stiffer penalties for fraud and tougher rules for recently incurred debts: A bankruptcy won't absolve you from debts you incur for luxuries you buy (or cash advances you take) within 60 days of filing for bankruptcy.

Your Rights as an Investor

This section discusses your legal rights as an investor, including your broker's legal obligations to you, and what grievances you can legally pursue—so-called actionable investment problems.

As an investor, you have the right to appropriate investment advice, suited to your financial situation and stated investment objectives, and proper handling of your money in any transaction. You do not, however, have the right to make money. If you knowingly sink your cash into a high-risk investment—and lose—you don't have the right to complain about your broker. On the other hand, you may have a case if:

- **You ask for a conservative investment** and the broker puts you into a high-risk one.
- **The broker misinforms or misleads you** about the risks of an investment he's recommending to you.
- **The broker trades excessively** on your behalf—buying and selling and thus racking up his commissions—in a manner that's inconsistent with your objective. This is known as churning an account.

■ **The broker trades without your authorization.**

■ **The broker "fails to execute" your trade** or delays so long that you miss an investment opportunity.

Under federal securities law enforced by the Securities and Exchange Commission (SEC), your broker must fully disclose the risks and rewards of any investment he or she recommends and must be sure that the investment is consistent with your needs.

The Complaint and Arbitration Process

As in most potential legal situations, if you think you've been wronged by your broker, you should first try to resolve the problem through negotiation. Talk to your broker to find out what happened. Don't be shy—after all, it's your money.

If talking doesn't work, complain in writing to the branch manager of the brokerage firm, and send copies of your complaint to both the broker and the firm's compliance department, asking that they take the necessary steps to resolve your problem. Request a meeting with the branch manager, and bring copies of

---

AVOID PROBLEMS WITH YOUR BROKER

You can in large part avoid having to tangle with your stockbroker or brokerage firm in arbitration if you follow these rules when your broker calls:

■ **Pay attention.** If it isn't a good time to talk, ask the broker to call back, or arrange to return the call. Don't get railroaded into a purchase.

■ **Consider whether the proposal fits your investment plan.** The final decision is yours. Though a broker can tell you about an opportunity he believes to be superior, but risky, if you buy it and lose big, it's no one's fault but your own.

■ **Ask for more information.** The broker should be able to send you written research, whether from her own firm or another. Read it. If you don't understand what you are reading, don't buy.

If you're going to pursue arbitration, do it sooner, rather than later. The statute of limitations is usually six years from the occurrence of the problem.

your monthly account statements and trade confirmations to support your case.

If the situation still doesn't get resolved to your satisfaction, you have to take it to the next step: arbitration.

Arbitration is likely to be the only option open to you; usually, when you open an account with a broker, the agreement you sign contains a clause that says you agree to resolve any complaints against the firm through binding arbitration. That means that you and the brokerage firm will abide by whatever decision the arbitrator reaches.

Most brokerage contracts require you to bring your case before the arbitration department of one of the industry's self-regulatory organizations (SROs): the New York Stock Exchange, the Municipal Securities Rulemaking Board, the National Association of Securities Dealers and several regional exchanges. Most complainants participate in arbitration programs run by the NYSE or NASD. A few are heard by representatives of the independent American Arbitration Association.

The various forums follow similar rules. Filing fees for AAA arbitration start at $500, whereas those of the industry-subsidized SROs start at $15.

For more information, contact either the National Association of Securities Dealers (33 Whitehall St., New York, NY 10004; www.nasd.com) or the New York Stock Exchange (11 Wall St., New York, NY 10005; www.nyse.com).

If you are going to pursue arbitration, do it sooner, rather than later. Under the rules of the exchanges, as well as state and federal laws, the statute of limitations is generally six years from the occurrence of the problem.

If you win—small investors who bring arbitration actions against brokers win on average more than half the time —you will be awarded monetary damages.

If you lose, it's virtually over. Because you agreed to binding arbitration when you opened your brokerage account, you have little legal recourse.

Tax Compliance

The tax law in the U.S. has come a long way since 1913 when Congress passed the 16th Amendment to the Constitution, allowing the federal government to impose an income tax. Today the Internal Revenue Code fills more than 2,000 pages of really fine print. It supports a whole industry of tax preparers, planners and lawyers who are out there slaving away to understand, apply and interpret the law for the rest of us so we can pay what we owe and no more. This book could hardly begin to cover all the issues that even an average taxpayer might be concerned with. But it will provide answers to some common questions about meeting the letter of the tax law and about what to do when the IRS says you haven't.

Deadlines and Extensions

Everyone knows the deadline for filing tax returns is April 15, unless that date happens to fall on a Saturday, Sunday or a legal holiday, which pushes the deadline to the next business day. If you have a refund coming, you don't really have to kill yourself getting to the post office by midnight of the due date; the penalty for filing late is a percentage of the tax due with the return, and a percentage of nothing is nothing. However, you won't want to leave your money languishing with the IRS or invite the agency's scrutiny by delaying too long.

You can get an automatic four-month extension just by filing Form 4868, "Application for Automatic Extension of Time to File U.S. Individual Income Tax Return." But be aware that this gives you only an extension for filing the return, not for paying the tax you owe. You still have to make a good-faith estimate of what your tax bill will be and send in a check for that amount along with the form asking for an extension.

If your estimated payment falls short of your final tax bill, you will be charged interest on the additional amount from April 15 forward.

If you underestimate by 10% or more, you'll probably be hit with a late-payment penalty, too.

If you have a refund coming, you don't have to kill yourself getting to the post office by midnight of the due date. However, you won't want to leave your money languishing with the IRS.

You generally have three years from the annual filing deadline to correct any errors—significant or otherwise, in the IRS's favor or yours—that you discover.

Divorce and Exemptions for Dependents

Around tax time, parents may thank their lucky stars for "Mommy and Daddy's little tax breaks." Parents can exempt a set amount of income for each child as long as they provide more than 50% of the child's support. When parents are divorced, however, the custodial parent usually claims the dependent-child exemption—with two exceptions.

If you were divorced before 1985, you might have written a provision into your divorce agreement allowing the noncustodial parent to take the deduction. If so, the noncustodial parent simply checks off a box on his or her Form 1040 indicating that a pre-1985 agreement is in effect.

If you were divorced after 1985 and want the non-custodial parent to have the exemption, the custodial parent must file Form 8332, "Release of Claim to Exemption for Child of Divorced or Separated Parents," every year the exemption is shifted.

Making Amends for an Honest Error

You generally have three years from the annual filing deadline to correct any errors—significant or otherwise, in the IRS's favor or yours—that you discover. That means for a 2002 return, you would have until April 15, 2006, three years from April 15, 2003, to file an amendment using Form 1040X. (You have seven years if the revision involves a bad debt or worthless security.)

If you owe money, send a check with the form. The IRS will bill you for the accrued interest that you owe. If it turns out that the IRS owes you, look for a refund check within two to three months of submitting your form.

What If My Tax Preparer Goofs?

If there is a mistake on your tax return, you are liable—even if you had an accountant or other tax preparer fill out your return. Most tax preparers worth their 1040s will pay any penalty that is levied on you for a mistake they made. Unfortunately, they needn't pay the additional tax that you owe. That's why it pays to take the following precautions when working with a tax preparer:

- **Go early.** Avoid the last-minute rush and get the attention you deserve.
- **Find out how much you'll be charged** at the outset, and ask what the tax preparer's policy is if he or she makes a mistake.
- **Ask the preparer** about qualifications and experience.
- **Be prepared.** Don't dump a paper bag full of documents on the tax preparer's desk and expect him to make sense of your disorganization.
- **Be suspicious of a preparer** who doesn't ask you a lot of questions, ensuring that he gets all the information he needs to get you all the breaks you have coming.
- **Check your completed return carefully** when you get it, making sure that all the forms and schedules the preparer discussed with you are included.

How Long Can They Get Me?

The statute of limitations for a tax return is generally three years from the date it's due to be filed. The limit is six years if the IRS can show that you failed to report 25% or more of the gross amount of income that you did report. And, if the IRS can prove you have acted fraudulently or you fail to file a return, it can investigate you at any time—there is no limitation.

Reporting Tax Cheaters

You are not legally obligated to report someone who is cheating on his or her taxes. However, if you do wish to let the IRS know that someone is shortchanging it (and the rest of us), you can call anonymously. If you're willing to give your name and the IRS finds your information is crucial to catching the cheater, you might be awarded a bounty of as much as 15% of the back taxes collected.

When an Audit Looms

The dreaded audit notice: your invitation to disaster? No, just an invitation to prove what you reported.

Less than 1% of taxpayers are audited each year. If you file a Schedule C or Schedule F, your odds increase.

> ## TAXPAYERS' BILL OF RIGHTS
>
> As enacted by Congress in 1988 and amended in 1996 to provide increased protection of taxpayers' rights, it provides that:
>
> - **If you send your representative to an audit,** you needn't go, too.
> - **If you give the IRS forewarning,** you can tape the proceedings of your audit.
> - **If you prove that you made a mistake on your return** by following written advice from the IRS given as a response to a specific request, it can't penalize you for the mistake.
> - **The IRS must work within certain limits** when it seizes your property to satisfy a tax bill.
> - **You can sue the IRS** if an IRS employee "recklessly or intentionally" disregards the law in collecting a tax liability.

Audits serve two purposes. They give taxpayers a compelling reason to comply with the law in the first place, and they help the IRS recoup some of the difference—estimated in the billions of dollars—between what taxpayers owe and what they voluntarily pay.

But take heart: Less than 1% of taxpayers are audited each year. If you file a Schedule C or Schedule F, your odds increase.

When notified of an audit, you may be asked simply to mail in proof of a specific claim on your return, or you may be subject to a field audit, in which an auditor comes to your home or business.

READY, SET, GO... In any case, your first reaction needn't be to call your lawyer. Instead, go find the files that you compiled when you prepared the return in question. Review your return and all your supporting documentation yourself. If your files are incomplete, fill in the gaps:

- **If your dog ate your copy of the return,** call the IRS office that contacted you and ask how you can get a copy.

- **Get copies of canceled checks from your bank,** duplicates of receipts or written statements from people who can back up your claims.
- **If all else fails,** prepare your oral explanation.

You'll probably have a couple weeks to get it all together, but if you need to reschedule the appointment—say, because the time is inconvenient or you need more time to gather your records—call the IRS promptly to request a new time.

HIRED GUNS? Whether you bring someone with you to the audit depends on the complexity of the issues you'll be discussing. If it sounds as if the audit will be pretty simple, you may want to go it alone. If someone else prepared your return, you might want to call him or her for tips on how to prepare.

One cost-saving strategy is to attend the first audit meeting by yourself to clear up any routine matters. If you disagree with the auditor's conclusions or you need more time to gather additional evidence, you can schedule a follow-up meeting. If you think the money at stake justifies the expense, you could pay your adviser to attend the next meeting. If the issues are more technical or require interpretation of the law, you'll probably want assistance in any case.

Of course, you needn't even go to the audit. You could hire a representative and give him or her written authorization to act for you via IRS Form 2848, a power-of-attorney form.

THE OUTCOME. If the auditor finds you owe money, you'll be asked to sign a form. Within a few weeks, you'll be billed for the extra taxes, interest and any penalties. If you disagree with the findings—and remember, auditors do make mistakes—you can ask the auditor to send a form explaining his or her reasoning. At that point, you'll probably want to hire professional assistance, and you can:

- **choose to meet with the auditor again,** say, to present additional evidence;

> You needn't even go to the audit. You could hire a representative and give him or her written authorization to act for you.

When naming beneficiaries, it's wise to identify a spouse by his or her given name or a premarital surname, if appropriate.

■ **informally appeal to the auditor's boss;**
■ **appeal to the regional IRS office; or**
■ **take your case to the U.S. Tax Court.** If your case involves less than $50,000 for any one tax year, there are simplified procedures. You can get information about these procedures and other matters from the Clerk of the Tax Court, 400 Second St. N.W., Washington, DC 20217.

Whatever the disputed amount of your tax, if you're willing to pay it in advance, you could also take your case to the U.S. District Court or the U.S. Claims Court in Washington, D.C. If you win, the court will refund what you were overcharged.

In addition, if you "substantially prevail" in court (that is, you win), the IRS is shown to have been unreasonable, and you initially tried to work out your differences with the IRS, you may be reimbursed for your legal costs.

Life Insurance

What's the most common legal concern about life insurance? Simply making sure that anyone you've chosen to provide for after your death receives your life insurance funds as intended.

You can start by making sure that you get a policy. When you apply, make sure to answer all questions honestly; the life insurance company may double-check the information you provide with the Medical Information Bureau (see page 184). If you lie—say, about an illness you said that you didn't have—the life insurance company doesn't have to grant you a policy.

After the fact, suicide (see page 54) and out-and-out fraud are the two big reasons that a claim would be denied.

Of course, for most people, these won't be issues, and there are other precautions you can take.

Choosing Beneficiaries

Generally, you can designate anyone you want as your

beneficiary—relative, friend, business associate, charity. Usually you will name a primary beneficiary and a secondary, or contingent, beneficiary in case the primary one dies before you do. You can also name a third beneficiary in case neither of the first two survives you. If you name two or more beneficiaries in the same rank—say, both primary or both secondary—the funds will be divided equally unless you provide otherwise.

When naming beneficiaries, it's wise to identify a spouse by his or her given name or a premarital surname, if appropriate. For example, Mrs. John Nelson would be described as "Mrs. JoAnne Nelson" or, alternatively, as "Mrs. JoAnne Smith Nelson, wife of the insured."

Children—current and future, biological and adopted—can be referred to collectively as "my children" or "children of the insured," but you might want to be more specific in the case of stepchildren.

If you name your minor child as beneficiary, you can avoid legal problems by naming a trustee who can accept the money upon your death and administer it for the child's benefit until he or she reaches the age of majority. Unlike a minor, the trustee can provide the insurance company with valid receipts for payments, protecting the company from future claims. State laws vary, but by selecting a guardian you'll avoid having the state appoint one to receive and take care of the funds. (For more on this, see Chapter 12, "Your Estate.")

Planning for an Uncommon Disaster

When you fill out the beneficiary forms, you will be asked how you wish to plan for a common disaster, in which both husband and wife die in or from the same accident. Legal and tax problems can occur when one spouse outlives the other briefly. One approach for handling this is to arrange for the surviving spouse to receive proceeds as needed, with the balance going to the contingent beneficiaries upon his or her death. Ask your insurance agent to discuss other suggested plans for handling common disasters. For more on the estate-planning aspects of designating life insurance

Children— current and future, biological and adopted— can be referred to collectively as "my children" or "children of the insured," but you might want to be more specific in the case of stepchildren.

beneficiaries, see Chapter 12, "Your Estate."

Changing Your Beneficiaries

Most policies also allow you to change your beneficiaries if you so choose.

There are, however, a few legal restrictions:

- **If you previously named someone as the irrevocable beneficiary.** This usually comes up in cases of divorce and separation settlements, and requires you to obtain the permission of the current beneficiary, typically your former spouse.

- **If you live in a community-property state and your spouse is currently one of your beneficiaries.** You may be required to get her consent to change the designation if she would lose out on that part of the proceeds to which he or she otherwise would be entitled. If you change the beneficiary without your spouse's permission, the court may find that your new beneficiary is entitled to only half the proceeds—or, possibly, that she has no interest at all.

- **If you take out a policy on another person's life,** you, the beneficiary, must have an insurable interest in that person, meaning that you stand to benefit or lose by the insured person's survival or death. In other words, you couldn't take out a policy on the life of your neighbor or, say, the queen of England, because in neither case would you directly benefit or suffer as a consequence of the person's death. However, you could take out insurance on your spouse or domestic partner, and your parent could take out insurance on your life.

The Subject of Suicide

Generally, if you kill yourself within two years of buying a life insurance policy, most insurance companies will not pay off on the policy. Insurance companies are vigilant against suicides disguised as accidental deaths, a form of insurance fraud.

Your Car

Your car represents legal liability on wheels. Your personal vehicle isn't just a means of transportation but a large and powerful moving object with tremendous potential to injure other people and damage their property. That's one of the reasons that governments at all levels regulate how we own and operate our vehicles, in an effort to keep cars parked and traffic moving without total chaos. It's also why nearly every state requires vehicle owners to purchase minimum levels of automobile liability insurance, as a means of protecting owners against the nearly inevitable.

This chapter addresses the legal limits to and possible consequences of owning and operating a passenger vehicle. It poses and answers many related questions, including: What are your rights if you're pulled over? What if you don't agree that your ticket was fair? What if someone besides you gets into trouble with your car, whether or not you gave that driver permission? How much and what kind of liability protection do you really need? If your car has an unreasonable problem, how can you get the manufacturer to help pay for its repair? How can you protect yourself when buying a used car?

Driving Is a Legal Privilege

Even though it may seem that driving a car is a God-given right, it is, in fact, a privilege dependent upon your obtaining and keeping a valid driver's license. In almost half the states, you must be at least 16 years of age before you can apply for a regular driver's license (the extreme is Montana, age 15). Every state has its own program and requirements for obtaining a license—usually some combination of training leading to a learner's permit, written and behind-the-wheel tests, and fees—whether it's a new license, a required renewal or a license for a new resi-

LEGAL AGES TO DRIVE

To qualify for a regular driver's license, you have to reach the age listed below for your state. This doesn't mean, however, that you can't drive at a younger age. Most states have restrictive driver's licenses that allow you to drive when you are between 14 and 17 years of age. Many states have implemented Graduated License Programs, three-tiered programs that require teen drivers to get a provisional license, then an intermediate license before they can be eligible for a regular license. Provisional licenses generally require drivers to have adult supervision, while intermediate licenses have restrictions such as no nighttime driving or no teen passengers. The state may require parental approval or completion of or proof of enrollment in an approved driver's ed course. To determine the requirements in your state, contact your local department of motor vehicles.

Age 18
Arkansas
District of Columbia
Florida
Georgia
Indiana
Massachusetts
Missouri
New Hampshire
New Jersey
Virginia

Age 17
Alabama
   (17 yr. 6 mo.)
California
Colorado
Illinois

Iowa
Louisiana
Maryland
   (17 yr. 7 mo.)
Michigan
Minnesota
Nebraska
New York
Ohio
Oregon
Pennsylvania
Rhode Island
   (17 yr. 6 mo.)
Tennessee
Utah
Washington
West Virginia

Age 16
Alaska
Arizona
Connecticut
   (16 yr. 4 mo.)
Delaware
   (16 yr. 10 mo.)
Hawaii
Idaho
Kansas
Kentucky
   (16 yr. 6 mo.)
Maine
Mississippi
Nevada
New Mexico
   (16 yr. 6 mo.)

North Carolina
   (16 yr. 6 mo.)
North Dakota
Oklahoma
South Carolina
   (16 yr. 3 mo.)
South Dakota
Texas
   (16 yr. 6 mo.)
Vermont
Wisconsin
   (16 yr. 9 mo.)
Wyoming

Age 15
Montana

dent of the state. Whatever your need for more information, call the local office of your state's department of motor vehicles.

Driver's License Restrictions

Most states will test your vision when you apply for a license and will specify on your license what kind of corrective lenses you'll be required to wear when you are driving.

They will also refuse you a license if your record shows that you habitually drive while intoxicated or are addicted to drugs.

You'll probably also be asked to specify any chronic medical conditions that might impair your driving and cause you to lose control of your vehicle, such as epilepsy or narcolepsy, as well as any mental or physical disabilities that might impinge on your driving abilities.

It's your obligation to report any such conditions, and in some states it may be your doctor's obligation, too. Depending on your condition, your state might deny you a license altogether or impose restrictions on when and how you can drive. If you misrepresent your condition, the state could consider that falsification of an official document and charge you with a misdemeanor. (If you are so charged, you can get a court-appointed lawyer to represent you if you can't afford your own and you're entitled to a jury trial. Punishment can include a sentence of up to one year in prison and as much as $2,900 in fines and penalties.) If you're caught ignoring a restriction on your license, it could be suspended.

Your Legal Rights and Responsibilities

Once you've got your license, you pretty much have the right to go where you please—as long as you go there safely and with due caution, following the rules of the road as set by the state or

Continued on page 60

If you misrepresent your condition when applying for a license, the state could consider that falsification of an official document and charge you with a misdemeanor.

LICENSE AND INSURANCE QUESTIONS

Americans Abroad

Q. *Will my U.S. driver's license be sufficient for driving overseas? What about in Mexico and Canada?*

A. Like international tourists in the U.S., you can use your driver's license in many countries overseas, including Mexico and Canada. However, many countries do not recognize a U.S. driver's license. Most countries accept an international driver's permit, which translates information from your driver's license into nine languages, and it's a useful tool to have in case of an accident or medical emergency. The U.S. Department of State has authorized two organizations to issue international driving permits to those who hold valid U.S. driver's licenses: the American Automobile Association (AAA) and the American Automobile Touring Alliance. To apply for an international driving permit, you must be at least age 18, and you will need to present two passport-size photographs and your valid U.S. license. Certain countries require road permits, instead of tolls, to use on their divided highways, and they will fine those found driving without a permit.

Visitors to the U.S.

Q. *My cousin is coming to visit from Brazil. Will his driver's license be valid here?*

A. Yes. Under the United Nations Convention on Road Traffic (1949) and the Convention on the Regulation of Inter-American Automotive Traffic (1943), tourists from many countries, including your cousin's, can use their own domestic licenses while driving in the U.S., in combination with an International Driving Permit they should get in their own country before coming to the U.S. (see question and answer at left).

If your cousin decided to come back as a student or resident, however, then he would have to obtain a valid U.S. driver's license.

If your cousin were a visitor from a country that is not a member of the United Nations, he would have to apply for a valid driver's license after arriving in the United States.

For more information, contact your state's department of motor vehicles.

Proving Your Identity

Q. *I don't drive and don't intend to get a driver's license. But I'm always being asked for one as identification. Is there a substitute for a license that I could get?*

A. Inquire with your state's department of motor vehicles to see whether it offers picture IDs for nondrivers.

Too Old to Drive

Q. *My dad was once a fine driver, but he's 88 now and not what he used to be. Our family is afraid he will have an accident and hurt someone else or himself. He has* *already made it clear that he won't give up driving voluntarily. What can we do?*

A. Not much. About the best you can hope for is that the next time he has to renew his license, he'll fail any required tests. No state has a maximum age limit for getting a driver's license, but some require older drivers to pass vision or road tests and to renew their licenses more frequently than younger drivers. For example, in Hawaii, people over age 72 get licenses for only two years, rather than the usual four. And in Illinois, drivers over age 87 are issued one-year licenses only.

Otherwise, in most states, your dad's ability to hold a driver's license can usually be challenged only because of his driving record, especially if it includes any traffic violations or collisions. So, if your dad does have an accident, the state can require him to retake the driver's test, and if he fails, he'll probably lose his license. In some states, a complaint by a police officer or a family member can cause his driver's license to be reviewed and he may be retested.

But I'm Just Renting It

Q. *What's my liability when I rent a car?*

A. You're responsible for any damage or injury you cause while driving a rental car, just as if you were driving your own. Usually your own car insurance policy will cover you when driving rental cars for personal—not business—reasons, so you probably will not need to buy the optional coverage rental companies offer. But check your policy before renting, just to be sure.

If you don't have car insurance of your own, you should take the collision and liability insurance you're offered. (In some states, such as Illinois and New York, collision damage coverage is automatically provided by the rental car company, so you'll need to buy liability coverage only.) Check with your credit card company, too; it may provide coverage when you rent a car using its card. If you are a frequent renter, you may consider purchasing a nonowner auto policy.

Crash, Boom

Q. *What if my car is totaled?*

A. If your car is totaled and you don't like what your insurance company is offering you for it, you don't have to settle for the claims adjuster's first offer. Make a counteroffer. If that fails, take your case to a senior adjuster at the company. Bring your insurance agent in as an ally. If that still doesn't work, you can take your case to arbitration (see Chapter 1, "Living With the Law") or consult a lawyer to file a lawsuit. Expect the battle to get more and more expensive. You may decide to settle for an offer that's only a little better than you got to begin with.

You usually register a vehicle when you purchase it or when you become a new resident of a state, and must periodically renew the registration thereafter.

locality you're driving in; even interstate highway speed limits and seat-belt laws are state, not federal, laws. You do not have the right to illegally park, drive above the speed limit or drive while intoxicated. And if you are involved in an accident, even a fender-bender, you must at least stop and see what damage has been done and then leave your name, address and telephone number. (For more on what to do in case of an accident, see page 66).

How You Can Lose Your License

If you don't handle your car responsibly, you can get into a lot of legal trouble. The law varies from state to state, but in most places, too many tickets for moving violations (those incurred while you're actually driving the car), a drunk-driving conviction, or driving without insurance can lead to having your license suspended temporarily or even revoked permanently.

Your license could be suspended or revoked by a state other than the one that granted it to you if you're visiting or living there temporarily. Either the judge who hears your case or state law, or both, will determine how long the suspension will last.

If you are caught driving after your license has been suspended or revoked, you will probably be arrested; you could be convicted of a serious misdemeanor or possibly a felony offense in some states, with corresponding monetary penalties or jail time.

At some point after revocation, you may be able to apply for a new license; a state hearing will decide whether one will be granted.

Registering Your Car

A licensed driver is legally entitled to drive; a registered vehicle is legally entitled to be driven. You usually register a vehicle when you buy it or when you become a new resident of a state, and must periodically renew the registration. You will probably be required to provide proof of your legal ownership (the vehicle title), and the car must meet your state's mechanical safety and environmental standards. In many states, you may also have to prove you have obtained necessary liability insurance (see page 68).

How frequently you must renew your vehicle registration varies by state. If you move to a new state, you usually have 60 to 90 days within which to register your car in that state and acquire new license plates.

Violations by Degree

Sooner or later, every driver is bound to break one of the rules of the road. There are a range of violations, from the minor ones such as driving through a stop sign and speeding, to more serious ones such as reckless driving and leaving the scene of an accident. Each state has its own laws, but most states allow a driver only a certain number or type of violations within a one- or two-year period before he'll lose his license. There are essentially four types of citations:

- **a parking ticket;**
- **a notice to correct violation.** This is issued for equipment violations or minor violations of license or registration requirements;
- **a notice to appear** issued by a police officer after investigating an accident he didn't witness; and
- **a notice to appear** issued by an officer after witnessing a moving violation, which might include speeding, driving under the influence of alcohol, disregarding a traffic control device (such as a stop sign or light), failing to yield the right of way to pedestrians or other vehicles, driving recklessly and fleeing from an accident (hit-and-run).

DRIVING WHILE INTOXICATED. Driving while intoxicated or driving under the influence of alcohol or other drugs is a criminal offense. Each state has its own drunk-driving laws, but usually a driver is considered intoxicated if his blood alcohol content ranges from 0.08% to 0.10%. Depending on the state, it's possible to be charged even if you're just sitting in the car, not actually driving it while intoxi-

Most states allow a driver only a certain number or type of violations within a one- or two-year period before he'll lose his license.

If you're stopped by the police, you can refuse to take a Breathalyzer test, but the state can then suspend your license and most will do so immediately.

cated. Many states also have made it illegal to carry open alcoholic beverages in a vehicle.

Many states have clamped down on driving while intoxicated: The offense used to bring probation and suspended sentences. Now it can really cost you: Many states require mandatory fines, jail time, the revocation or suspension of the driver's license, community service work, or drug and alcohol rehabilitation programs.

If you're stopped by the police, you can refuse to take a Breathalyzer test, but the state can then suspend your license and most will do so immediately; in some states you're considered to have given your implied consent to taking a Breathalyzer test when you get your driver's license. If you are charged with driving under the influence in a state that has enacted an administrative suspension law, you can have your license automatically suspended if you fail to give a blood, urine or breath sample. The suspension will actually remain in effect even if you are found innocent of the charges against you.

If you're pulled over in a police roadblock designed to catch intoxicated drivers, remember that these have been found to be constitutional as long as they're not discriminatory. That is, troopers can stop everyone or every third person, but they can't, for example, stop just whites, African Americans or Hispanics.

RECKLESS DRIVING. Under the Uniform Vehicle Code, a national set of guidelines that states can follow when passing their own codes, reckless driving is driving with gross, willful or wanton disregard for the safety of persons or property. For example, a reckless driver is one who, though he may not have any desire to do harm, chooses to race down a residential street at 80 miles per hour—a choice that presents the possibility of causing an accident. The penalties for reckless driving vary from state to state. Reckless homicide—causing the death of another person while driving with reckless disregard—is a felony (a serious crime that carries more than a one-year prison sentence).

LEAVING THE SCENE OF AN ACCIDENT. If you are involved in a crash—if you hit someone or they hit you—and you leave without identifying yourself to the other motorist or the police (this is also known as hit-and-run), then you have broken the law. This is a serious violation. The consequences vary from state to state and depend upon the damage done, but you might have your license suspended, serve time in jail and receive a heavy fine.

Your Rights Regarding Search and Seizure

Because the Fourth Amendment of the U.S. Constitution protects citizens from unreasonable search and seizure, police usually need a warrant to search your home or other private property. They must request the warrant from the appropriate court and must show sufficient reason why the warrant should be issued. Cars, however, are an exception; the U.S. Supreme Court has ruled that citizens expect less privacy in a car.

Police officers cannot search your car unless they have a reasonable suspicion or probable cause to believe that you have committed a crime, have charged you with an offense and have taken you into custody (a custodial arrest).

■ **Reasonable suspicion** means there are facts that can establish that someone in the vehicle is involved in violating the law.

■ **Probable cause** is the suspicion of direct criminal involvement.

So a search could be legally made if the officer believes you are carrying a weapon, or are under the influence of drugs or alcohol. In most states, police can usually search both the passenger compartment and the trunk. The police might have probable cause if your car fits the description of one seen leaving the scene of an accident or crime, or one that has been stolen.

In recent years, the courts have become more liberal about what constitutes reasonable suspicion or probable cause.

Police usually need a warrant to search your home or other private property. Cars are an exception; the Supreme Court has ruled that citizens expect less privacy in a car.

In many states even if you have a permit to carry a firearm, you can't carry it in a vehicle.

WHAT ELSE CAN THE POLICE DO IF THEY STOP ME? They can confiscate anything that would serve as evidence. In a number of states, if you're arrested for driving under the influence, the police can impound your car and conduct an inventory search, listing its contents for purposes of evidence and to prevent theft (you'll eventually get your belongings back). But if they find something illegal, they can use it against you.

CAN THEY RESTRAIN ME? Yes, if you are charged with something and taken into custody. At that point, you can be handcuffed and you must receive the Miranda warning (see page 297 of the Appendix).

WHAT SHOULD I DO IF I THINK I'VE BEEN SUBJECTED TO UNREASONABLE SEARCH AND SEIZURE? If you believe that a police officer wasn't justified in stopping your car in the first place—he or she had no reasonable suspicion nor probable cause—call a lawyer.

CAN I CARRY A WEAPON IN MY CAR? State laws vary tremendously regarding your right to carry a firearm in your vehicle. In many states even if you have a permit to carry a firearm, you can't carry it in a vehicle. In others, you may be allowed to carry the weapon in your vehicle so long as it is unloaded, or you may be able to carry it in the trunk if the firing mechanism has been dismantled and the gun is unusable. If you hide the weapon in your glove compartment, purse or your basket of dirty laundry, that would be unlawful concealment of a weapon. Contact the attorney general's office to find out the laws governing transportation of weapons in your state.

Challenging a Citation
If you want to challenge a ticket or moving violation, you can go to court and argue your case. But before you fight, ask yourself: Is it worth the effort? You could end the whole thing by just paying the fine. On the other hand, the fine might involve a lot of money. And if you've received a moving citation, paying the fine is

an admission of guilt. Your charge will go on your record and might increase your chances of losing your license, not to mention pushing insurance costs up.

If you choose to proceed, you'll have to send in the appropriate form or appear in person for an arraignment. This is a legal proceeding at which you will be told the charges against you and given your rights, and you can "enter" your plea—in this case, not guilty. Check your ticket: It will show either an arraignment date or a deadline by which you have to decide how you'll plead. If you're far from home when you're charged, you will usually have to return to the distant location for your day in court.

If you do go to court, be aware that the judge is more likely to believe the police officer than you, so unless you have an independent witness—that is, preferably (but not necessarily) someone not involved in the accident—who can corroborate your versions of events, you shouldn't expect to win.

Do you need a lawyer? Generally not, if it's just a parking ticket. Parking tickets don't go on your driving record and don't affect your insurance premium, so the worst that can happen is that you lose your time and money if you're found guilty. For more serious cases, like reckless or drunk driving that could result in jail time, however, you should definitely call in a lawyer as soon as possible.

WHEN YOU'RE AWAY FROM HOME. What if you're charged with a moving violation—say, speeding— when you're far from home and you don't have sufficient funds or a credit card with which to pay your fine on the spot? In theory, the local police can put you in jail until you can obtain the funds; nowadays, however, most locales and states will release you with the expectation that you will pay the fine.

What if you get, say, a parking ticket outside your home state and simply ignore it? In theory, you could be extradited (arrested by officials of your own state and turned over to officials of the state in which you were charged with an offense), but in practice, for mis-

Unless you have an independent witness who can corroborate your versions of events, you shouldn't expect to win.

A witness's help is strictly voluntary; they're not obliged to report what they saw unless a police officer asks them to.

demeanor and traffic violations, you won't be. However, an arrest warrant could remain outstanding, and if you go back to that state you could be arrested.

Some states will consider you automatically guilty if you fail to respond to the ticket. In that case, your offense could be reported to your home state, where it will appear on your record and you'll be subject to your state's penalties—for example, points against your license.

In Case of an Accident

If you are involved in an accident, there are certain steps you should be sure to take. First, if someone is hurt or you think the damage is more than minor (about $100 to $200, depending on state law), you're required to contact the police. Without a police report of the accident, most insurers won't pay your claim.

More important, failure to report such an accident or leaving the scene can leave you open to criminal charges (see the preceding discussion).

Be sure to exchange pertinent information with the other driver if possible, including name, address, telephone number, driver's license number and license-plate number; year and make of the car; and name, address, and telephone number of the insurance company and agent. (Your auto insurance company may be able to provide you with copies of a standard accident report you can keep in your glove compartment.)

Ask any witnesses for their names and addresses, but be careful not to discuss the accident—or whose fault it was—with them or anyone else. This could come back to haunt you later—say, if you admitted to the witness that you thought the accident was your fault and you later deny it. Remember that the witnesses' help is strictly voluntary; they're not obliged to report what they saw unless a police officer asks them to.

Remember to contact your insurance company about the damage, regardless of whether you want to file a claim.

STATES THAT SHARE WHAT THEY KNOW

Forty-eight states and the District of Columbia belong to an agreement called the "Driver's License Compact." (The only states that don't belong are Michigan and Wisconsin.) When you get a ticket in one of these states, the department of motor vehicles will relay the information to your state—and the violation will add points to your driving record as if the ticket had been given at home.

If someone's been hurt, it's a good idea to get in touch with a lawyer for guidance concerning your rights and liability.

Also, see a doctor yourself as soon as possible. Even if you don't think you're injured, your doctor could spot minor symptoms that could lead to long-term health problems. (See page 75 for more information about reporting accidents to your insurer.)

WHEN YOU'RE THE WITNESS. Generally, if you are a witness to an accident, you have no legal obligation to volunteer information, but if an officer asks you what you saw and you fail to respond with what you know, you could be charged with obstructing justice or as an accessory to the crime. So, if you see an accident, your safest strategy is to stay and talk to the police.

WHEN YOU'RE THE GOOD SAMARITAN. Most states have Good Samaritan laws that place responsibility on licensed emergency medical technicians to act to help an injured person—and protects them if anything goes wrong while they are trying to help.

If you stop and help someone as a private citizen, you are not necessarily protected by this law. Unlike an EMT, you are under no obligation to help, so if you do undertake to actively help the person, you do so without automatic protection from liability. If you begin to help someone, continue until an ambulance or trained medical technician arrives. If you stop administering aid before help arrives and the person is

Most states require their drivers to have liability insurance, the cornerstone of any car insurance policy.

in worse shape than when you first arrived, you could be liable.

Liability Insurance Is Legal Insurance

If you (or someone else driving your car with your permission) cause an accident in which someone is killed or injured, or damage is done to someone else's car or property, you could suffer legal and financial catastrophe. The injured party could take you to court and sue you for damages, which in the worst case could amount to millions.

That's why most states require their drivers to have liability insurance, the cornerstone of any car insurance policy; the remaining states don't require this insurance if you can prove you can cover certain losses. (See the discussion of financial responsibility laws, below.) (Other kinds of optional coverage protect you in other circumstances, which we'll describe later.)

Say that you're clearly responsible for causing a car accident: You run a red light, hit another car and injure its driver. Your liability coverage obligates your insurance company to defend you against the injured party—in court, if need be—and pay claims to the other driver for vehicle damage and bodily injuries, including medical and hospital costs, rehabilitation, nursing care, and possibly lost income and pain and suffering.

Then again, say you're in a collision in which it would be difficult to pin the blame on either driver. Again, your insurance company must defend you against most proceedings the other driver might bring against you.

Required and Suggested Limits: How Much Coverage Is Enough?
The following primer should help you cover your legal liability if you're buying a new-car insurance policy, think you might need to revise the limits of an

existing policy, or are uncertain how your liability might be affected by upcoming changes in your life.

States legislate how you manage your liability in one of two ways: All states have financial-responsibility laws, meaning that you must show that you're able to cover any financial consequences of your liability after an accident, up to certain amounts. Most people meet this requirement with an insurance policy, though it may not be illegal to operate a vehicle without it. Some states also have compulsory auto liability insurance laws, meaning that it's illegal to drive without insurance, period.

Either way, state requirements for coverage of a driver's liability are modest: typically $10,000 to $50,000 for bodily injury suffered by one person, no more than $100,000 for all people hurt in the same accident and up to $25,000 for property damage resulting from that accident. Those amounts may sound like plenty, but not when you consider that damage claims can sometimes be settled in the millions.

Experts instead recommend a minimum of $100,000 in bodily-injury coverage per person, $300,000 in bodily-injury coverage per accident and $50,000 in property-damage coverage, or a minimum of $300,000 on a single-limit policy, which sets one liability limit for all expenses arising from the same accident.

Your insurance company need pay only up to the limits you selected when you chose your policy. Over and above the liability limit, the insurer is also responsible for the cost of any bail bonds (money put up to get you released from police custody and to ensure your appearance at your trial) and earnings that you give up when you attend hearings and trials at the insurer's request. However, many policies free the insurer from any obligation to continue your legal defense for sums above the liability limit you have chosen.

Filling Gaps Left by Liability Insurance

COLLISION COMPLICATIONS. Okay, so you can pursue compensation from a driver you believe is liable for causing damages to your car. But ask yourself, what if:

If the other driver is at fault, but his insurance company contests your claim, it may take a long time for you to collect.

The big drawback to liability coverage is that you have to prove someone was to blame for the accident in order to qualify for compensation.

■ **You cause the accident?** In that case, you can't collect for damage to your car by taking action against the other driver. Your own collision coverage will pay for the damage.

■ **The other driver is at fault,** but his insurance company contests your claim? It may take a long time for you to collect. With collision coverage, your insurance company can repair your car and take over your claim against the other driver (a procedure known as subrogation). Your insurer is ethically, but not legally, bound to fight for enough money to pay you back part or all of the deductible amount you had to pay before your coverage kicked in.

■ **The other driver is at fault** but has no liability insurance? Suing could get you involved in a long-term, fruitless legal tangle. The other driver's uninsured motorist coverage won't necessarily protect your car in these situations (see below). Your collision coverage does.

■ **You're the sole participant in the accident?** If you run your car into a tree or overturn it, there's no one to take action against. Only collision coverage will pay for the damage to your car.

THE OTHER GUY IS UNINSURED OR UNDERINSURED. An accident may clearly be the other driver's fault, but what if he or she doesn't have any liability insurance? There are plenty of drivers who go without, even where it's legally required. Uninsured/underinsured motorist coverage protects you against such drivers and will also protect you if you are injured by a hit-and-run driver. In some cases, it will protect you from a driver who is insured by a company that becomes insolvent.

Before you can benefit from this coverage, the other driver must be declared legally responsible for the accident. In most states, when the party to blame is in doubt or the amount payable is contested, you and your insurer have to submit to arbitration to settle your differences over how much the insurer should pay.

This kind of insurance usually covers only costs arising from bodily injuries, though in some states it covers property damage, too.

Generally, companies must pay claims up to the minimum amount fixed by your state for liability insurance, though you can often purchase higher limits for an additional premium.

The big drawback to liability coverage is that you have to prove someone was to blame for the accident in order to qualify for compensation. Proving fault, which is not always possible, can delay payment for your damage and lead to expensive legal action.

No-fault insurance (or personal-injury protection) is designed to take the fault out of liability. That way your insurance company will pay for your medical expenses regardless of who is to blame for the accident.

Twenty-six states and the District of Columbia have enacted plans that reduce the fault element in some way. Generally, these plans provide that:

■ **Your insurance company** has to pay you and others

STATES REQUIRING UNDERINSURED OR NO-FAULT COVERAGE

Underinsured Coverage		No-Fault Coverage
Connecticut	Oregon	Colorado
District of Columbia	Rhode Island	Florida
Illinois	South Carolina	Hawaii
Kansas	South Dakota	Kansas
Maine	Vermont	Kentucky
Maryland	Virginia	Massachusetts
Massachusetts	West Virginia	Michigan
Minnesota	Wisconsin	Minnesota
Missouri		New Jersey
New Hampshire		New York
New Jersey		North Dakota
New York		Pennsylvania
North Dakota		(Puerto Rico)
Ohio		Utah

STATES REQUIRING UNINSURED COVERAGE

Connecticut	Minnesota	Rhode Island
District of Columbia	Missouri	South Carolina
Illinois	New Hampshire	South Dakota
Kansas	New Jersey	Vermont
Maine	New York	Virginia
Maryland	North Dakota	West Virginia
Massachusetts	Oregon	Wisconsin

covered by your policy for medical bills, lost wages, the cost of hiring people to do household tasks you can't perform, and funeral expenses up to a certain limit.

■ **Property damage is excluded** from no-fault protection.

■ **Compensation for pain and suffering claims** aren't included and must be pursued by going to court in a liability action.

■ **You usually can't bring a liability suit** until expenses of the type covered by the no-fault insurance exceed a certain amount. Conversely, you are immune to suits by others until their costs exceed that limit. To protect themselves against fault-based suits permitted under no-fault regulations, drivers in some states where the limits are especially high must continue to buy traditional liability insurance. But liability payments may be reduced by compensation received under the no-fault provisions.

More What-Ifs of Liability

WHO'S LIABLE IF SOMEONE STEALS YOUR CAR AND HAS AN ACCIDENT OR COMMITS A CRIME? If you've taken all due precautions to protect your car, such as taking the key and locking the doors, you will not be liable if a thief steals your car and gets into an accident or commits a crime while in possession of your car. However, if you are found negligent—say, you left your car running and someone hopped in, drove off and ran over a pedestrian—you could be held liable. No, the police won't give you a ticket or throw you in jail for being irresponsible, but the victim's family could make a claim against your liability insurance or choose to sue you for damages over and above what your policy would cover.

WHO'S LIABLE IF YOU LEND YOUR CAR TO SOMEONE? Bottom line: You should never lend your car to anyone if you're not prepared to be legally liable for injury or damage caused by that person to himself or someone else.

At the very least, never lend your car to someone you know is an unsafe driver with a history of fender-benders, reckless driving, driving while intoxicated or other infractions. If he has an accident, and his victim can prove that you should have known better than to lend the car to him, you could be held liable.

If you lend your car to someone you believe to be a good driver, your liability for any accident he has may hinge on where you live. In some states, you may not be liable if you lend a car that's in good working condition to a friend who's in good driving order and who gets into an accident. In other states, you would be liable if you gave anyone permission to drive your car and he or she had an accident.

Most insurance policies will pay a claim if you've lent your car to a good driver for a one-time pleasure purpose. But if the company finds out that she or he regularly uses your car and isn't listed on the policy, it may not cover your claim.

If, for example, a nanny who cares for your children in your home uses your car regularly for family or personal business, you should add her to the list of drivers on your insurance policy to be sure you're covered for any accidents she has.

For more information on this aspect of liability, call your insurance agent or other company representative, or your state's department of insurance.

WHAT IF YOU DRIVE IN A CAR POOL OR DRIVE OTHER PEOPLE'S KIDS TO THE WEEKLY GAME? Some car owners decline to participate in either of these activities for fear

Bottom line: Never lend your car to anyone if you're not prepared to be legally liable for injury or damage caused by that person to himself or someone else.

EXTRA MEDICAL COVERAGE

If you participate in a car pool or chauffeur other people's kids, it might make sense (see the discussion in the text below) to purchase medical-payments coverage. This will cover you, your family members and guests in your car for reimbursement of medical costs resulting from auto accidents regardless of who is at fault. This coverage, however, may duplicate coverage already provided under your other medical policies, and you may not want to pay for it unless you're regularly carrying nonfamily members.

of being sued by carpoolers or parents in the event of an accident. That's unnecessary avoidance if you have the following insurance coverage:

Medical-payments coverage. If your passengers suffer injury in an accident while riding with you, you could be liable for any medical expenses they incur. Depending on the accident and without proper coverage, that could break you. Chances are your employer-provided group health insurance coverage (as opposed to a policy you purchase yourself) will cover only your own family members. Of course, your passengers may already be covered by their own health insurance, in which case you may be off the hook—unless their medical costs exceed their own coverage, or they or their insurer are particularly concerned about the issue of fault. If you don't want to take the chance, you can protect yourself by making sure that you have medical-payments coverage in your automobile insurance plan. Medical-payments insurance, optional in most states, will pick up the bill for all those injured in your car up to the limits of the coverage, typically $1,000 to $5,000 for each person.

Liability coverage. You could also be liable for any expenses, including claims for pain and suffering, over and above what the medical-payments coverage takes care of. For example, the parents of an injured child could sue you for negligence if they questioned your decisions as a driver. In this instance, your liability coverage would protect you up to the limits that you've chosen.

Depending on the degree of your exposure—the frequency or duration of your carpooling trips, the number of people you carry, or the degree to which others might perceive you as having significant financial resources (you can "afford" to be sued)—you may want to consider purchasing additional umbrella liability insurance, which typically boosts your coverage to $1 million. (See page 127, in Chapter 6, "Your Home and the Law.")

Uninsured/underinsured motorist coverage. Even if it's not required in your state, be sure to get uninsured (or underinsured) motorist coverage, which will protect you and your passengers from costs incurred if your car is hit by an uninsured driver (see the discussion on page 70).

Consult with your insurance agent to make sure you have sufficient coverage for your situation.

If you're driving others as a volunteer for an organization, see the box on page 132 of Chapter 6, "Your Home and the Law."

WHAT IF SOMEONE HITS YOU AND HAS NO INSURANCE?

If you have uninsured motorist coverage, which some states require (see page 72), then your insurance company will pick up the bill for any injury or damage the uninsured driver causes you. If you don't, an accident with an uninsured motorist could end up being extremely costly to you, depending on the limits and deductibles of your own auto-collision, medical-payments and health insurance coverage.

Dealing With Your Auto Insurance Company

When you file a claim with your insurance company or that of another driver, you may hit a wall of bureaucratic inertia. Your best strategy is to keep good

> **Even if it's not required in your state, be sure to get uninsured (or underinsured) motorist coverage.**

If you think your insurance company hasn't met its legal obligation, contact the commissioner of insurance in your state to complain.

records of all proceedings (including the names of company representatives, their phone numbers and extensions, and notes from your phone conversations with them) and to be assertive—tell the adjuster what you need, and if he or she can't solve your problem, ask to speak with a supervisor.

If your insurance company denies your claim, you may be able to sue and win. But first be sure you have a case. Double-check your policy's provisions to see that it covers your claim and that you submitted it within the allotted time limit. You're protected in other ways, too. In most states:

- **The insurance company must by law** investigate and pay claims within a reasonable time and promptly offer a reasonable explanation if it turns you down.
- **It can't delay settling on one part of your claim** in order to influence settling on another part; otherwise it could, for example, resist paying for car repairs to pressure you into settling quickly and possibly for less on bodily-injury costs.
- **Once liability (fault) has become clear,** the company must attempt to make a prompt, fair and equitable settlement.
- **It can't force you to begin legal action** by making an unreasonably low settlement offer; that is, the company can't just say, "So, sue us."

If you think your insurance company hasn't met its legal obligation, contact the commissioner of insurance in your state to complain. In most states, that office can't necessarily force the company to settle with you to your satisfaction, but it can throw its weight around and influence the outcome. You may also want to seek the advice of a lawyer about how to handle the situation and to see if you should sue your insurance company.

Should I pay for it myself?

Filing a claim under your car insurance may result in being penalized by your insurer with higher premiums (loss of preferred-customer discounts or add-ons for insurance surcharges) or a cancellation, depending on the terms of your policy. That's why drivers sometimes choose to pay for any damages themselves.

That's probably okay if the accident involved you, your car and an old stump. But it's legally risky if another car or person was involved and you could be considered at fault. Even if damages were minor and you don't want to file a claim, inform your insurance company promptly about the accident, as your policy most likely requires. That will protect you if you pay the victim for the damage but he comes back weeks or months later—having had time to think about it—and claims hidden damages or personal injuries. In that case, you'll end up having to refer him to your insurance company, anyway. And on top of that, key evidence might by then be lost. Whether the company would ultimately pay up would depend on the circumstances, company policy and state law.

What If You're Injured?

If you're seriously injured in an accident, you might want to hire an attorney, even if only to discuss whether you have reason enough to sue. The decision depends on how badly injured you were, whether you suffered any permanent damage and the type of claim, such as for medical and hospital costs, nursing care, lost income or pain and suffering. Sometimes the only way to get the other driver's insurance company to pay up is to sue it. Attorneys usually charge a percentage of the recovered amount in personal-injury cases, usually 30% to 40%. Plus, you might have to pay court costs if the case goes to trial. Few cases go that far. Usually the parties agree on a settlement out of court.

Look for an attorney with experience in injury claims. Start by asking your personal contacts for references, try a legal referral service or check the Yellow Pages.

The good news is that claimants typically get a bigger settlement with the help of a lawyer. The bad news

Even if you don't want to file a claim, inform your insurance company. That will protect you if the victim comes back later and claims hidden damages or personal injuries.

> ## LIFE'S LITTLE DISASTERS
>
> It would be hard to sue a deer for running into your car, and who do you blame when you find that your stereo has been ripped out of your car during the night? Comprehensive coverage protects you from such things as collision with an animal, falling objects, theft of the car or its contents, vandalism, earthquakes, floods, fire and civil commotion, such as if your car had been damaged in the World Trade Center bombing in New York City.

is that after paying the lawyer's fees, the net settlement may be less, in some cases, than the claimants could have gotten for themselves.

Car Repairs You Don't Think You Should Have to Pay for

With today's cars, you're less likely than ever to suffer ownership of an out-and-out lemon, the kind of car that fueled creation of many states' lemon laws in the 1970s and early '80s. But as a car owner, you may still occasionally have to deal with a recurring problem that isn't covered by your new-car warranty and that you think you shouldn't have to pay for. As with most consumer problems, you could sue the manufacturer in small-claims court or elsewhere. But that may not be necessary if you take strategic steps for getting your problem solved in the first place.

Here's a strategy for getting the dealer or carmaker to pay for all or part of a repair.

STAY COOL, CALM AND COLLECTED. Make your case politely but forcefully. Calmly insist that you're entitled to the company's consideration. Point out that you're a loyal customer, if that's the case. Don't threaten to take your business elsewhere: That leaves the manufacturer and the dealer little or no incentive to help because it's going to lose your business anyway.

IS IT JUST YOUR CAR, OR IS IT OTHERS, TOO? Determine whether a problem is unique or whether it's part of a widespread problem with that make and model.
- **Talk with other owners** who have cars like yours.
- **Contact the Office of Defects Investigation** of the National Highway Traffic Safety Administration (NHTSA, Office of Defects Investigation, NSA-Room 5319 Seventh St., S.W., Washington, DC 20590; 888-327-4236; or check your car's make and model on their Web site at www.nhtsa.dot.gov).

If NHTSA has complaints like yours on file, that may confirm that your problem isn't an isolated one.

NHTSA also keeps files of technical service bulletins, which carmakers send to dealers, describing new procedures for handling common repairs. For a fee, NHTSA can tell you whether service bulletins covering your car's problem have been issued and send you copies.

TELL THE DEALER HOW MUCH YOU WANT. Decide what you think is fair compensation by checking the cost with other dealerships. Then, talk with the service manager at the dealership or a salesperson, whomever you've had the most contact with. Most dealers can make free repairs without prior approval from the manufacturer, but if the cost is too high or the car is out of warranty, the dealer may have to get approval. The carmaker will want to settle the claim quickly to promote customer satisfaction.

ESCALATE IF NECESSARY. If the dealer ignores your request, call the carmaker's zone office—its regional management office—and insist that a representative discuss the matter with you. (You can call the manufacturer's "800" number listed in your owner's manual to find the nearest zone office.)

CALL IN THE CAVALRY. If all else fails, you can com-

You may be able to avail yourself of your state's lemon law. Nearly all states and the District of Columbia have them.

It's hard to know what kind of life a used car has led, and you don't want to end up with a dud or a stolen car, or entangled in a legal mess with the previous owner.

plain to your state representatives or your attorney general's consumer-protection office.

You may be able to avail yourself of your state's lemon law. Nearly all states and the District of Columbia have them, but their provisions vary. Many require the disputing parties to participate in arbitration. And in New York, for example, a car that has been declared a lemon by arbitrators will have that fact noted in its title. Most manufacturers don't want the headache of trying to sell a lemon, so they're often eager to settle a case before going to arbitration.

For more information about your state's lemon law, contact your state attorney general's office. (See also the discussion of arbitration in Chapter 1, "Living With the Law.")

For safety-related problems, contact the federal regulatory officials at NHTSA or the Center for Auto Safety (1825 Connecticut Ave., N.W., Suite 330, Washington, DC 20009-5708; 202-328-7700; www.autosafety.org) and ask to be included in any class-action suits it decides to pursue against a manufacturer.

GO TO COURT. You could take the manufacturer to small-claims court if the damages you're seeking are below your state's small-claims limit (see the list of state limits on page 10). You'll do best if you can show documents indicating that your case is not an isolated one. The threat of a court case may be enough to get the company rep to take another look.

AT EVERY STEP OF THE WAY. Keep well-organized files of your service records and receipts, related correspondence, supporting documents and research.

Protect Yourself When Buying Used

I t's hard to know what kind of life a used car has led, and you don't want to end up with a dud or a stolen car, or entangled in a legal mess with the previous owner. Regardless of whether the seller is a private owner or a used-car dealer, you can save yourself a lot of trouble by taking the following steps when buying used:

IF YOU'RE LOOKING FOR A PARTICULAR MAKE AND MODEL, DON'T BUY THE FIRST ONE YOU SEE. Test-drive several of the same car to learn about normal—and abnormal—characteristics.

DON'T BE OVERLY IMPRESSED WITH EXTERIOR LOOKS. Cars may be "detailed"—cleaned inside and out, painted or touched up—and the engine compartment even steam-cleaned. Outside, check for rust or leaking fluids. Inside, look for wear and tear on rugs, armrests, seats and pedals. Stained carpeting may indicate water leaks. Check to see that everything works—lights, signals, wipers and radio.

LOOK FOR REPAIRED ACCIDENT DAMAGE. Check for wavy sheet metal and mismatched paint. Even with the best masking, some paint adheres to chrome edges and logos. Because the body of most cars today also serves as the frame, it's important for all damage to be properly repaired. If you see evidence of repainting, investigate further. Otherwise, the car may not be safe to drive.

FIND OUT WHETHER THE CAR HAS EVER BEEN RE-CALLED FOR A SAFETY DEFECT. If it has been recalled, don't assume that the previous owner had it repaired. You can call the National Highway Traffic Safety Administration's hotline (888-327-4236) to find out whether the model you're interested in has ever been recalled by the carmaker or by NHTSA. Ask the owner of any recalled car for copies of the appropriate repair records.

TAKE A SERIOUS PROSPECT TO YOUR MECHANIC AND HAVE IT INSPECTED. In addition, many jurisdictions require a safety inspection, an emissions inspection or

If the seller doesn't know the true mileage (say, he claims that the odometer has been broken), you should probably look elsewhere for a car.

If you're buying a passenger vehicle from a used-car dealer, look for the "Buyer's Guide" sticker.

both at regular intervals during the car's lifetime. (Maryland requires an inspection upon transfer of ownership of a car.) Though these tests are valid only at the moment of testing, their successful completion does give some assurance of basic roadworthiness. Be sure to get copies of the inspection results and any reinspection confirming repairs.

GET EVERYTHING IN WRITING. Read all the car's papers and get copies of everything, including a signed mileage statement. Federal law requires disclosure of true mileage at every change in ownership. If the seller doesn't know the true mileage (say, he claims that the odometer has been broken), you should probably look elsewhere for a car.

HAVE A TITLE SEARCH MADE IF YOU HAVE DOUBTS ABOUT OWNERSHIP. At a private sale, the title should be in the seller's name. If you're buying from a dealer, the title should be in the previous owner's name or the dealer's name. You may have reason to suspect monkey business if: the previous owner's address is out of state; the title is in the name of a wholesaler or an auction company, especially with a post office box for an address; the odometer reading is obscured in any way; or the vehicle identification number (VIN) plate (visible through the windshield) appears to have been altered.

State motor vehicle offices sometimes, for a charge, can do a title search on a vehicle if you have the full serial number or VIN. Chances are you would pursue this only if the car in question is a very expensive or special one. Otherwise, pick another car.

Look for the Buyer's Guide

If you're buying a passenger vehicle from a used-car dealer, look for the "Buyer's Guide" sticker. Used-car dealers selling more than six passenger vehicles a year must display the sticker on a window of any vehicle other than a motorcycle or recreational vehicle. Required by the Federal Trade Commission's Used

Car Rule, the Buyer's Guide will tell you:

■ **Whether the vehicle comes with a warranty** and, if so, what specific protection the dealer will provide. If you negotiate any change in warranty coverage with the dealer, that change must be specified in the buyers guide, which will become part of your sales contract and override any provisions to the contrary.

■ **Whether the vehicle comes with no warranty—** "as is"—or with implied warranties only. If a car comes as is, you must pay for any problems yourself. An implied warranty says, basically, that the car will do what it's supposed to do. If a serious problem occurs, you may have some recdourse to get the dealer to take care of it—even if the problem was not apparent when you bought the car.

A NOTE ABOUT WARRANTIES FOR PRIVATE SALES. If you buy a car through a private owner, it will usually come as is and won't be covered by any implied warranties. One way to protect yourself is to ask the owner to write and sign a statement about the car's condition at the time of sale. Also, ask whether the car is still covered by the manufacturer's warranty or an extended service contract. You should ask to see any such warranties, get copies of them, and find out whether there are any limitations to or costs for transferring them to a new owner.

Buying and Selling a Home

Chapter 5

This is a mighty long chapter dealing with one legal transaction. There are good reasons for that: Chances are a home is the biggest asset you will ever own. And buying or selling a home is probably the most complex legal, contractual and financial transaction in which you'll ever take part. It's a stressful time, and the last thing you want is any legal headaches, now or later—possibly long after you've forgotten the details of the deal. This chapter will help you protect yourself by outlining your legal rights and responsibilities, and those of the other parties involved. For example, both buyer and seller may use the services of the same real estate agent, but only one can legally claim the agent's allegiance.

Bottom line: As a buyer you have the legal right to choose the house you want in a place you want without being discriminated against. You also have the right to expect the seller to accurately represent the house's condition to you at the time of the sale.

And as a seller you have the right to sell your home to whomever you wish, as long as you don't illegally discriminate (see "Discrimination Against Buyers," on page 98). You also have an obligation to be honest with the buyer about any material defects in the home. Concealing any problems with the house, such as faulty heating or electrical systems or a leaky roof, can come back to haunt you later (see "Telling the Truth About a House," on page 93.) Double-check to see that there are no liens on your house (see "Getting Good Title to Your New Home," on page 105) and that you have all

---

SORTING OUT AGENTS

You may hear agents referred to as brokers, sales agents and Realtors. Here's the difference:

A real estate broker is licensed by the state to conduct real estate business and to negotiate transactions for a fee.

A real estate agent represents the broker, usually as an independent contractor. He or she can sell real estate under the supervision of a licensed broker.

Both brokers and their representatives can call themselves agents, because both act as agents for their clients.

Not all brokers and agents are Realtors or Realtor Associates. These titles are reserved for members of the National Association of Realtors, a trade and lobby organization, which through its local boards of Realtors regulates the professional behavior of its members through voluntary compliance with its rules.

---

the proper permits and certificates of inspection for any improvements made to the home.

Paying attention to such issues will enable both the buyer and seller to get to the final settlement— or closing—faster and hassle-free. At that meeting, you'll sign final documents and exchange funds, even as a real estate attorney makes sure that all the legal i's are dotted and the t's crossed (see "The Act of Settlement," on page 109). If both buyer and seller have clearly specified what they want in the contract in the first place, there should be no surprises at the final walk-through inspection or at the closing table. The buyer won't find the refrigerator gone when he moves in, and the seller won't be shocked when the buyer asks where it is.

This chapter will cover these topics and more, fully explaining the legal ins and outs of buying or selling a home. The last part of the chapter discusses special legal concerns that buyers will have depending on the type of home they're buying, whether condo, co-op, new home or manufactured home. The next chapter discusses one of the greatest of legal liabilities—homeownership.

Hiring an Agent: Who Works for Whom?

You'll probably choose to work with a real estate agent while you're looking for a home or a buyer, negotiating, and bringing a deal to a successful close. Though the process begins with just you and an agent, as time wears on many more players may enter the picture. It's critical that everyone involved is aware of who owes whom allegiance—and that, in large part, depends on who pays whom.

How They're Paid

If you've never bought or sold a home, this brief rundown of how the process works will help you understand the "who owes what to whom" situations described later.

Most real estate agents are paid a sales commission—usually a percentage of the price of the property being sold—by the seller. It's possible that the same agent will list the house for sale ("put it on the market"), show the house to prospective buyers, find the buyer, negotiate the deal and follow the sale through to the end. If an agent both lists and sells a house, he or she will earn 100% of the commission.

However, the agent frequently doesn't get the whole pie because buyers who come to see the house may already have enlisted another agent to help them find a house. In that case, the seller's broker and the so-called selling broker, who brings in the buyer, will split the sales commission. And those brokers in turn will split their share of the commission with their respective agents, who probably did most of the work.

If You're the Buyer

No matter how warm, caring and helpful an agent seems to you, the buyer, remember that his job is to try to get the highest price he can for his client, the seller. This is true whether he listed the seller's house himself or is only bringing in the

> No matter how warm, caring and helpful an agent seems to you, the buyer, remember that his job is to try to get the highest price he can for his client, the seller.

It's not smart to tell a seller's agent too much about your strategies and intentions— all of which agents are duty-bound to tell sellers.

buyer (that is, working as a subagent). Since his obligation to the seller (also called dual agency) is in direct conflict with the buyer's interest, a broker cannot by law represent both sides of a real estate deal without both parties' written consent. And in most states and the District of Columbia, agents must disclose their legal and financial arrangements with sellers, whom they represent, to the buyers they help. That's why it's not smart to tell a seller's agent too much about your strategies and intentions—all of which agents are duty-bound to tell sellers.

Ultimately, legalities aside, this arrangement between a buyer's and a seller's agent is risky business. The agent gambles that in return for her time and service, you will be loyal enough to buy a home through her. You gamble that your loyalty will reward you with good service and a great home. But, of course, the agent and the buyer aren't contractually obligated to each other.

Buyer What-ifs With Agents

The question of who owes whom what, whether service or payment, can sometimes get a little complicated. Here's a rundown of how it works in several situations.

WHAT IF AN AGENT TAKES YOU TO A HOUSE AND TOURS IT WITH YOU THE FIRST TIME YOU SEE IT? You should submit your purchase offer through him or her. If you don't, that agent may still be entitled to a share of the sales commission from the seller if you ultimately buy the house—even if by that time you've hooked up with an agent of your choice. The more agents involved, the more diluted the power of the sales commission in your negotiations with the seller. That's why it's a good idea to hook up with your agent of choice before you begin looking at houses.

WHAT IF AN AGENT MERELY MENTIONS THAT A PARTICULAR HOUSE IS FOR SALE, BUT YOU FIRST TOUR IT BY YOURSELF OR WITH ANOTHER AGENT? The first agent will probably not have any claim to part of the commission. (That's why an agent won't give you the address of a listing when you call but will offer to take you there instead.)

WHAT IF YOU USE MORE THAN ONE AGENT TO HELP YOU WITH A HOUSE HUNT? You should make it clear that you will remain loyal to whichever agent shows you the house you ultimately want to buy. (You might want to do this if the house you're looking for is really special or if the market is really hot and houses are moving fast.)

WHAT IF THE HOUSE YOU WANT IS FOR SALE BY OWNER (A "FISBO")? This means that the seller is working alone without the benefit of a seller's agent. If you are also working without an agent, you should seek the advice of a good attorney or hire an agent to help you negotiate.

WHAT IF YOU FIND A FISBO WHILE WORKING WITH AN AGENT YOU HAVEN'T COMMITTED YOURSELF TO?
- **You could abandon the agent** and deal directly with the seller, with no compensation to the agent. An agent knows she'll be paid only if you buy a listed house that you first saw with her.
- **You could deal directly with the seller** but pay the agent a modest fee for the time and effort spent on you. You're probably not legally obligated to do so.
- **You could persuade the seller to accept your agent** and pay the agent, say, a 3% commission (about half the usual 6% or 7% commission) or a sum you agree on. The agent can then help get everyone to closing without a hitch.

Hire Your Own Buyer's Broker
If you want absolute loyalty, you could hire your own buyer's broker. In this single-agency relationship, you pay the agent by the hour or with a set-in-advance fee. The compensation preferably wouldn't be tied to the selling price of the house because that could create a conflict of interest.

If you want absolute loyalty, you could hire your own buyer's broker. In this single-agency relationship, you pay the agent by the hour or with a set-in-advance fee.

If you're the seller, once you've selected an agent, you'll work out an employment contract—the real estate listing.

However, some so-called buyer's brokers engage in fee-splitting. They contract with you to represent your interests and they must disclose this to sellers, but their fee is paid by the seller and tied to the sale price of the home—a potential conflict of interest. If you consider working with an agent this way, raise your concerns about conflict of interest and address them in writing in any contract you sign with him or her. Ask what will happen if you buy a property soon after your agreement with the buyer's broker ends. Will the broker get a commission? If so, under what conditions?

To find a buyer's broker in your area, contact the Buyer's Broker Registry, a free referral service, at 800-729-4663 or www.thebuyersbroker.com.

The Risk of Representing Yourself

If you feel confident about your abilities, you may choose not to hire a real estate agent, or to hire one only for her negotiating skills and administrative help in getting the deal to the closing table.

Either way, you will want to find a real estate lawyer who can represent your interests, decipher the contract form, suggest contingency clauses and help with any final negotiating. You can get the names of experienced lawyers from friends or the local bar association, listed under "Lawyers Referral Services" in the Yellow Pages. Ask for an estimate of the fee, whether for just reviewing a contract or for actually being present at settlement.

If You're the Seller

Once you've selected an agent, you'll work out an employment contract—the real estate listing—with the agent's broker. The contract appoints the broker (and his agents) as your agent for locating a buyer for your home who meets the conditions set out in the listing. This agreement, whether oral or written, exclusive or nonexclusive (as defined on page 91) is a legally enforceable contract—that is, an agreement a court would force you to uphold. Keep in mind that you can adapt the standard real estate agency contract to your needs.

With any kind of listing, if the agent brings you the deal that the listing calls for—the full price and exact terms offered by a buyer who is ready, willing and able to buy—then you are legally obliged to pay a commission whether you accept the deal or not.

HOW YOU WILL PAY. Most commonly you and your agent will enter into a contract specifying that the agent has the exclusive right to sell your property. But your situation may call for another arrangement for paying the broker and his agent that is better suited to your needs. Your options are:

> **IF YOU'RE BEING TRANSFERRED**
>
> What if you're being transferred and your employer has guaranteed to buy your home at a discount if you can't get a better offer on the open market? In that case, make sure you amend an exclusive-right-to-sell agreement to keep an agent from claiming a commission if your company ends up buying the property.

- **Exclusive right to sell.** This entitles the listing agent to a commission no matter who sells the property, including you. If another agent produces the buyer, you still owe only one commission, which both agents will share.

- **Exclusive agency.** You don't pay a commission if you find your own buyer without help from the agent.

- **Open.** You agree to pay a commission to any agent so long as he or she is the first to produce an acceptable buyer. You don't owe any commission if you are the first one to find a buyer. This is the kind of listing often used by sellers who want to do most of the selling work themselves but want an agent's cooperation in finding buyers. The commission is typically half of the standard rate, about 3%. You can sign such an agreement with each agent who expresses an interest in bringing a buyer to see the home. But make sure to specify an expiration date on each agreement because you can't sign an exclusive listing with one agent if you have any open listings still in force.

WHAT IF YOU FOUND A BUYER EARLY ON?

What if you have a good prospect who entered the picture before you listed the property with an agent? Ask for an exclusive-agency agreement and add a clause that says you may sell the house to this named party—or any other that you find yourself—without paying a commission to the agent. Be prepared for rejection, though—some agents won't agree to this type of listing. If you do sell on your own, they will not be compensated for their time and marketing efforts.

PROVISIONS TO AVOID OR INCLUDE

■ **Don't sign an agreement** that automatically extends the listing beyond the usual three to six months. Designed to protect the agent, that provision could obligate you to continue working with an unsatisfactory agent.

■ **Do consider adding a clause reinforcing your right to cancel** the contract if you think the agent has failed to do a good job. You could still end up liable for certain expenses incurred by the agent, and some listing contracts may require you to pay a penalty for having canceled.

■ **Do make sure the so-called protection period** protects you, not just the agent. Protection periods typically last 90 to 180 days after a contract ends. If the listing expires and you sell your home to someone your former agent helped find, you may still owe a commission to that agent. In fairness to you, the provision should also require that the agent give you the names of any prospective buyers before the contract ends and that any written purchase offers be presented within a reasonable time after the listing expires.

■ **Do see that the listing agreement** describes the general condition of the property. It should show what items or features are being sold "as is" and what, if anything, will be repaired, removed, substituted or altered prior to settlement. The agreement should list every fixture that will be sold with the house, as well as those that will not. If the agreement doesn't adequately describe the current condition of the structure, appliances, and electrical, mechanical and plumbing systems, have it corrected or write a letter to the agent setting out the information (see the discussion of disclosure, beginning below).

■ **Do ask the agent to attach a marketing plan** as an addendum to the contract. This describes how the agent plans to advertise and sell your home, and it can serve as documentation if you think the agent isn't living up to her promises. (Some agents don't use formal marketing plans, so you may find they are unwilling to provide one. If that's the norm in your area, okay; but if not, you may want to seek an agent who can and will provide one.)

Your Liability for Misrepresentation

What happens if you, as a seller, don't hire an agent and a buyer believes that you have misrepresented the situation? You could end up in arbitration, as most sales contracts require, or you could be sued. Your settlement lawyer could try to step in and negotiate a way out or remedy the situation. If you represent yourself, be sure to keep a diary documenting thoroughly all disclosures and information shared with the buyer. If there are problems later, this could help verify what you have said to the buyer.

If you work with an agent from the beginning, however, you somewhat lessen your liability if there's a suit because the agent and the brokerage firm will probably be named with you as defendants. That's because under the law governing agencies, it's assumed that client and agent are privy to the same knowledge.

Telling the Truth About a House

Buyers have a right to know about the true condition of your house and property. While "caveat emptor"

If you work with an agent from the beginning, you somewhat lessen your liability if there's a suit because the agent and the brokerage firm will probably be named with you as defendants.

BUYERS' AND SELLERS' QUESTIONS

Exclusions Old and New
Q. *I used the old once-in-a-lifetime $125,000 exclusion in the past. Am I eligible for the $250,000 exclusion?*
A. No matter. You can still use the new exclusion.

His-and-Her Tax Breaks
Q. *My fiancé and I each own a home. We plan to sell one after the wedding. How does this effect our exclusion?*
A. Assuming that each of you lived in your houses for two of the five years before you decided to sell the house, you can each exclude up to $250,000 of profit. A similar rule holds that if you marry someone who has sold a home and excluded the gain prior to the marriage, that sale doesn't prevent you from claiming a $250,000 exclusion if you sell your home within two years.

Divvying up the Profit
Q. *After our divorce my spouse wishes to sell the family home. Can we each exclude $250,000?*
A. Assuming both of you pass the two-out-of-five ownership and residency tests, you can each deduct up to $250,000 of the gain on your individual returns. If ownership of a home is transferred to you in a divorce, the time your former spouse owned the place is added to your period of ownership before the sale for the purpose of the two-year-test.

Counting the Years
Q. *My widowed mother has to go into a nursing home and her home is being put up for sale. Is she entitled to the $250,000 exclusion?*
A. Your mother would qualify for the $250,000 exclusion, assuming she owned and lived in the house for at least one year and when time spent in the nursing home is included she meets the two-out-of-five-year tests.

Exclusions on Inherited Property
Q. *My spouse died and I did not sell my home until the following year when I no longer qualified to file a joint return. How much of the gain can I exclude?*
A. Your maximum exclusion would be

(buyer beware) used to be the rule of thumb in real estate, these days the law usually comes down on the side of the buyer. If you don't disclose problems and the buyer later discovers them, in most states the buyer can sue you, your agent, and his or her broker—and will often win.

PATENT DEFECTS: EASY TO SEE. If you're selling your home in a state that still has a "buyer beware" philosophy, you may have less liability for easily detectable

$250,000 not $500,000. But if your spouse jointly owned the home, the half of the profit built up before his or her death would be forgiven because the tax basis on that half would be whatever it was worth on the spouse's date of death. (See the discussion of tax basis of inherited property in Chapter 12.)

If the Seller Dies
Q. *What if I have a contract to buy a house and the seller dies before settlement?*
A. Your contract should bind the executors of the estate to proceed with the sale of the house to you. But you'll need an attorney's help to establish your claim and keep the process on track.

Cooling Off on a Timeshare
Q. *I've heard that there's a cooling-off period after you decide to buy a timeshare unit. What is it, and how does this protect me?*
A. Most states with resort areas have enacted laws designed to protect buyers of timeshares. To avoid unnecessary legal hassles, most states mandate that the buyer have at least three days after signing a purchase contract to reconsider the deal and cancel the purchase contract without penalty. This not only gives you an out if you've made an impulse purchase but also gives you time to have a lawyer who specializes in timeshares review the contract and to be sure that the resort is financially sound.

Keep Track of Your Home's Cost Basis
Q. *Do the new tax rules mean I don't have to keep records of improvements so I know what my basis is?*
A. You should still keep track of your home's cost basis, which is the cash you've invested in your home, in case you ever need to figure depreciation deductions for a home office or for a room you've rented out. Those portions of the house don't qualify for tax-free gains. Keep invoices for any major home improvements you make over the years, too. The cost adds to your cost basis and cuts potential tax gains. When you sell your home you can't take deductions for points you agree to pay on the buyer's behalf.

defects (*patent* defects), unless you make misleading comments about them. Agents should also tell buyers about problems they're aware of; they can be held accountable for giving buyers misinformation about things they should have known.

MATERIAL DEFECTS: INVISIBLE FLAWS. If you are a seller, most states require you and your agent to warn buyers of any problems that wouldn't be picked up during a routine inspection and that would change a

You're responsible for any hidden defects that a responsible buyer couldn't discover.

buyer's assessment of the value of the house (material defects), such as a bad septic tank, a cracked foundation, a leaky basement or the presence of radon (see the discussion of environmental hazards, below).

You should tell buyers about known structural deficiencies or building-code violations and any work done without a permit.

You're also responsible for any hidden defects that a responsible buyer couldn't discover. That could be a problem that's seasonal, such as a well that goes dry in the summer or a basement that leaks when the snow melts in the spring.

You can probably be held responsible for problems that have been covered up—say, a water stain covered over with paneling.

ENVIRONMENTAL HAZARDS. Depending on your state's law, you may be required to reveal known problems, including radon, lead-based paint and asbestos.

■ **Radon.** You can check with your real estate agent about radon-disclosure requirements and with your state or local environmental office about testing methods. Some home buyers are including contingency clauses in sales contracts that require testing for and sometimes correction of radon problems before they buy. You can also request a copy of the Environmental Protection Agency's *Home Buyer's and Seller's Guide to Radon* from your state's radon, radiation control or radiological health office, or request it from the EPA (National Service Center for Environmental Publications, P.O. Box 42419, Cincinnati, OH 45242-2419; 800-490-9198; www.epa.gov; single copies are free).

■ **Lead.** Several states have lead-based-paint disclosures as part of their mandatory property-condition reports (prepared by homeowners, not home inspectors). Your local real estate agent should be able to tell you if your state requires such disclosure. When you sell a home built before 1978, federal law requires that you tell all prospective buyers about known lead-based paint used in and around the property.

PROTECT YOURSELF. As a seller, you should shift as much liability as you can from yourself to the real estate professionals who help you sell your home. Any agent should inform you of your responsibilities and assume his or hers, too. Buyers should use home inspectors who carry errors-and-omissions insurance, which is liability protection against malpractice or business mistakes. The fact that they're protected protects you in turn. You can discuss any potential liability with your lawyer.

Many states require that sellers fill out written disclosure forms. Practically speaking, the more you disclose, the better. It's better to get a lower price for your house now than to be sued for fraud and misrepresentation later.

> **Practically speaking, the more you disclose, the better. It's better to get a lower price for your house now than to be sued later.**

If You Have a Beef With Your Agent—or Vice Versa

As a buyer or seller, you should expect that the agent will meet the letter of state and federal laws regulating real estate transactions, many of which this chapter discusses. You should expect that he or she will also comply with the professional and ethical standards set by the real estate industry, as represented by the National Association of Realtors (www.realtor.org), as well as any promises made in a listing contract.

Before hiring any agent you can check his or her reputation and any record of complaints with your state's agency regulating the real estate profession.

You should also ask how any disagreements will be handled. As mentioned previously, most sales contracts require that both parties agree to submit to binding arbitration, using a neutral third party, in situations that might otherwise result in a lawsuit.

If a problem arises once you've signed a contract, try to talk to your agent first. If you're left unsatisfied,

If a problem arises once you've signed a contract, try to talk to your agent first. If you're unsatisfied, speak with his or her broker.

you can speak with his or her broker. Both have a vested interest in keeping your business and preserving their reputations in the community.

If that fails, you could take your complaint to the local real estate board, which will hold a hearing and listen to both sides. It may give the Realtor a warning, impose a fine, or remove him or her from the board, but it can't suspend or revoke a real estate license.

If you believe that the Realtor is not meeting the letter of the law, you should also contact the state agency regulating the real estate profession, which will be interested in any license violations. The state regulatory agency could fine the Realtor, force him or her to take a certain number of continuing-education credits, provide restitution to the buyer, or suspend or revoke the Realtor's license.

Discrimination Against Buyers

Federal fair-housing laws, as well as many state and city laws, prohibit discrimination because of race, sex, color or nation of origin; some state laws forbid discrimination against buyers because of sexual orientation or marital status. That doesn't mean that you won't be discriminated against when trying to buy a house.

A broker might claim that a house in a particularly exclusive neighborhood is sold or has just been taken off the market, or might refuse to show you anything at all in the neighborhood or new development. You might be told that you couldn't afford anything there. Though he might not tell you directly, a seller might refuse to sell a home to you because he thinks your race or religion would make a neighbor angry. When it comes time to get a mortgage, a discriminatory lender might turn you down to prevent you from purchasing a house in a particular neighborhood only because you are a person of color, or a woman, or a member of a religious group. All these actions are illegal. A lender must assess only your financial qualifications, including past, current and future earnings. (For more on discrimination and what to do about it, see the reference

---

FOR MORE INFORMATION

If you think you've been discriminated against, you can contact a civil rights or real estate lawyer, or:

■ **The National Fair Housing Alliance** (1212 New York Ave., Suite 525, Washington, DC 20005; 202-898-1661; www .nationalfairhousing.org), through its local offices, conducts "testing." Someone will pose as a buyer or renter to see whether he or she experiences the same type of discrimination as you did. This information can prove very helpful if you take your case to court.

■ **The HUD Housing Discrimination Hotline** (Office of Fair Housing and Equal Opportunity, Department of Housing and Urban Development, Room 5204, 451 Seventh St., S.W., Washington,

DC 20410-2000; 800-669-9777; www.hud.gov/hdiscrim.html) provides information on fair housing and will investigate individual complaints of discrimination.

■ **The U.S. Department of Justice** (U.S. Department of Justice, Civil Rights Division, 950 Pennsylvania Ave., N.W., Housing and Civil Enforcement Section, NWB, Washington, DC 20530; 800-896-7743; 202-514-1116; www.usdoj .gov/crt/housing/) will investigate cases that indicate a pattern or practice of discrimination, such as cases of suspected discrimination by large property owners or a city housing authority. The department shares information with HUD.

---

to the Federal Truth in Lending Act in Chapter 3.)

The Rules for Real Estate Professionals

Under federal fair-housing laws, agents and mortgage lenders must not:

■ **refuse to sell, rent, deal or negotiate** with you because of your race, color, religion, sex or national origin, or because you are disabled or have children under 18;

■ **deny that housing is available** for inspection, sale or rent when it really is available;

■ **persuade owners to sell or rent their homes** by telling them that minority groups are moving into the neighborhood—a practice called block busting; or

■ **set different terms or conditions** for mortgage financing based on race, creed, religion, sex, national origin, disability or pregnancy.

What to Do in the Face of Discrimination

If you think you're being discriminated against, keep a

You have the right to add or delete any contingencies or clauses to protect your interests or meet your special needs.

record of meetings and phone calls with all the details, including what happened and what was said. Keep any other appropriate documents, such as business cards, copies of applications, and so on.

Confront the person and demand an explanation. If you don't get a good answer from a real estate agent, write a letter to the agent's broker-supervisor and send a similar letter to your state's department of real estate.

You should also complain in writing to the fair-housing agency in the city, county or state where you are house-hunting. It must begin an investigation within 30 days and proceed with "reasonable promptness." You can contact the National Fair Housing Alliance (see box on page 99) for the number of a fair-housing group near you.

Alternatively, you can file a complaint with the Department of Housing and Urban Development (HUD) within one year of your encounter, or you can consult a lawyer, who could take your complaint directly to a state or local court within 180 days or to federal district court within two years.

A Good Purchase Contract

Prospective buyer and seller have found each other. Now it's time for the buyer to make the seller an offer, in writing. Whether it's called a contract to purchase, an offer, a binder or an earnest-money agreement, a written and signed (ratified) purchase offer binds both buyer and seller to the deal. Any offer, including the first one, should be comprehensive; once the seller has agreed to it, it may be too late to add anything.

Protecting the Buyer's Interests
You can have your attorney or buyer's agent draw up a purchase contract, or, if you're working with a seller's agent, he or she will probably provide his or her broker's standard contract form. This form, however, will be written from the point of view of protecting the seller. You have the right, of course, to add or delete

any contingencies or clauses to protect your interests or meet your special needs.

Here are some ideas for provisions you might wish to include; your lawyer or buyer's broker may suggest others.

EARNEST-MONEY DEPOSIT. You're not required by law to make a deposit of a certain size, or any deposit at all, except in cases of court-ordered sales (foreclosure). But sellers almost always judge the seriousness of an offer by the size of the deposit.

Find out whether the earnest-money check will be deposited in a trust account or with a neutral third party, such as a title company, escrow service or attorney acting as an escrow agent. If not, insert that requirement. You can also require that the funds be held in an interest-bearing account and that you be credited with any interest at settlement. Set out any conditions for return of your money, including how quickly you'll get it back if the offer expires or you withdraw it, or if for some reason the seller decides not to sell. This will help protect you from having to sue to get your money back from an unregulated private individual if the deal goes bad.

Keep in mind that the contract could specify that the seller keep the earnest money as compensation for his time or any lost opportunities if you pull out or don't meet the terms of your offer. One strategy is for the seller to try to label the earnest money "option

> **Find out whether the earnest-money check will be deposited in a trust account or with a neutral third party. If not, insert that requirement.**

SAFEGUARD YOUR DEPOSIT

When you make out your earnest-money check, you'll be asked to make it out to the real estate agent's firm, his or her managing broker, the escrow or title company, or the lawyer. Add the words "trustee," "fiduciary agent," or "escrow agent" after the name on the check, and never make the check out to the seller. This will prevent anyone from being tempted to cash the check and carelessly or maliciously abscond with the funds.

The contract could specify that the seller keep the earnest money as compensation for his time or any lost opportunities if you pull out or don't meet the terms of your offer.

money," giving you an option to buy the house for, say, six months (which may be longer than the period prior to settlement noted on your contract, usually 45 to 60 days). If you don't buy the house for whatever reason within that period, the seller keeps the money.

DEED AND TITLE CONDITION. You'll want to make the deal dependent on your receiving an unencumbered deed and clear title to the property (see the discussion beginning on page 105).

SETTLEMENT DATE AND POSSESSION. Settlement usually occurs 30 to 60 days from the date of signing. If you need to move in before closing or the seller needs to move out a day or two after closing, a separate rental agreement will be necessary. Make sure all documents are prepared and reviewed by an attorney before you accept them.

But even better, do your best to avoid renting because these arrangements can have horrendous consequences. One issue is the potential liability for damage while living in a place you don't own—in the worst case, the house burns down. The seller may also face tax consequences having do with whether the house is viewed as investment property or a personal residence.

You could address liability and other renting questions in the sales contract. You'll find, however, that if you are planning to rent for only a few days, the time and energy it takes to reduce liability, as well as the money it takes to get proper insurance in this arrangement (not to mention the potential for aggravating the overall transaction) are too much. It's probably cheaper to stay in a hotel.

SETTLEMENT AGENT. The contract usually specifies the attorney or title company that will perform final settlement services.

RESPONSE-TIME LIMIT. This requires the seller to respond to your offer in writing within, say, 48 hours, or the offer will be void. The deadline helps protect you from having your offer shopped—that is, used to push a slower buyer into topping your offer. You can withdraw and cancel your offer at any time before the seller has accepted it and you have received notice of it according to the contract.

HOME INSPECTION. This gives you the right to have the property inspected and to withdraw your offer if the inspection report isn't satisfactory to you for any reason. And, it may allow for price adjustments to pay for any necessary repairs. The contract specifies who will do the inspection, usually "a recognized professional," and how long you have to get it done. If some part of the house is off-limits, say, because of the weather or season, you can retain the right to get that part inspected before removing the contingency, but not after closing. If the inspector finds something catastrophic, you're out and off the hook.

ENVIRONMENTAL TESTS AND TERMITE INSPECTIONS. You might want to have the property inspected for radon, lead paint, asbestos, or urea formaldehyde insulation. Make sure the appropriate contingency clauses, similar to the one for home inspection (see above), are added to your contract. (See also the discussion of seller disclosure, "Telling the Truth About a House," on page 93.) If termite (or pest) inspection is not required, be sure that there is a clause adding it.

WHAT GOES WITH THE HOUSE. The more specific the list, the better. Don't make any assumptions about appliances or what appear to be built-ins, such as bookcases, carpeting or cabinets.

CONDITION OF THE HOUSE. Specify what must be in apparent working order on the day of settlement, to be verified by a walk-through inspection. That's no guarantee they'll work later, though. Anything you'll get "as is," should be noted. You can ask that the house be empty of all left-over stuff, especially in the attic, basement or garage, and that it be left in broom-clean condition.

You have the right to have the property inspected and to withdraw your offer if the inspection report isn't satisfactory to you for any reason.

Specify what must be in apparent working order on the day of settlement, to be verified by a walk-through inspection.

The Ratified Contract

Once you've presented your purchase offer and the seller has considered it, he or she may come back to you with a counteroffer, which may simply be revisions to your original contract form. The seller will sign it and note a time limit for your consideration. If it's okay with you, you sign, too. If a counter to the counter is in order, you may want to start with a clean agreement to avoid any confusion over multiple changes. Once you've both agreed and signed, you have a binding contract.

Breaking a Contract to Buy or Sell

Whether you're a buyer or a seller, if you try to back out of a contract it will probably cost you. If the seller breaks the contract, he must be willing to reimburse the buyer for the money she's put out during the process. That might include the earnest-money deposit, the cost of a home inspection, and any fees associated with applying for a mortgage. More likely, however, the buyer may sue him for specific performance and make him adhere to the contract. If the buyer ends up having to purchase a more expensive home, say, because she has already sold her previous home, she could conceivably sue the original seller for the difference. Or, if the buyer insists on buying the house, she could take the seller to court where he could be compelled to live up to the deal.

But the buyer isn't the only one who's protected if the deal does not close. If the buyer backs out, the seller can keep the earnest money if the contract says so. If the seller ends up having to sell to someone else for less money, say, because he's already bought another home, he could conceivably ask the original buyer to make up the difference in price and to pick up any expenses he's incurred during the process. He, too, can go to court and try to compel the buyer to actually purchase the property according to the terms agreed upon.

Getting Good Title to Your New Home

Basically, holding clear title to property means that you, as its owner, have the right to own, possess, use, control and dispose of the property, free of any legal "encumbrances"—that is, impediments or claims by other people against the property. A faulty title may result from long-ago or recent fraud, forgery, conflict between heirs, unpaid liens from contractors (see the box on page 107) or the IRS, or just a goof—a mistake or omission—when one of the previous owners' title was written.

Title Search and Title Insurance

Customarily, an attorney, title-insurance company or other title specialists will conduct a title search or examination prior to closing, though states typically don't require it. But it may fail to turn up a problem that can come back to haunt you later. If that's the case, your secure ownership and your ability to resell the property may be threatened.

The best way to make sure you are getting clear title to any property you are buying is to buy title insurance. That one-time purchase protects you from a faulty title and from anyone who lays claim to your home or tries to put a lien on it based on actions that occurred before you purchased it.

Your title insurance will protect you up to the purchase price of the property; in some areas, you can purchase a rider that will increase your coverage as the property increases in value (appreciates). (Your mortgage lender will probably require you to also purchase a policy to protect its interest, the decreasing amount of the mortgage on the home.) If someone does challenge your title, the insurance company will pay to defend you, and, if you lose, it will pay you off.

WHEN TITLE PROBLEMS ARISE BEFORE CLOSING. If any problems show up in the title search, they must be cleared up before settlement or they could force a

The best way to make sure you are getting clear title to any property you are buying is to buy title insurance.

WHAT TITLE SEARCHES WILL TURN UP

A title search can tell you if there are any:

- **Unpaid taxes,** which, if unpaid by the current owner prior to settlement, could become your responsibility.
- **Restrictive covenants or easements** that tell you where and what you can and can't build on the property—or what the town or county can build there, such as a utility or highway right-of-way.
- **Nonconforming structures** on the property that don't comply with existing community standards.
- **Encroachments**—that is, anything on your property that runs over into your neighbor's property, or vice versa.

---

delay. Some problems, such as those arising from record-keeping errors, may be simple to solve. But others, such as a contested will, can be nightmares forcing you to void the contract.

That's why you should ask for a title-insurance interim binder. This is the title-insurance company's preliminary commitment to insure, based on search and examination of the public records. If problems are discovered, the company may still agree to insure the title if certain conditions have been met by the closing date. Or, it could make the insurance coverage subject to specified exceptions. Basically, the interim binder, along with the title-search contingency in your purchase contract, gives you the chance to decide whether you want the seller to fix the problem or whether the problems merit trying to cancel the purchase. If it comes to that, don't try canceling without skilled legal advice.

Taking Title: Who Owns What?

Before you can take title to your new home, you'll have to decide what form of ownership you want. (See Chapter 12, "Your Estate," for a discussion of ownership as it concerns estate planning.)

IF YOU'RE SINGLE. You'll probably buy the house in your name alone.

LIEN ON ME

When you owe money because of a debt, back income taxes, a court judgment (say for child support) or an unpaid mortgage and you fail to pay, those you owe can slap liens on your house. A lien is a charge against your property; it guarantees that you will pay what you owe— if worst comes to worst, upon the sale of your home. A mechanic's lien is placed by a contractor who makes a claim on your home's title in lieu of an unpaid bill. A lien will be removed when you pay up. If you don't, it can remain attached to the title of your home and cause legal hassles if you try to sell.

IF YOU'RE MARRIED. Husband and wife generally own property through joint ownership, in the form of joint tenancy with the right of survivorship (another variation of this is called tenancy by the entirety). The choice can affect how property might be divided in case of divorce (see Chapter 10, "Ending a Marriage") and how the surviving spouse and the couple's estate will fare when one or both spouses die (see Chapter 12, "Your Estate").

IF YOU'RE UNMARRIED PARTNERS. If you're buying with a partner who isn't your spouse, the usual forms of ownership probably won't serve your purpose. Here's why:

■ **If you own the property together** as tenants in common, each owner has separate legal title to an undivided interest in the whole property. That means that each owner is allowed to independently sell, mortgage or give away his or her interest. That may be good for the seller, but not necessarily for the remaining partner. For example, when one share changes hands, the lender may declare the mortgage loan due, in which case the remaining partner may have to pay off the mortgage and refinance if she wishes to keep the property. Also, if one owner dies,

> **The best strategy for unrelated individuals may be a limited partnership, whereby the partnership, not the individual owners, takes the title.**

the other doesn't automatically get the deceased's share unless that person specifically made that arrangement in his or her will. And if the person dies intestate (without a will), the state will determine who gets the share.

■ **If you own the property together** in joint tenancy with right of survivorship, each person has an equal interest in the property regardless of how much he or she contributed at purchase. However, if one owner dies, that person's share goes automatically to the other without going through probate.

FORM A LEGAL PARTNERSHIP. The best strategy for unrelated individuals may be a limited partnership, whereby the partnership, not the individual owners, takes the title. In this case, a deceased partner's heirs would acquire the interest in the partnership; the other partners could be among the heirs if the deceased willed it so. This avoids problems if one person goes into bankruptcy or has other legal problems that could cloud the title, because the partnership is separate from any legal problems of the individual partners.

If you choose to set up a limited partnership you'll want to consult with an attorney experienced in partnerships who can help you draw up the partnership agreement. Points to address include:

■ **How ownership will be divided,** which in turn determines who pays how much of the down payment, monthly payment, maintenance and repairs. The contract should also describe how any profits or losses from rent or sale of the place will be divided and how tax benefits will be distributed.

■ **How use of the house's space is to be divided.**

■ **What constitutes a deciding vote** and under what circumstances such a vote is considered necessary.

■ **Which owner will act as managing partner** and thus be responsible for signing checks and paying routine expenses.

■ **How much advance notice** a withdrawing partner

must give and how the buyout price will be set.

The Act of Settlement

Depending on where you live, this procedure is known as title closing, settlement or closing of escrow. It entails the final exchange of legal documents and funds and the signing of statements and disclosures required by the federal Department of Housing and Urban Development (HUD). Chances are the buyers will feel as if they're signing away their lives.

The closing office in your area may be a title company, an abstract attorney or a regular real estate attorney. Occasionally, it is a broker or lender.

When closing involves an actual meeting, it's called settlement. If no meeting occurs, it's often known as escrow and is handled by an escrow agent.

In escrow cases, the buyer and seller typically sign an agreement requiring each party to deposit certain funds and documents with the agent. When all the papers and money are in, the escrow is "closed." The agent records the documents and pays out the funds as appropriate.

What Buyers Should Know About Closing

Though you usually have the option of choosing the settlement agent, if your seller has done the picking you should take along your own attorney or have an attorney of your choice review the documents before you sign them.

Prior to settlement, when you apply for a new loan from a lender covered by the federal Real Estate Settlement Procedures Act (RESPA), as most are, you must be given a "good faith" estimate of settlement fees or be sent one within three business days. You must also be given the HUD pamphlet, *Settlement Costs and You*, which describes how the closing process works and explains terms you'll encounter.

Under RESPA, the day before settlement you're

Chances are the buyers will feel as if they're signing away their lives at settlement.

entitled to see the Uniform Settlement Statement, a duplicate of what you'll see at settlement. (If there is no meeting, the escrow agent is required to give you a copy when escrow is closed.) This statement will outline all the costs associated with getting your loan.

Your real estate agent or settlement attorney will make sure that you show up with any other necessary documents, such as your loan commitment, as will the seller. Bring a copy of the purchase contract, just in case.

Because the house must be handed over to you in the condition specified by the contract, a final walkthrough inspection should be scheduled shortly before closing. If anything needs fixing or more cleaning, other than those items conveyed "as is" in the contract, you should tell the seller immediately. No one wants to postpone closing, but make it clear you won't proceed until a second walk-through is satisfactory.

TITLE DOCUMENTS YOU'LL SEE AT CLOSING

Warranty deed

This officially transfers title to the buyer. The seller signs it and agrees to protect the buyer against losing the property because of claims against it. When the deed is recorded at the local courthouse, the buyer usually keeps the original deed.

Different states may use different kinds of deeds, such as bargain and sale, security, grant, or special warranty. Whatever kind your state uses, be sure you understand what rights it will convey to you.

Quitclaim deed

This is often used to deal with title problems. Anyone with a claim against the property who signs it releases any rights he or she might have had, though this alone isn't enough to ensure a clear title for the new owner.

Mortgage deed or deed of trust

Either of these secures your mortgage loan. When a debt is secured by a mortgage, the borrower signs a document that gives the lender a lien on the property.

Owner's affidavit

The seller swears that there are no unpaid liens, assessments or other encumbrances against the property. If the seller is lying, he or she can be sued for damages by the purchaser, the lender or the title company.

Purchaser's affidavit

The buyer swears to the lender that there aren't any existing or pending suits, judgments or liens against him or her. If the buyer turns out to be lying, down the road the lender can foreclose on the property.

Special Considerations for Home Buyers

New-home, condo, co-op and manufactured-home purchasers face all the same challenges that buyers of older single-family detached homes do—and then some.

Homeowners Associations

Condos and co-ops are governed by associations, and townhouses and homes in new developments are likely to be, too. Not all states require such associations to offer you information about their role and rules, so be sure to ask for it—and to understand the bottom line—before buying.

Check to see whether the association is incorporated and insured. This will limit your liability in case the group is sued. Find out how much dues and assessments are, and how often they can be raised. Make sure that there is enough cash flow to pay for expenses and that you can live with any ground rules the association might have.

Most states require that buyers be given a "cooling-off period," usually three to five days, after they've

---

WHAT YOU'LL PAY AT CLOSING

Be prepared to pay these items at closing:

- **Expenses** required to be paid in advance at closing, such as mortgage interest (for the period—between the date of closing and the end of the month—preceding the month for which you'll make your first mortgage payment) and property taxes;
- **Reserves** for insurance, taxes and assessments;
- **Title costs;**
- **Recording and transfer charges** associated with recording of your loan and property documents at the county courthouse; and
- **Any other fees,** such as attorney fees and pest-control inspection.

A condo association may be relatively inactive, but it still has power over how you live.

signed a purchase agreement and have been given condo or association documents. This gives an out to buyers who learn something they can't live with.

An association may be relatively inactive, but it still has power over how you live. Among other things, it can assess you for emergency expenses and put a lien on your property if you don't pay your dues (see the discussion on page 123 in the following chapter).

If You're Buying a New Home

In most states, contracts for new homes favor the builder. But you can exert some control.

A deposit on a new home is typically 5% of the selling price. Insert a clause in the contract protecting your right to get the deposit back if the deal falls through. You will also have to pay for all extra, non-standard items up front. The money deposited for extras is generally not refunded in the event you cancel the contract.

You should be able to get the builder to give you a delivery date. To protect against late delivery, make sure that there is a daily-penalty clause added to the contract, charging the builder a set amount for each day past the delivery date. You can add a clause to your contract demanding that your house be built to the quality standards of the model. That's a good idea because developers sometimes give themselves escape clauses that, for example, permit them to change to a cheaper house if the market changes.

You should also insert a clause in your purchase offer giving you the right to have ongoing inspections done (at your expense) as construction proceeds, plus a final walk-through inspection.

The builder must give you a list of disclosures about the subdivision and a copy of the development's homeowners association bylaws.

Have an attorney review the bylaws and everything else in the contract before you sign.

NEW-HOME PROBLEMS AND MAKING THE MOST OF ANY WARRANTIES. What do you do if, two years after you buy your new home, the foundation begins to crack or the fireplace pulls away from its supporting wall? If your builder won't fix the problem, you will have to sue the builder to get it to cover the cost of repairs.

Many states and localities hold builders and developers to an implied warranty on the habitability of their homes. That generally means that a builder should replace or repair anything that threatens a home's soundness and the safe functioning of its basic structures and components within one or two years of building it. You'll have to go to court to get an implied warranty enforced.

That's why builders frequently offer long-term protection plans backed by insurance. These ten-year warranty plans protect member builders and their buyers against catastrophic losses arising from major design and structural defects. The ten-year warranty stays with the home for ten years regardless of how often its owners change.

If a member builder can't or won't fix a covered defect, the insurance will cover the cost of repairs exceeding the owner's deductible, typically $250. A built-in dispute-settling process is usually available to mediate between builder and buyer if they can't agree on a solution. The neutral third party can decide the issue, based on the warranty documents. The builder is bound by this decision, but the buyer can reject it and go to court if he or she chooses to.

The biggest problems that homeowners typically have with warranties is that:

■ **they don't know what the warranty covers,**
■ **they don't give the builder a chance to fix the problem, or**
■ **they wait too long before filing a claim.**

Here's how to make the most of this warranty protection:

■ **Find out before you make a purchase offer** or sign a contract how state warranty law could affect you. For example, your state's law may permit you to sue or

To protect against late delivery, make sure there is a daily-penalty clause in the contract, charging the builder a set amount for each day past the delivery date.

Find out before you make a purchase offer or sign a contract how state warranty law could affect you.

file a claim against a warranty company. And if you sue, your builder's extended warranty (an express warranty) could stand in the place of any implied builder warranty. That's why it's smart to find out what your state's law might make a builder do to fix a problem—and for how long—so you can judge the value of promises in an extended warranty plan. It's also a good idea to find out how your state courts have treated homeowners who sued builders.

■ **Ask your attorney to assess the warranty.**

■ **Read all the terms and conditions** of any ten-year warranty. Have those terms entered in your contract. Be aware of what household features and systems will be covered (warranted) during your first year of ownership only, your second year only, and during the remaining eight years.

■ **Make contractors unambiguously responsible** for everything and for everyone they choose to hire.

■ **Keep records and act quickly.** If you have a warranty and problems show up within two years, write directly to the builder. Send copies of all correspondence to the warranty administrator. Hire an independent inspector to support your claims. Keep a diary and copies of correspondence.

■ **Give the builder or warranty administrator** a reasonable period of time to review your claims and make repairs, but be prepared to fight—and put them on notice that that's what you'll do.

■ **If you bought a new home** with a mortgage guaranteed by the Department of Veterans Affairs or insured by the Federal Housing Administration, and if you meet certain strict requirements, you may be covered under the agency's own four-year structural-defect plan. Complain to the nearest field office, probably the one that processed your loan.

If You're Buying a Condo

The mention of the word "condo" probably brings to mind an apartment that's individually owned. That's only partially correct. Fact is, the word "condominium" really refers to a legal form of ownership that could apply to a variety of housing situations. Owners of each individual dwelling unit—typically an apartment or townhouse—in a housing development also own "undivided proportional interests" in such common areas as the grounds, hallways, elevators and recreation areas. In other words, everyone owns these areas collectively and in proportion to his or her percentage of actual ownership in the development, which might be determined by the number of apartments he or she owns or the size of the unit.

Most condo developments are run by a condo association, with a board of directors elected by the condo owners. The board is much like a miniature government, with ultimate authority to run the condominium even if it turns day-to-day operations over to a resident manager or outside management company. It can have a lot of power: A condo board may be able to spend thousands of dollars on a repair or improvement without the prior approval of other owners. It can put a lien on your unit if you don't pay your monthly condo fee or are late with money for a special assessment.

That's why, with a condo, you should get answers to the following questions about the condo association's financial soundness:

- **What debts does the condo association owe,** and to whom?
- **Are there adequate funds in the condo association's** reserve fund to handle replacement of expensive items, such as the roof and plumbing system, and emergency needs?
- **What will happen** if funds are stolen or mishandled?
- **Will you and the other owners** be adequately insured?
- **Are funds in an insured account,** and if not, what would happen if investment losses occurred?
- **Can the association provide evidence** of liability and

The mention of a "condo" probably brings to mind an apartment that's individually owned. That's only partially correct. Fact is, the word condominium really refers to a legal form of ownership.

CONDO DOCUMENTS YOU SHOULD RECEIVE

The master deed

Also knowen as the enabling declaration, plan of condominium ownership, or declaration of condominium. This is key. When recorded, it establishes the project as a condo. Among other things, it authorizes residents to form an operating association and describes individual units and commonly owned areas.

Bylaws

These spell out the association's authority and responsibilities, authorize the making of a budget and the collection of various charges, and establish the association's parliamentary procedures. They may give the association power to hire a professional management firm. The by-laws may set forth insurance requirements and authorize liens against property owners who fail to pay monthly charges if the condo master deed doesn't.

House rules

These are the do's and don'ts for owners, including restrictions on pets, children, decorations on the outside of units, use of facilities, and so on. They may be incorporated into the bylaws or set out separately. Though it may seem unfair and possibly discriminatory if you have kids, Congress has allowed a special exemption to the federal Fair Housing Act to places whose residents are all over age 62 or who meet a very rigid 55-plus standard.

Sales contract or purchase agreement

This won't be much different from other real estate sales contracts, but when you sign a condo contract, you probably will be acknowledging that you've received the other documents just described. The contract may provide for a cooling-off period during which you can study the condominium documents and back out if need be. If there is no such clause, insert one to that effect.

If the project isn't yet completed, ask for written assurance that it will be— and as promised.

Other papers

You'll want to see a copy of:
- **the operating budget,**
- **any recent budget reports,**
- **a schedule of current and proposed assessments,**
- **a financial statement** for the homeowners association, including a balance statement for the reserve fund with information about how it's invested,
- **any leases or contracts,**
- **a plan or drawing of the project and your unit,** and
- **an engineer's report,** if one was done, that discusses the physical condition of the building, including projections for major repairs.

property insurance, which protect you from the usual legal risks and other perils of homeownership, and a fidelity bond? The bond protects the owners from officers, directors and board members who might embezzle the condo association's funds or who might decide to take an early retirement in the tropics.

On the face of it, these may not sound like legal issues, but they could cost you plenty if the condo runs into financial problems and has no protection. That's also why you'll want to make sure that you get copies of the condo documents before you buy, whether or not your state requires that you receive them. In some states, developers are required to give potential buyers a prospectus with relevant facts about a condo offering. Take special care to read and review the documents with the help of an attorney who can interpret any legalese and identify issues that you should investigate.

If You're Buying a Co-op

Unlike a condo, which gives you title to a particular unit and an undivided interest in the common areas (see the preceding section), buying a cooperative apartment, or co-op, unit entitles you to a share in a corporation. Stock ownership or certificate membership in the corporation gives you the right to live in a particular unit. You become a tenant-stockholder. Typically, the corporation owns and manages the co-op, pays the property taxes, and finances the project with a "blanket" mortgage.

Because a tenant is a fellow shareholder in the whole building, current co-op members tend to be choosy about prospective owners. They can require interviews, personal references and financial statements. They can reject prospects they believe could be noisy, reclusive, sloppy or likely to throw big, noisy parties. But state and federal laws prohibit them from rejecting or discouraging a prospective buyer on the basis of race, gender, creed or national origin (see the

CO-OP DOCUMENTS TO STUDY BEFORE YOU BUY

Articles of incorporation

A cooperative is incorporated under state law, and the corporation's purpose, powers and obligations are described in the articles of incorporation.

Bylaws

These spell out the duties and responsibilities of the shareholders, officers and directors. This is where you'll probably learn how many of the cooperative's units may be rented out to nonshareholders. It's possible that a majority of the units could be occupied by tenants (or "nominees" of partnerships, trusts, estates and corporations) rather than by shareowners who have joined together as "cooperative homeowners." In the extreme case, that could change the nature of cooperative living and change the co-op into a general partnership, having tax and resale consequences for individual tenant-stockholders

and making lenders less likely to lend to you.

Stock, shares or membership certificates

Shares or membership certificates are your proof of ownership in the corporation.

Occupancy agreement or proprietary lease

The lease sets up the terms and conditions by which you occupy your co-op unit. It obligates you to pay your pro rata share of the corporation's expenses, including real estate taxes, operating costs and debt. This is where you'll find rules on using your unit, subleasing and maintenance.

Recognition agreement

When you buy a co-op, you'll probably try to obtain a "share loan"—that is, a mortgage that will be secured by your occupancy

discussion of discrimination on page 98 and the list of co-op documents above).

Buying a Manufactured Home

As with any other home purchase, protect yourself by studying the purchase contract or lease, bylaws, rules and regulations, and all other pertinent documents before you settle. Don't commit yourself to a lot or to a home until you've consulted with an attorney. And don't sign anything you don't understand. Read and keep any warranties you receive from the retailer, transporter, installer and appliance manufacturer.

rights and your stock in the corporation.

The single largest originator of share loans for co-ops is the National Cooperative Bank, through its affiliate, the NCB Savings Bank. To participate, a co-op project must meet the NCB's, as well as the Federal National Mortgage Association's, underwriting and legal standards for such things as structural soundness, restricted residential and commercial use, fiscally responsible operating budget, and appropriate management.

When a share-loan lender and the co-op corporation enter into agreement, they document the lender's rights as well as the corporation's responsibilities and obligations to the lender. A co-op corporation may enter into recognition agreements with more than one lender.

Security agreement

This confirms your agreement with the lender and pledges your share of the co-op in exchange for the loan.

Regulatory agreement

This document is issued by the lender or government agency that has provided the blanket mortgage. It sets out requirements for such things as reserves, reporting and budget approval. Like condominiums, co-ops must establish reserve funds to pay taxes and debt, as well as to replace structural elements and major components such as heating, cooling, plumbing and electrical systems.

A general operating reserve must be established for other contingencies and for resale problems. Income for these funds typically comes from the tenant-stockholders, commercial use such as parking, and income earned on the reserve funds. These reserve funds are established under the co-op's regulatory agreements.

RENTING A HOME SITE MEANS YOU'LL HAVE LESS LEGAL CONTROL. About half of all buyers put their manufactured homes on land they own. Your best bet is to select a lot before you buy the home and make sure the zoning ordinances will allow you to place your home there. While zoning restrictions that keep manufactured homes out of residential neighborhoods still exist, many states have passed legislation that prevents such discrimination. Check local zoning ordinances before making plans to situate your new home.

If you plan to rent the land, you must clearly understand that you're about to place a valuable piece of property on someone else's land. Of course, you can expect to have certain activities controlled by the management of a manufactured-home land-lease community, as well as by a group of neighbors. As a tenant, there may be little you can do if a community is sold or if the management becomes lax. In a dispute with the landowner, you may have no recourse but to sell or move. For a move of less than 50 miles, you could end up paying thousands of dollars to dismantle, move and reassemble a luxury multisection home.

LEGAL STANDARDS FOR QUALITY. Manufactured homes aren't subject to local building codes. But units built after June 14, 1976, are covered by the National Manufactured Home Construction and Safety Standards Act of 1974. If you're buying a new mobile home, be sure that you get a certificate from the manufacturer stating that the home is in compliance with Department of Housing and Urban Development standards, and look for a permanent label, located at the outside rear of each section, stating the same.

Be aware that HUD has amended its building standards to require all manufactured homes that will be sited in severe weather zones, such as near the Gulf of Mexico or on the southeastern coast of the United States, to meet the same wind-safety standards as are required of site-built homes in those areas. This information now appears on the permanent label affixed to each new manufactured home.

A significant number of structural problems have been traced to improper installation of units on their

FOR MORE INFORMATION

- **The National Association of Housing Cooperatives** (1707 H. St., N.W., Suite 201, Washington, DC 20006; 202-737-0797; www.coophousing.org)
- **The National Association of Home Builders** (1201 15th St., N.W., Washington, DC 20005; 800-368-5242, 202-822-0200; http://nahb.com)
- *How to Buy a Manufactured Home,* by the Manufactured Housing Institute, in cooperation with the Federal Trade Commission's Office of Consumer and Business Education (Manufactured Housing Institute, 2101 Wilson Blvd., Arlington, VA 22201; 703-558-0400; www.mfghome.org; available free online or for $2 per copy)

sites, which HUD doesn't regulate. States set standards and regulations governing installation. Check with your local building inspection offices (or your state's Manufactured Housing Association) for more information.

Tax Considerations for Sellers

Tax legislation written in 1997 included an almost unbelievable deal for homeowners: In almost all cases, Congress has banned the taxation of profit from the sale of a home. Generally, if you file a single return, up to $250,000 of profit will be tax-free; double that to a cool half a million if you file a joint return. The tax-free amounts are so large that only owners of the most expensive homes, or those who remain in the same house for decades, are likely to ever pay tax on profit from the sale of a home. It gets even better: You can use this break over and over during your lifetime, too, protecting the profit from one home to another. There's no lifetime limit on how much profit you can claim tax-free and there's even a way to pull a vacation home under the tax shelter.

In a nutshell, here are the new rules:

■ **Up to $250,000 of home sale profit is tax-free;** $500,000 if you file a joint return.

■ **To qualify,** you must own and live in the house for two of the five years before the sale.

■ **Generally,** you can use this break once every two years.

New Temporary Regulations

At the end of 2002, the IRS issued temporary regulations on the subject of excluding gain, but with a reduced maximum amount, when the seller does not satisfy one of the time rules. The tax law provides an exception to the two-year rules for use, ownership and claimed exclusion when the primary reason for the sale is due to:

■ **Change of health;**

■ **Death;**

■ **Divorce;**

> Generally, if you file a single return, up to $250,000 of profit will be tax-free; double that to a cool half a million if you file a joint return.

- **Becoming eligible for unemployment compensation;**
- **A change of employment that leaves the taxpayer** unable to pay the mortgage or reasonable living expenses;
- **A change of employment where the qualified person's new place of work** is at least 50 miles farther from the old home than the old workplace was from that home;
- **Multiple births** resulting from the same pregnancy;
- **Damage to the residence** resulting from a natural or man-made disaster, or act of war or terrorism; or
- **Condemnation, seizure or involuntary conversion** of the property.

If your situation appears to qualify, check with your local IRS office to be sure these "temporary" regulations are still in effect.

Your Home and the Law

Chapter 6

Your home may be your castle, but the law has a lot to say about how you run it, especially how what you do affects your neighbors and community. It even covers the extent to which you can protect you and yours from intruders.

In the course of homeownership, you'll have contractual business relationships with a whole cast of characters. Over time, a stream of people will come and go from your home, and you could potentially be liable for any injury or damages they suffer while on your property. The law enters into all these relationships.

This chapter will tell you what you need to know about protecting yourself from liability, meeting your legal responsibility as an employer in your own home or as a landlord when you rent your home, and more.

The Rules of Homeownership: How Serious Are They?

Zoning laws, environmental regulations, neighborhood covenants, neighborhood associations and condo and co-op rules: If you're a home or property owner these days, you're bound to encounter such boundaries to home and property ownership. At their best, they're meant to ensure public health and safety, regulate community growth and development, promote certain aesthetic standards and a pleasant living environment, and maintain home values. At their worst, they can inhibit you from doing what you want with your property and from living the way you

Once the purchase has been made, you've explicitly and contractually agreed to abide by all the community's rules.

please. If you come up against them, you may feel that they're arbitrary and foolish. But the reality is, they are all legally binding, so it's important to understand what they are and what they mean before you buy a home that falls under their jurisdiction.

Be sure to check the bylaws of the condo, co-op or neighborhood association, or the deed to your home, or ask neighbors about the local neighborhood association. State or local law may require that the appropriate person or entity provide you with all the documentation you need to be fully informed about any pertinent rules and regulations before you agree to purchase your home; once the purchase has been made, you've explicitly and contractually agreed to abide by all the community's rules (see the discussion of buyers' special concerns beginning on page 111 of Chapter 5, "Buying and Selling a Home"). Talk to current owners to find out how strictly the rules are enforced and whether the regulatory board can be persuaded to change them.

WHAT IF I MOVE IN AND FIND THAT I CAN'T LIVE WITH ONE OF THE RULES? In the case of a local zoning regulation, you could ask for a variance, typically by applying to your local planning and zoning department. This might be necessary if, say, you wanted to add on to your home but the addition would extend too close to the street or property line. Depending on your town's or city's rules, a public hearing might be required before your request would be granted. If you go ahead and build the addition without the necessary approval, your local government could at least require you to make the corrections necessary to bring it up to code, or at worst force you to remove the addition.

Or, say that your condo or neighborhood association won't let you hang window boxes, paint your house yellow, or park a recreational or commercial vehicle outside your home. You could start by asking your governing board for an exception, or you could even propose that the association change its rules, which would probably require a vote by all the owners.

If you simply decide to do whatever you want to,

FOR MORE INFORMATION

To learn more about handling legal hassles with your neighbors, consult *Neighbor Law: Fences, Trees, Boundaries and Noise*, by Cora Jordan (Nolo Press, 800-992-6656; $26.99). This book explains how to maintain neighborly relations while still resolving such problems as noise, boundary disputes, obstruction of views and trespassers. It also gives solid advice on the proper legal channels to pursue if a friendly solution can't be found.

Another excellent resource is *Neighbor Vs. Neighbor: Over 400 Informative and Outrageous Cases of Neighbor Disputes* (Comprehensive Self-Help Law Guide) by Mark Warda (Sphinx Publication; $16.95)

---

come what may, your community's governing body could force you to comply: It could impose a financial penalty, take out your new basketball hoop and send you the bill for the work, sue you or, if your offense was bad enough, even force you to sell your place.

WHAT IF THE NEIGHBORHOOD ASSOCIATION OR CONDO ASSOCIATION DOESN'T LIVE UP TO ITS PART OF THE BARGAIN? Say you believe the engineering work on your condo was done incorrectly and so unwanted puddles form outside your house. You've complained to the condo board to no avail. You could threaten legal action, but check your condo documents first. You may have agreed to resolve any such disagreement via alternate dispute resolution (see the discussion of mediation and arbitration in Chapter 1, "Living With the Law").

Defending Yourself, Your Home and Your Family

You have a right to protect your property from trespassers. You needn't hang a sign on your property declaring "no trespassing"; it's understood in the law that it's your right to determine who

The law does not consider the fact that someone was stealing your property enough reason to use deadly force.

can or can't set foot on your property for any reason.

If an unwanted person enters your home or property, you can warn him off or throw him off bodily, so long as you don't hurt him. But the smart thing to do is call the police, who will make an arrest if necessary.

While you also have a right to own a registered gun and threaten someone with it to protect your property, be aware that you can shoot a trespasser only in self-defense or in defense of your family. The law does not consider the fact that someone was stealing your property enough reason to use deadly force. If you do injure an intruder who demonstrated no intent to hurt you or your family, you may be sued for damages. If you kill him, you could be charged with homicide. This is true whether you use a gun, a baseball bat or any other weapon.

That's why you may want to avoid setting yourself up for this disaster by choosing other, safer means of protecting your home and family. Your local police can probably help you assess your home's security and give you some ideas on measures you should take.

Homeowners Insurance: A Legal Safety Net

Homeowners insurance protects you from what others do to you, and what you or your family members do to others.

It comes in six basic flavors: HO-1, HO-2 and HO-3 differ in the number of perils that they cover and the degree of protection that they offer; HO-3, an "all-risk" policy, covers everything that isn't specifically excluded. Renters would want HO-4, condo owners HO-6, and in some states, owners of unique older houses may be insured with a special HO-8 policy.

Whatever kind of home you own, house or apartment, there are two parts to a homeowners insurance policy: property protection and liability coverage. The extent of your coverage in each area depends on the specific policy and extra features you choose.

Use It to Protect Your Property

Depending on the specific coverage you choose, the property-protection part of your homeowners insurance will typically reimburse you for loss of or damage to your house and its contents as well for cleanup costs afterward. It also covers the cost to live elsewhere if your house is uninhabitable or is being repaired.

Property protection even covers your household belongings when you take them with you off the premises. Personal property insurance typically also covers your credit cards for up to $500 of unauthorized use (see the discussion of credit card rights beginning on page 27, in Chapter 3, "The Law and Your Finances"). It does not, however, compensate you for lost pets or damages to your car, though it would cover stuff stolen from inside your car.

Generally, business property in the home—such as home-office equipment—is not covered, or its coverage is limited.

When buying homeowners insurance, be sure to ask for replacement-cost coverage, which lets you replace lost items for their current cost, not their actual cash value, a depreciated amount they were worth at the time you lost them. (The standard policy will automatically pay set amounts—even for replacement-cost coverage—on personal property, unless you "schedule" the item with your agent, that is, turn over the original receipt and ask for that specific amount of coverage. A separate schedule is a good idea for your valuables, such as jewelry, art or antiques.)

Use It to Cover Your Liability

Liability coverage protects you against personal liability for injuries to others and damage to other people's property. It will pay for your defense if someone sues you and cover the cost of damages you must pay if a court finds you careless or negligent. Liability coverage usually pays up to $100,000 per incident (sometimes more, depending on the policy) for injury or damage that you or a family member might have caused or for an accident that occurs around your home. Most

Property protection even covers your household belongings when you take them with you off the premises.

WHAT'S A NUISANCE?

Most people think of a nuisance as something that is simply annoying, but in legal terms, it's something that may cause harm or injury. There are two types of nuisance of concern to homeowners:

■ **A private nuisance** is something that keeps you from using and enjoying your property, such as a neighbor's overhanging tree or a rodent infestation.

■ **An attractive nuisance** is an existing condition that poses a danger and "attracts" children to it. A typical example is a swimming pool (see page 130). In many areas this legal concept has been replaced by "duty of reasonable care"—that is, if a dangerous condition exists, the homeowner is responsible for repairing it or warning others of its existence.

---

policies also cover damage or injury by pets, but be sure and check whether yours does. Injuries to someone by a family member who is away from the home may also be covered.

If your liability policy includes medical-payments coverage, then even if someone is injured at your house, their medical bills will be covered. For example, if a neighbor takes a shortcut through your backyard and falls over your child's toy, then your medical-payments insurance could pick up her medical bills. (If you're renting your home, see the discussion of renter's insurance in the box on page 147.)

Remember, though, all policies vary, and all have exclusions. So it's a good idea to read the policy carefully and know exactly what it covers.

It's also important to know that one of the conditions of coverage is that you give your insurance carrier prompt notice of any sort of accident or any lawsuit someone is filing against you. For example, if you have a wild party and someone tries to hold you liable for injuries they suffer there, contact your carrier. True, the company may not renew your policy or they may increase your premium, but if you don't report an accident and someone sues you, you risk losing your coverage.

If You Need Extra Liability Protection

Does the value of your assets exceed the liability coverage on your home and auto insurance policies? If so, for a little extra cost, "umbrella" liability insurance will give you even greater dollar coverage, usually measured by the million, and may include protection from things not covered in your underlying policy, such as the following:

■ **Libel, slander and character defamation.**

■ **Emotional harm or injury.**

■ **False arrest.**

■ **Wrongful entry or eviction.**

■ **Malicious prosecution.**

For $1 million worth of coverage you can expect to pay between $125 and $250 per year, more if you're insuring more than one house, car or driver, or if you own a recreational vehicle. You may also have to pay a higher premium for your underlying coverage to meet the umbrella policy's required limits. Most insurers require that you purchase your home and auto insurance from them before they'll sell you an umbrella policy, so start your shopping with your agent. Take note of any exclusions, such as for business or professional liability.

Home Building, Repair and Contract Work

Any time you make a major structural change in your home, such as adding a room or even a bathroom, you may need a building permit from your city or county building inspector's office. Essentially, a building permit says that you've had your plans approved and that they meet the requirements of the local building code for a minimum standard of safety.

Any time you make a major structural change in your home, such as adding a room or even a bathroom, you may need a building permit from your city or county building inspector's office.

continued on page 132

WHAT-IFS OF LIABILITY

This section covers some of the legal problems that homeowners are vulnerable to and neighbors are likely to encounter.

The Perils of Pools

Q. *I'm thinking about buying a house with a swimming pool. What will my liability be if people other than my family use the pool?*
A. You're wise to think about this before you buy. When you have a pool on your property, you have heightened exposure to risk and you have a duty to exercise reasonable care for things concerning it.

Local laws typically govern what you must do to be sure that your swimming pool is not a danger to the neighborhood. Some localities require pool covers; others mandate fences of certain heights and materials. If your locality doesn't require such precautions, install them anyway to reduce your risk of liability. Check with your insurance agent; he or she will know what your locality requires.

It's important for you to follow these laws. If you don't and an accident occurs, you could be held liable—subject to a claim for damages, say, by the parents of an injured child—and be charged with breaking the law or with negligence. Even if your kids and their friends are using the pool without your permission when you're not around, you're still potentially liable if someone gets hurt. That's because the pool is an attractive nuisance, and it's your fault if kids are drawn to it and get hurt. An attractive nuisance is a legal term describing an existing and dangerous condition that "attracts" children to it, such as a swimming pool. If homeowners think children will trespass, they must take special action to eliminate a dangerous condition.

A Negligent Neighbor

Q. *My neighbors' old maple tree has one huge limb that extends out over my yard. I'm afraid that one of these days a storm is going to send it crashing down and through my garage. They seem unconcerned, and I've considered having someone come to cut down the part hanging over my yard.*
A. Talk to your neighbors and ask them to take care of the problem. If they won't, you may be within your rights to cut off the limb—but if you happen to kill the tree in the process, your neighbors could sue you. If trying to discuss the situation reasonably doesn't work, another alternative would be to tell your neighbors that you will take them to court and claim that the overhanging limb is a private nuisance—something that is preventing you from enjoying the use of your property. A court may demand that your neighbors rectify the problem. And, if you choose to wait for the limb to come through your garage, you can ask your neighbors to pay for the damages. If they're at fault, their homeowners liability insurance will reimburse you for any damage the tree caused to an insured structure on your property. If they don't have homeowners coverage and refuse to pay, you could sue.

A Rat's Nest Next Door

Q. *My neighbor has an old cottage on his property that is an eyesore, attracts rodents, and*

caused more than one prospective buyer of my house to change his mind. What can I do?
A. Being an eyesore isn't enough to trigger any action unless there is a neighborhood covenant or local ordinance that governs appearances. However, if rodents are involved, you can call and complain to the health department, which will investigate and may force your neighbor to take action. And if the house is what is called a private nuisance—it creates extreme noise, odor or hazards—then you may have the basis for a lawsuit.

A Dog-Eat-Dog World
Q. *What if my dog bites someone?*
A. Many states have dog-bite statutes—laws that hold a dog owner responsible if his or her pet bites someone, regardless of whether the owner is at fault. If your state has no dog-bite statute, or if the particulars of the dog-bite statute don't apply in your case, then common law (often called "the one-bite rule") may. It works like this:

If your dog is normally a loving, docile animal that doesn't bite, you may not be liable if he sinks his teeth into someone. After all, if it's never happened before, it will be hard for someone suing you to show that you were careless in how you handled the situation.

If, however, your dog has a history of biting people without provocation, or if you were obviously careless in the way you handled the dog, then you may be liable. But you might be less responsible if the dog was at home where he was supposed to be, not wandering the neighborhood,

and someone came onto your property and harassed the dog. In that case the person might be a trespasser and you would have less responsibility to them.

After a biting incident, your dog could be removed from your possession if you were violating local ordinances about caring for animals or if the dog needs to be quarantined and watched for rabies.

If your dog bites someone and you are held responsible, the injured person may be able to get some or all of the following paid for under your homeowners insurance liability coverage: medical bills, lost income, pain and suffering, loss of services and punitive damages.

Check your insurance policy to be sure it covers actions by your pet. Because various breeds of dogs, such as pit bulls, have in some cases proven themselves to be dangerous pets, dogs aren't always covered by homeowners policies.

When You're the Bartender
Q. *What's my responsibility as a host if I serve my guests alcoholic beverages?*
A. It depends where you live. State laws on what is called social-host responsibility are in flux. Some states have ruled that hosts are not liable for drunk driving accidents or related injuries incurred by their guests after they leave the host's home, and some states hold the hosts liable. To find out the law in your state, check with your state department of insurance or ask your insurance agent.

If someone drinks at your house and then has an accident and sues you, in most

continued on next page

WHAT-IFS OF LIABILITY, continued

cases the injured party's own carelessness may be some type of defense for you. Things get more complicated, however, when a drunk driver leaves your home and injures a third party. If the third party sues, you could be found at fault and be liable for damages.

Be sure to report the incident to your insurance agent as soon as possible, when you hear of the accident or when a claim is made.

In the meantime, when you're hosting a party, do what bars do: Serve food and nonalcoholic beverages, not just alcoholic drinks, and arrange rides with other friends or call cabs for those who need it.

Shoveling Your Sidewalks

Q. *What's my legal responsibility for shoveling my sidewalks, and what's my liability if I don't?*
A. In most states, you have no duty to shovel your walk. If you go ahead and shovel it, though, be sure to do it well. If a pedestrian mistakes your halfhearted job for a safe sidewalk, abandons caution, falls and is injured, then you can be found at fault and liable for damages.

Crime at Home

Q. *What's my responsibility for illegal acts committed on my property?*
A. This book deals primarily with civil law, not criminal law. If you think you need that kind of advice, you should consult a lawyer immediately. But, in a nutshell: If you know about an illegal act and gave your consent to it, you will be criminally liable.

If you knew about the illegal act, but neither gave your consent nor objected to the action, your consent might be implied and that could make you criminally liable, too.

If there are illegal activities going on at your house that you don't know about—your relative or household help is selling drugs on the premises while you're out of town, say, or your neighbor is growing marijuana in the farthest corner of your property—you probably won't be criminally liable.

When You Volunteer

Q. *It is true I could be sued for something that happens while I'm working as a volunteer?*
A. When you volunteer to help your favorite charity or serve on your church or condo board, you open yourself up to

If you are doing the work yourself, you will need to obtain the permits. However, if a contractor is doing the work for you, he should get the permits. Don't volunteer to do this for him; whoever gets the permits will be liable if the work does not conform to the local building code.

If you don't have the proper permits, the building inspector may not approve the addition, and when you potential legal liability. Say that you coach Little League, and one of your players falls on a piece of glass in the outfield and is severely injured. Both you and the group could be sued. If you lose and insurance doesn't pay damages and legal fees, the money could come out of your pocket.

Each state and the District of Columbia has enacted volunteer protection laws. If you're covered, an accuser would have to show that your conduct was grossly negligent, reckless or intended to cause harm, rather than simply "unreasonable," in order to win a case against you. But how these laws apply varies with the state. State laws don't provide protection from claims made under federal law, for example, those related to employment or civil rights.

To learn how your state's volunteer protection laws apply to your group, check with a local volunteer clearinghouse or agency.

Find out whether your group has purchased general liability insurance, auto insurance or directors' and officers (D&O) insurance that specifically covers volunteers in their work for the organization and to what extent.

Your group's insurance policy should advance funds to hire a lawyer and defend your case instead of reimbursing you for those costs. Check your group's bylaws to see if it includes a broad indemnification provision to protect volunteers, including officers and directors, if a claim exceeds insurance limits.

Find out whether your personal home-owners, auto and umbrella liability insurance policies will cover you in your volunteer role. For example, if you're driving, will your policy protect you if you drive a vehicle owned by the organization, if you are paid other than reimbursement, or if you drive a van or bus rather than a car?

For more information, send for:

■ *The Responsibilities of a Charity's Volunteer Board,* from the BBB Wise Giving Alliance, 4200 Wilson Blvd., Suite 800, Arlington, VA 22203; 703-276-0100; www.bbb.org. ; $4.00 per copy

■ *No Surprises: Harmonizing Risk & Reward in Volunteer Management,* from the Nonprofit Risk Management Center; 1001 Connecticut Ave., N.W., Washington DC 20036; 202-785-3891; www.nonprofitrisk.org; $15.00 plus shipping costs.

go to sell your house the illegal addition may reduce rather than enhance the home's value. Depending on local requirements, you or the inspector must schedule inspections at critical points throughout the project.

Failing to acquire a building permit for your do-it-yourself project could mean having to make any corrections necessary to make it conform to the local building code, or—worse, having to tear it down.

In most states, a contractor who is licensed is also bonded, meaning he has insurance guaranteeing you some compensation if he fails to live up to his end of the deal.

Licensed, Bonded and Insured to Build

Licensing protects both you and the contractor. To get a license in some states, the contractor must demonstrate a certain amount of experience, pass an exam and carry insurance that will cover any damage to your property or to his workers during the course of the work. In other states, no test or experience is required for a license, and a few states require no licensing of contractors at all. Most states require plumbers and electricians to be licensed, to prove their competence in these critical areas that can affect the public health and safety, and about half require the same for home remodelers. To find out what your state requires, contact the contractor's licensing board or the state licensing board for general contractors.

In most states, a contractor who is licensed is also bonded, meaning he has a special type of insurance that guarantees you some compensation if he fails to live up to his end of the deal, as set forth in the contract, or does substandard work. By adding the appropriate clauses to the contract, you can also protect yourself from the following problems:

- **failure to build** according to the plans or specifications that you agreed on;
- **failure to finish** in a reasonable or agreed-upon amount of time;
- **costs that greatly exceed** the estimated cost of the project;
- **failure to clean up your property** after finishing the project, hauling away refuse and so on;
- **damage to your property**—say, to trees or other landscaping—in some way during construction; or
- **failure to correct problems** discovered during the final walk-through (called a builder's "punch list").

If you then experience a problem, the contractor will be in breach of contract.

If there is no licensing requirement in your state, it's all the more important that the contractor be bonded. Don't hire one who isn't. Ask to see proof of his bond and get a copy of it for your records.

Even if he's bonded, ask what the contractor's bond covers. Chances are pretty good that a residential contractor's bond will not protect you against his going into bankruptcy or failing to complete a job. If you request this kind of coverage, you will probably have to pay for it; it will generally cost you about 2% to 3% of the job price. To obtain a performance bond, which is more typical of commercial work, the contractor must have a long track record and a stable financial background.

If you ultimately think you need to make a claim against the contractor's bond, contact the company that insured him.

Similarly, before work begins, be sure the contractor carries liability and workers' compensation insurance that protects you, your home, your neighbors, passersby and all workers in case of an accident on the job.

If the worker works for an insured contractor, then

FOR MORE INFORMATION

■ *How to Hire the Right Contractor,* by Paul Bianchina and the Editors of Consumer Report Books (1991; out of print, but check at your public library or buy a used copy on Amazon.com).

■ **American Homeowners Foundation** (6776 Little Falls Road, Arlington, VA 22213; 800-489-7776; www.american-homeowners.org). This nonprofit education and research organization represents homeowners, buyers and sellers. Publishes books and sample contracts on subjects including building a home and remodeling.

■ **National Association of the Remodeling Industry** (780 Lee St., Suite 200, Des Plaines, IL 60016; 800-611-6274; www.nari.org) Check

their Web site for information on choosing and working with remodeling contractors.

■ **National Association of Home Builders** (1201 15th St., N.W., Washington, DC 20005; 800-368-5242, 202-266-8200; www.nahb.org).Check their Web site for information on buying, building or remodeling a home.

■ **American Institute of Architects** (1735 New York Ave., N.W., Washington, DC 20006; 800-242-3837; www.aia.org). The AIA Bookstore offers a wide variety of educational materials including the video *Investing in a Dream: A Guide to Getting the Home You Really Want* ($29.95).

By law, if the contract involves more than $500, the contractor must put his fees in writing.

the contractor's liability insurance will cover the injury. If the worker is employed by you as an independent contractor, however, your homeowners insurance will cover you.

Protect Yourself With a Good Contract

By law, if the contract involves more than $500, the contractor must put his fees in writing. Your contract should describe your project, include start and finish dates, and set out a payment schedule (with final payment contingent on your approval; see the discussion of withholding payment, below). It should also include the contractor's warranty, a promise or guarantee that he'll stand behind his work if something goes wrong (see the discussion on the opposite page).

Even after you've paid in full, subcontractors and suppliers can file a mechanic's lien (or construction lien) against your home if they haven't been paid by your general contractor, and you might end up having to pay for the same work twice. So ask the general contractor to provide proof that workers and suppliers are being paid with each installment you pay, and include a release of all liens in your contract. A release of lien means that workers must sign a lien waiver form saying that if they've gotten any payment they can't put a lien on your property. And to be double sure that the money trickles down to subcontractors, make your checks jointly payable to contractor and subcontractor—their endorsements on the canceled checks prove that they've been paid.

WITHHOLDING PAYMENT. You have the right to withhold payment for poor work if you have a clause in the contract that gives you the right to inspect the work before making the last payment (or to inspect work-to-date prior to each partial payment). If you have no such clause and you don't pay, you may wind up in court with the contractor seeking the balance of payment, legal fees or damages, and threatening to slap a lien on your home.

Another way to avoid this kind of problem is to

specify in the contract that you and the contractor agree to binding arbitration if you lock horns in a disagreement.

How Does a Warranty Help Protect You?

When a contractor gives a warranty, it means that he promises to stand behind his work, typically for some limited period of time. It's a good idea to get such a guarantee in writing. That way, if your new heating or air-conditioning system doesn't work properly, for example, you can demand that the contractor solve the problem. A good warranty will provide that the contractor fix or replace whatever is necessary immediately and free of cost.

A warranty covering materials and workmanship for a minimum of one year should be written into the contract, and the warranty should be identified as a full or limited warranty: In a full warranty, all faulty products must be repaired or replaced or your money returned. In a limited warranty, replacements and refunds are limited in some regard. Be sure to include the name and address of the party (contractor, distributor or manufacturer) who will honor the guarantee and see that the time limit is specified.

If you discover a problem for which the warranty has just expired, you can try appealing to the contractor's sense of responsibility, but the contractor has no obligation to fix it.

What If Your Builder or Contractor Goes Bankrupt?

If your builder or contractor goes bankrupt before completing your project, you may have to sue in order to get at least some, or possibly all, of your money back. If he is covered by a performance bond (see page 134), however, you are guaranteed to be reimbursed some of your deposit—money that you have invested but that hasn't yet been put into the project— usually up to about $5,000. Of course, on a big project, $5,000 may not be much, and you may wish to sue for anything over what the contractor's bond cov-

You have the right to withhold payment for poor work if you have a clause in the contract that gives you the right to inspect the work before making the last payment.

You need to know whether you have hired a self-employed businessperson or an employee. The difference determines the extent of your legal obligations.

ered. Even then, there may be nothing left to get.

Try to avoid the problem in the first place by hiring a builder or contractor whose business is financially sound. When getting references from previous clients, ask whether the builder was slow to fix anything; this may be a sign that the builder delayed paying or didn't pay his subcontractors, who are typically responsible for making repairs. When hiring a remodeler, you'll usually be asked to pay a deposit of one-third up front, one-third during the work in progress, and one-third on completion. If the remodeler asks for an unusually large deposit—say, one-half up front—his credit with suppliers may not be good.

Household Help

When you hire someone to help you with child care in your home, cleaning, yard work, gardening or other household chores, you need to know whether you have hired a self-employed businessperson or an employee. The difference determines the extent of your legal obligations to the person.

As several would-be Supreme Court justices and Cabinet secretaries have learned to their dismay, if the worker you hire is legally your employee, you'll have to do one or more of the following: withhold federal and state income taxes from his or her pay, contribute to state and federal benefit programs including unemployment insurance and social security, and be certain that he or she is legally entitled to work in the U.S.

If the worker is an independent contractor or he works for one, then he is not considered to be your employee and you will not be stuck with the associated paperwork or costs. You will, however, have to file an IRS Form 1099, "Miscellaneous Income," if you pay him $600 or more in a calendar year. It's then up to the contractor to declare this money as part of his income and to pay income and social security taxes accordingly.

Employee or Independent Contractor?

So, how do you tell the difference between an employee and an independent contractor? Someone you hire to care for your kids in your home, for example, is almost sure to be your employee. A part-time housekeeper may or may not be. If the housekeeper supplies the equipment and materials and works in numerous homes, he or she might qualify as a self-employed, independent contractor, who is responsible for his or her own tax liabilities. When you hire someone through an agency that treats the person as its employee, you're clearly off the hook. But if you control what must be done and how it will be done and you supply the necessary materials, the person is probably your employee. It doesn't matter whether you exercise this control; the point is that you have it. It also doesn't matter whether the person works full-time or part-time, or whether you call the person an independent contractor.

That's the federal law. For state income tax and other tax purposes, most states additionally define an employee as someone who works for you more than 60 hours a quarter.

If You Ignore the Law

What if you are, in fact, the employer of your household help and you choose not to comply with these regulations? If the IRS finds out—which may not be likely—it can impose stiff financial penalties and require payment of back taxes, as well as interest on those taxes. The issue may arise if you are audited, or if your employee files for social security or unemployment benefits and shows that you failed to pay taxes on his or her behalf.

If you decide to come clean and pay the back taxes before the IRS catches up with you, the IRS may waive the penalties, but you'll still owe the interest on the back taxes.

WHAT IF YOUR EMPLOYEE ISN'T LEGALLY ELIGIBLE TO WORK IN THE UNITED STATES? If you wanted to meet the letter of the law, you would have to hire someone

> If the worker is an independent contractor or works for one, then he is not considered your employee and you won't be stuck with the associated paperwork or costs.

The issue may arise if you are audited, or if your employee files for social security or unemployment benefits and shows that you failed to pay taxes on his or her behalf.

else. If you wanted to continue employing an illegal who expects to become legal in the future, then you may want to go ahead and pay any back taxes. But you'll be in a gray area: The Social Security Administration will report illegal workers when it knows about them, but it doesn't assume that the lack of a social security number means the employee whose taxes you're paying is illegal (see the opposite page).

The Taxes You Must Pay

Social security and medicare taxes. If you pay your household employee $1,400 or more in 2003 (indexed for inflation in the future), you must pay part of his or her social security taxes and medicare taxes annually with your income-tax return. The combined tax rate, as before, is 15.3% of wages.

Although your employee is supposed to pay half of that amount, you must submit the full amount to the IRS with your own income-tax return. You can withhold half of the 15.3% tax (7.65%) from the employee's wages, or you can pay the full amount yourself.

You're off the hook if, for example, your babysitter is a high-school student; you needn't pay the tax as long as your employee is under 18 and doesn't list his or her principal occupation as household employment.

Federal unemployment taxes. If you're paying the employee more than $1,000 cash during any three-month period, you're also liable for federal unemployment taxes (FUTA). This amounts to 6.2% of the first $7,000 of wages, but you'll probably be eligible for a credit

---

A CAREGIVER TIP

One way to arrange for in-home caregiver help while avoiding tax obligations is to trade room and board for dependent care. Under such an arrangement, the IRS does not consider you liable for medicare, social security or any other taxes, nor would the room and board be taxable for you as the employer or the caregiver as employee.

---

against this for paying your state's unemployment tax.

State unemployment taxes. Most states use the federal $1,000-a-quarter test to determine who must pay state unemployment tax, but the trigger point is $500 in New York and the District of Columbia.

Check with your state's department of labor or employment, or the local unemployment claims office. Ask about payment schedules and any other state taxes you might owe, such as training and disability taxes.

What about income-tax withholding? It's up to you and your employee to decide whether you will provide withholding of the employee's wages for income-tax purposes. If you withhold on your employee's behalf, you can pay in the appropriate amount when you pay the social security and medicare tax.

The tax forms and publications you'll need are listed in the box on page 142.

Is Your Employee Legal?

Before you can hire an alien worker, you have to meet these requirements of the U.S. Immigration and Naturalization Service (INS):

- **You must show** that you tried to find an American worker but that no one was right or available for the job. The Department of Labor requires that you advertise a job in a local paper and interview all applicants before hiring the alien worker.
- **You state that you will pay** that worker the going rate in your neighborhood for comparable work.

In addition, it's up to you to make sure anyone you hire has a legal right to work in the U.S. You're supposed to fill out Form I-9 (which you can order or download from the the INS Web site at www.ins.gov), listing the documents your employee presented to verify his or her eligibility to work. These might include an alien registration receipt card (known as a "green card"), an unexpired temporary resident card or a certificate of U.S. citizenship. You keep the form, available

If you're paying the employee more than $1,000 cash during any three-month period, you're also liable for federal unemployment taxes (FUTA).

from the INS, with your employment records.

For more information, contact your INS office (www.ins.gov) or the Department of Labor and request *Application for Employment Authorization* (Form I-765).

IF YOU EMPLOY AN "ILLEGAL". If your employee is an illegal alien, as his or her employer you could petition the Immigration and Naturalization Service to have the person work with you legally. While awaiting approval your employee should go back to his or her country of

---

PAPERWORK FOR HOUSEHOLD EMPLOYERS

You can get any of these forms and publications by calling the IRS at 800-829-3676. Most can be downloaded from the IRS Web site at: www.irs.gov.

- *Application for Employer Identification Number* (Form SS-4). With this complicated form, you can apply for your federal employer identification number. But if you don't apply for one, the IRS will simply assign one to you upon receiving your first estimated tax payment.
- *Household Employer's Tax Guide* (IRS Publication 926). A helpful guide.
- *Employee's Withholding Allowance Certificate* (Form W-4) and *(Circular E) Employer's Tax Guide Publication 15.* Ask for this if you're going to provide withholding for your employee.
- *Wage and Tax Statement* (Form W-2). Like any other employer, you provide this statement of annual earnings to your employee by January 31 and to the Social Security Administration by the end of February.
- *Earned Income Credit Advance Payment Certificate* (Form W-5) and *Notice of a*

Possible Federal Tax Refund Due to the Earned Income Credit (IRS Notice 797). Your employee is eligible for this tax credit if he or she has a dependent child and earns less than $29,666 a year (for 2003). The employee gives you the W-5, which requires you to pay the credit in installments each payday. The money comes out of the taxes that you would otherwise send to the IRS with Form 941 *(Employer's Quarterly Federal Tax Return).* If your employee is eligible for this credit and you don't make the appropriate arrangements, you can be penalized.
- *Employer's Annual Federal Unemployment Tax Return* (Form 940-EZ). Due by January 31 for the previous year.
- *Child and Dependent Care Expenses* (IRS Publication 503).
- *Employment Eligibility Verification* (Immigration and Naturalization Service Form I-9). This confirms that you verified your employee's legal right to work in the U.S. It's available from the INS Web site at: www.ins.gov or by calling your local or regional office of the INS (check the blue pages in your phone book).

origin and later re-enter the U.S. legally. The reality is that such illegal employees often stay in the U.S. while the employer's petition is being approved. Chances are no one will check on the illegal's whereabouts, so you'll probably get away with it. If you are caught, your illegal employee will be sent home. You'll be warned the first time and fined the second time.

For more information, see *How to Get a Green Card; Legal Ways to Stay in the U.S.*, by Loida Nicolas Lewis (Nolo, $29.99; 800-992-6656; www.nolo.com).

If Your Employee Is Injured

About half the states require household employers to buy workers' compensation insurance, which covers on-the-job injuries and pays benefits while the employee is unable to work. A few states require that the insurance be purchased through a state fund; the rest let you buy through private companies. You may be able to get coverage through your homeowners insurance policy—in fact, in New Hampshire, New Jersey and New York, most domestic workers are covered under your homeowners policy. For more details, contact your state's department of labor or employment, as well as your insurance agent.

When You Become the Landlord

You may sometime have reason to rent out your home—perhaps because you're going away on a temporary work assignment, you've given up trying to sell your property in a down market, or you don't need to sell it but want to use it as an income-producing property. It's not a decision to enter into lightly, because when you become a landlord you take on a whole new slate of legal obligations. Here are the basics you need to know.

The Landlord's Obligations

As a landlord, you must do your best to be sure that the premises you rent—your apartment, your house, or even a room in your house—are safe and hazard-

If your employee is an illegal alien, as the employer you could petition to have the person work with you legally.

As a landlord, you must do your best to be sure that the premises you rent are safe and hazard-free.

free. Almost all states require landlords to offer an implied *warrant of habitability*—that is, to make their premises suitable for living or other appropriate purposes by complying with all state and local housing, building, health and safety codes. This can also appear as a provision in a lease. It means that the tenant can expect such essentials as heat and hot water, light, plumbing, lockable doors, sanitation and proper maintenance. If a tenant is injured because you did not take proper precautions, he can sue you.

Finding Renters

As a landlord, you can refuse to rent property to anyone for any reason as long as your decision isn't based on sex, religion, race, color, handicap, familial status or national origin. Federal and many state and local laws prohibit such discrimination. Some state and local laws prohibit discrimination based on sexual orientation.

Drawing Up a Good Rental Contract

Leases are usually preprinted forms that you can buy in stationery stores and fill in. A lease should include:

- **a description of the property** (street address and apartment number);
- **the names of the parties** involved and how many people will live there;
- **a requirement of notice** if someone other than the person who signed the lease moves in or out of the property;
- **the amount of monthly rent;** and
- **the length of lease** (monthly, yearly, and so on).

The lease should also spell out the tenant's and landlord's rights and responsibilities for repairs, including:

- **the amount of security deposit** (the allowable amount that a landlord can require varies by state, as do rules on whether a deposit must be kept in an escrow account);
- **a pet clause,** specifying whether pets are allowed, and, if so, whether additional rent or security deposit is required;

- **a provision for an inspection,** with a checklist, required within ten to 14 days of moving in and of moving out;
- **a clause concerning assigning and subletting** of lease rights (see the discussion on page 147);
- **a clause concerning the landlord's right to entry,** typically requiring 24 to 48 hours' notice in advance; and
- **what the landlord can do if the rent is late or isn't paid,** or some other element of the contract is violated. Late-payment fees and other means of enforcing the terms of a lease are usually regulated by contract law and local statutes.

Especially if a professional property manager isn't involved in the deal, it's a good idea to have your lawyer review any lease before you sign it.

An Effective Inspection

During the moving-in or -out inspection, the landlord and the tenant usually inspect the property together and make a checklist of anything that is damaged and requires repair. This might include such features as blinds, lights and other fixtures, the floor, the condition of appliances, and so on. You or a tenant might want to take photos of the appliances before moving in or out to show that there's been no change.

Dealing With a Bad Tenant

In principle, a landlord has the right to evict a tenant who has fallen behind in his rent, used the apartment for illegal purposes such as drug dealing, refused to maintain the premises or broken the lease agreement by having a pet. However, procedures vary from state to state, making eviction more or less easy to carry out. So call your local clerk of court handling eviction cases and ask for manuals or information on the subject. You can also check with your community development office, city housing division or landlord-tenant agency and ask who can help you.

Especially if
a professional
property
manager isn't
involved in
the deal, it's
a good idea
to have your
lawyer review
any lease
before you
sign it.

FOR MORE INFORMATION

For more on your state and municipal landlord-tenant law, contact a local tenants union or landlord support group. If you're thinking of becoming a landlord, you can consult the following sources:

■ *Landlording: A Handy Manual for Scrupulous Landlords and Landladies Who Do It Themselves,* by Leigh Robinson (Express Press, $27.95).

■ *Landlord's Handbook: A Complete Guide to Managing Small Residential Properties,* by Daniel Goodwin, et al (Dearborn Trade, $29.95). This hands-on guide for landlords provides instruction on the use of active management techniques that maximize tax deductions and increase bottom lines.

If You Are the Tenant

For starters, a good rental contract will protect you as much as your landlord. Review any lease for the items listed on pages 144-145, and make sure you can live with the terms.

If the landlord volunteers neither an inspection nor some other opportunity to create a checklist of already-damaged items, do your own inspection when you move in and write the landlord a letter documenting any problems that you find. That will help ensure that you're not eventually charged for something you didn't do.

Getting Your Landlord's Attention

Chances are if you're renting an apartment or home from a private individual, he'll do his best to make repairs in a timely fashion, if only to maintain the value of the property. So, if you need your landlord to fix something, ask him promptly in writing and give him a chance to take care of it. But be sure to keep a record of your calls and copies of letters and other documents.

If your landlord doesn't respond, you can call the landlord-tenant agency in your city or another appropriate local or state agency to see whether it can intervene and help resolve the problem (see the box at the top of this page).

If he continues to breach the warrant of habitability

(see page 143)—that is, he is not making your apartment or home livable:

- **Subject to state and local laws, withhold your rent,** pay your rent into escrow, ask for a reduction in rent or deduct the cost of repairs from your rent;
- **Terminate the lease;** or
- **Sue,** say, in small-claims court, to recover damages or the cost of repairs that you've paid for.

If the owner of your home has hired a professional property manager who is falling down on the job, talk to the owner, who will want to know that he or she isn't getting the service paid for.

What If You Want to Break Your Lease?

First, see whether your lease allows you to assign the lease or sublet your apartment. If you assign the lease, someone else takes it over entirely and you are free from all responsibility for the apartment. If you sublet, another tenant moves in, but you are still ultimately responsible for paying the rent and for any tenant problems that arise.

If you must move and can't assign or sublet the apartment, then you will have to break your lease. Check your lease to see whether there is a clause detailing this process, or consult your local landlord-

---

PROTECTION FOR RENTERS

Renters need insurance as much as owners do because damage to your personal possessions is not covered by your landlord's insurance. Renter's insurance protects all your possessions—your stereo, jewelry, bikes, TVs, computers—if they are stolen or damaged or destroyed by fire, smoke, explosion, lightning, windstorm or water damage from plumbing.

This kind of insurance also protects you from liability if someone injures himself in your home, and it covers your legal-defense costs if you are sued as a result. (See the discussion of homeowners liability beginning on page 127.)

Generally, if you break your lease, a landlord is entitled to collect the rest of rent due. However, you probably won't have to pay him for all of those future months.

tenant agency. Generally, if you break your lease, a landlord is entitled to collect the rest of the rent due to him under the contract. However, you probably won't have to pay him for all of those future months: Before he can collect it from you, he must make a good faith effort—run an advertisement or post a sign—to find a tenant to replace you. You may have to pay for lost rent, covering the time before the unit is rented to a new tenant, and marketing costs incurred while trying to find a new tenant.

If Your Landlord Wants to Evict You

Laws concerning eviction vary from state to state, but generally, landlords must give you written notice (a demand notice or notice to pay) that they intend to sue for eviction, and tell you why. Then you will receive a summons from the court and a copy of the complaint for eviction filed by the landlord, and a trial will ensue, usually within about two weeks. The landlord will have to prove that you didn't live up to the terms of your lease. When you receive the summons, you could nip the whole thing in the bud by simply agreeing to move out and correct the problem. If you feel you must stay in your apartment—because, for example, it's close to your child's school, or because you feel you are being unfairly discriminated against—then you might want to fight an eviction. But if you lose and are evicted, the eviction will appear on your credit record and haunt you for years to come.

If you need more information or advice, you can contact your local tenant's union or Legal Aid office:

- **To search for tenant's organizations in your state,** visit "The Tenant Resource Directory" at www.directory.tenantsunion.org.
- **To locate a local legal aid office,** look under "Legal Services" in your local Yellow Pages, or contact the National Legal Aid and Defender Association to request a referral (1625 K St., N.W., Suite 800, Washington, DC 20006-1604; 202.452.0620; www.nlada.org).

Your Workplace Rights and Retirement

When it comes to your rights in the workplace, you may be surprised to learn just how few you have. For example, unless you've signed a contract that lists your rights as an employee, your employer is free to set whatever policies it wishes, change them as it likes and, in most states, fire you for almost any reason, without even telling you why. But that doesn't mean you have to go quietly. Referring to this section throughout your tenure with an employer—before and after you've been hired, and if necessary, after you've been fired—will help ensure that you and your employer are operating on a level playing field. Knowing the laws of the workplace and using them to your advantage will give you confidence and a greater measure of control over your fate.

Getting Hired

The biggest legal issue you face in the workplace is the possibility of being discriminated against before you're ever hired. That's illegal in principle and in practice, and is the subject of the next section. We'll then discuss what you should do if you encounter discrimination on the job. The box on page 154, provides a rundown of the federal laws designed to protect you from discrimination in the hiring process and beyond. Later on in the chapter, you'll find discussions of the Americans With Disabilities Act, the Family and Medical Leave Act, and your rights with regard to your pension and social security.

There are rare cases when a personal characteristic, such as sex, age, race or religion, would count as a bona fide occupational qualification.

Off-Limit Interview Questions

A prospective employer should ask questions that relate directly to an applicant's job qualifications, which wouldn't usually involve:

- **your age or date of birth;**
- **your spouse's occupation,** ages of your children or plans to have children;
- **your ancestry, national origin, native language** or language you speak at home, parentage or birthplace;
- **the naturalization status** of your parents, spouse or children;
- **your religion;**
- **your political affiliations;** or
- **the existence, nature or severity of a disability** (see the discussion of the Americans With Disabilities Act, on page 161).

There are rare cases, however, when a personal characteristic, such as sex, age, race or religion, would count as a bona fide occupational qualification (BFOQ). For instance, a hospital might hire men only for an all-male maximum-security ward, or a theatre might have specific requirements for actors and actresses in certain parts. You could be asked whether you're over 21 years of age if it's pertinent to the job—say, if you were applying to be a bartender.

If You Are Asked Illegal Questions

You have a choice of strategies if an employer asks you an illegal question during an interview:

- **You can deal with the question by replying** that you don't believe it is relevant to your ability to do the job or by asking the interviewer to explain its relevance.

- **If you otherwise like the company,** you could give the interviewer the benefit of the doubt, presuming his or her ignorance, and deflect the question with a light touch and a sense of humor.

- **If you want to formally complain,** ask for a business

HOW PRIVATE IS YOUR EMAIL?

Not very. Although email seems private, it is not, especially in the workplace. Your boss has a legal right to monitor it, as well as the Internet sites you frequent. Your personal email sent from home is also not as private as it seems. It can be intercepted by hackers, and if you are suspected of a crime, law enforcement officials with a warrant can seize your electronic correspondence. Even your Internet service provider may legally be able to scrutinize it.

It is possible to use software to encrypt your email messages. Still, the best advice is, don't send anything in an email that you would not want to see published on the front page of your local newspaper.

---

card from the interviewer and indicate that you are filing a complaint with the Equal Employment Opportunity Commission (EEOC) and considering legal action. You might even be offered the job on the spot as a result. But would you really want to work for an employer who operates like that?

■ **If you feel that your response**—or lack of response—to the question was used against you and cost you the job, you could contact a lawyer who specializes in employment law or file a charge with the EEOC (for more on the EEOC, see page 153). You might seek to simply prove that the company discriminated and should be subject to appropriate penalties, or you might also seek to win the job or promotion plus any back pay and punitive damages. The down side of taking action is that, win or lose, you may find yourself labeled a troublemaker and consequently find it difficult to find employment elsewhere or to function well where you are. Deciding whether to proceed is a highly personal decision.

Non-Compete Clauses
When you are offered a job, your prospective employer may want to ensure that you won't work for any of

If you intend to sign a non-compete agreement, hire a lawyer to help you review it beforehand and negotiate the terms if possible.

the business's competitors within a specified period of time after you leave its employ. Such an agreement will also likely prohibit you from starting a similar business within a specified geographic area and for a certain number of years. The point of non-compete clauses or contracts is to prevent you from competing for your employer's customers or clients after you leave.

Avoid signing such a document if you can. In general, a non-compete clause does not benefit the employee. Because of that, most states have laws limiting non-compete clauses to some degree.

If you live in a state where such contracts are allowed, your employer may be able to make signing the contract a condition of your employment.

If you do intend to sign a non-compete agreement, hire a lawyer to help you review it beforehand and negotiate the terms if possible.

If you sign such an agreement and then later violate it, your employer may sue both you and your new employer. Your former employer may try to stop you from working for your current employer and seek payment for the value of lost clients or customers.

But if the agreement is overly stringent, a court may rule in your favor or amend the contract to make it more reasonable: Usually an employer can prevent a former employee from competing only within the same geographic area—say, the same metropolitan region or county. The broader the geographic boundaries and the longer the time limit, the less legal clout the employer will have if it attempts to enforce the agreement. For example, at the extreme, most courts would not uphold an agreement that prevents you from working in a certain business in any part of the country for the rest of your life. Your case will be stronger if you are engaged in honest employment clearly not intended to hurt your former employer, if a reasonable time has passed since your employment there or if you have moved to a different city.

CONFIDENTIALITY AGREEMENTS. In addition to non-compete contracts, you may be required by your employer or by state law to keep your company's secrets to yourself. Its proprietary information could include business plans, technical information, pricing and discounts, products and inventions, copyrights, computer programs and more.

Your company may state its policies regarding proprietary information in its employee handbook, or it may ask you to sign a confidentiality agreement when you are hired. The agreement typically defines what information is included, specifies limits to your ability to disclose, copy or disseminate the information and to whom, and the consequences for doing so. For example, your company could seek a court's injunction to restrain you from disclosing the information or sue you for any losses or damages that it suffered because of your breach of confidentiality.

Before you sign such an agreement, make sure that you understand what, if any, restraints would be imposed upon you after you leave the company; consult a lawyer if necessary (see also the earlier discussion of non-compete contracts).

Before you sign a confidentiality agreement, make sure that you understand what, if any, restraints would be imposed upon you after you leave the company.

Discrimination on the Job

The first thing to do if you feel that you're being discriminated against on the job is to take the matter to your employer. This is important because it may not know about the occurrence of discrimination within the organization, or the actions or attitudes of a particular supervisor. If, once informed, your employer takes no action to resolve the problem, you should file a claim with the Equal Employment Opportunity Commission (EEOC), the federal agency charged with enforcing the equal-employment laws described above. It is illegal for an employer to fire you for bringing a complaint to the EEOC. If it does, you can sue for damages, including reinstatement to your job if you want it and lost pay.

Filing a Claim of Discrimination

To file a claim with the EEOC, locate the office nearest

you in the federal government section of your telephone directory, contact the EEOC headquarters in Washington (800-669-4000), or call your city hall and ask whether your community has an equal-opportunity office that represents the federal EEOC. You must file your complaint within 180 days of the most recent act of discrimination.

Be prepared with evidence, including any relevant documents such as performance evaluations and records of incidents that took place. Any time you believe you've been subject to discrimination, it's wise to note names of participants, dates, details of the incident and names of any witnesses.

If, after investigation, the EEOC finds reasonable

LAWS THAT PROTECT YOU AT WORK

There are several laws that either alone or in combination protect most workers from discrimination.

- **Title VII of the Civil Rights Act of 1964,** commonly known as Title VII, prohibits employment discrimination based on race, color, religion, sex or national origin. Title VII applies to hiring, firing, promotions, raises, benefits and most other aspects of employment. However, businesses with fewer than 15 employees are not bound by Title VII or its provisions.
- **The Pregnancy Discrimination Act,** part of Title VII, makes it illegal for an employer to refuse to hire a pregnant woman, to terminate her employment or to compel her to take maternity leave.

Employees who feel that they have been discriminated against may also use Title VII in conjunction with several other federal laws, including the:

- **Equal Pay Act of 1963,** which outlaws discrimination in wages on the basis of gender.
- **Age Discrimination in Employment Act of 1967** (ADEA), which outlaws workplace discrimination on the basis of age if the employee is 40 years of age or older. The Age Discrimination Act applies only to private employers with 20 or more employees; federal, state and local governments; and employment agencies with 25 or more members. Many states have laws banning age discrimination no matter what the person's age—check with your state department of labor to find out about the law where you live.
- **Americans With Disabilities Act** (ADA, see page 161), which prohibits employers from discriminating against qualified people with disabilities, including AIDS.

cause to believe there has been discrimination, it will contact your employer and first attempt conciliation. It may ask your company to hire, rehire or promote you, or to award you back pay for the time since you were let go. Your employer might also be subject to other fines and penalties for its employment practices, which it may be forced to change. If conciliation fails and your case is approved for litigation, the EEOC will file a lawsuit on your behalf in federal district court.

Your State's Role

Many states also have their own laws concerning discrimination in the workplace. If your state has an employment-discrimination agency or a human rights commission, you may file a claim there. (Ask the nearest EEOC office whether your city or state has such an agency, or look in the blue pages of your telephone directory under state government.) If your state does have such an agency, you will probably have up to 300 days from the date of the discriminatory action to file a charge.

Most states have a workshare agreement with the EEOC. In other words, if you file a charge with the state agency, your complaint is also lodged with the EEOC. And if you lodge a complaint with the EEOC and there is a state agency that can handle your case, the EEOC will turn it over to them.

Sexual Orientation

Although Federal workers are protected from workplace discrimination on the basis of sexual orientation, no federal law specifically outlaws such discrimination in the private sector. Eight states (Colorado, Deleware, Illinois, Indiana, Montana, New Mexico, Pennsylvania and Washington) have laws prohibiting sexual-orientation discrimination in public employment. Thirteen states (California, Connecticut, Hawaii, Maryland, Massachusetts, Minnesota, Nevada, New Hampshire, New Jersey, New York, Rhode Island, Vermont and Wisconsin) and the District of Columbia have laws prohibiting such discrimination in both private and public jobs.

Most states have a workshare agreement with the EEOC. In other words, if you file a charge with the state agency, your complaint is also lodged with the EEOC.

Only about 1% of the cases filed with the EEOC are taken to court.

Most other large cities, including Atlanta, Chicago, New York and Philadelphia, have laws protecting gays and lesbians from discrimination in the workplace.

Your Right to Sue

In theory, once you file your claim with the EEOC, the agency will first try to work out a settlement with your employer; if that fails, it may file a lawsuit. In practice, because the agency doesn't have sufficient staff, it may take months or even years to respond to your complaint, much less bring suit. Only about 1% of the cases filed with the EEOC are taken to court.

So you may end up hiring a lawyer and pursuing the matter yourself. If the EEOC doesn't act within 180 days, you can ask for a right-to-sue letter, authorizing you to sue your employer in federal court.

If you decide to request a right-to-sue letter, be sure you have an attorney lined up to take your case: You must file a lawsuit within 90 days of receiving the letter. If you win your case, you will probably be granted attorney fees and back pay if you were fired, but don't get too hopeful. It could take years—and lots of money—to win such a victory. Again, as described previously, you may find yourself labeled a troublemaker and have difficulty finding employment elsewhere. You may choose to proceed based on principle, or you may decide to put it all behind you and move on. Only you can decide which is the best strategy for you.

FOR MORE INFORMATION

For more information about your rights in the workplace, call your state department of labor or state human-rights commission. Or write to or call the following agencies:

- **U.S. Department of Labor,** 200 Constitution Ave., N.W., Washington, DC 20210; 866-4-USA-DOL; www.dol.gov.
- **Equal Employment Opportunity Commission,** 1801 L St., N.W., Washington, DC 20507; 800-669-4000; www.eeoc.gov.

Stopping Sexual Harassment

Considered a form of sex discrimination under Title VII, sexual harassment is against the law. And, with the creation of the Civil Rights Act of 1991, victims of sex discrimination can sue for compensatory damages. How is sexual harassment defined? The EEOC has established the following guidelines.

Sexual harassment occurs when:

- **employees are made to believe they will lose their jobs** if they don't submit to sexual overtures;
- **employees are made to believe they will lose a promotion** or good work assignments if they don't submit to sexual overtures; or
- **sexual overtures interfere with the employee's work performance** or create a hostile or offensive work environment.

Sexual harassment is an equal-opportunity offense—women can be harassed by men, men by women, and each by the same sex. It can include not only physical conduct but verbal advances, such as requests for sexual favors, vulgar or lewd comments, and sexual propositions. It can also include displaying sexually suggestive objects.

While some extreme behavior need only occur once to constitute sexual harassment—if your boss says "sleep with me or you're fired," or touches you on a private part of your body, for example—the inappropriate behavior usually must continue over time to be considered harassment.

SEXUAL FAVORITISM. Sexual favoritism is also a form of sexual harassment. For example, a court could rule that you are a victim of sexual harassment in the following cases:

- **If your boss trades pay raises for sex** and you are denied such benefits for refusing to submit.
- **If your boss has an affair with a staff member** and she gets a raise and you don't for equal work performance.

> Sexual harassment is an equal-opportunity offense—women can be harassed by men, men by women, and each by the same sex.

You're the only one who can define whether someone has stepped over your limits.

INDIRECT HARASSMENT. Sexually oriented activity need not be targeted directly and personally at you for you to be a victim of harassment. For instance, if your boss or co-workers hang calendars featuring near-naked men or women or they make "dirty" jokes that offend you, you can claim harassment so long as the behavior creates a hostile work environment and interferes with your ability to do your job.

This provision is one of the stickiest for employers and the courts to deal with because defining what's hostile or disruptive is so subjective. A joke that you find offensive another person might find off-color but amusing. That's why courts try to apply the reasonable-person standard—that is, would a reasonable person find the behavior offensive or are you being overly sensitive? If it's the latter, the court would be less likely to rule in your favor.

What if It Has Happened to You?

What should you do if you think you are the victim of sexual harassment? You're the only one who can define whether someone has stepped over your limits. Depending on your degree of comfort and control over the situation, you may want to immediately and clearly tell the person where you draw the line and how you expect his or her behavior to change in the future.

If that's not an option or if the person persists, your first move is to see whether your employer has a policy against sexual harassment and a grievance procedure designed to resolve sexual-harassment claims. (Look in your employee manual or ask your company's human-resources or personnel department.)

If your company has no formal procedure, try confronting the harasser and emphatically telling him or her to stop. Also notify your supervisor. If your supervisor is the person doing the harassing, then go to her supervisor. Or write a letter of complaint to your company's highest-ranking executive, and send a copy to your supervisor. Let them know that you are prepared to take legal action.

Keep a copy of the letter in a file, along with any

documents you receive from the company in response and any evidence of harassment, including sexually suggestive notes or photos sent to you by the harasser. Also keep a log of the incidents of harassment and make note of any witnesses to them. Find out whether this has happened to other people.

To be sure you're protected from being fired, you should also file a claim with the Equal Employment Opportunity Commission (see page 153). It is illegal for an employer to retaliate against an employee—say, by claiming that your job performance is substandard and then firing you or demoting, failing to promote, or otherwise harassing you—for claiming discrimination.

Several states have laws that specifically prohibit sexual harassment of employees; most others have laws that prohibit sex discrimination without directly referring to harassment. If your state specifically prohibits sexual harassment, you can also file a complaint with the appropriate state agency.

If you feel you've suffered great distress from the harassment, you can also file a personal-injury lawsuit claiming intentional infliction of emotional harm or defamation. Consult a lawyer who specializes in employment law or civil rights if you are considering this option. Such cases can result in very large money rewards, but they may take years and thousands of dollars to resolve.

> **If you feel you've suffered great distress from the harassment, you can also file a personal-injury lawsuit.**

Getting Fired

In general, if you work for the private sector (a non-governmental organization), unless you have a contract stating the terms of your employment and termination, you are considered an "at will" employee and your employer can fire you for almost any performance-related reason. An employer cannot, however, fire you for a reason that violates state or federal anti-discrimination laws (relating to sex, race, religion, national origin, disability or sexual harassment).

Nor, under the federal Age Discrimination in Employment Act (ADEA), can an employer force older workers of any age to retire or fire them and replace them with younger, less-well-paid workers. There is an exception to this rule, however. An employer may force an executive or other corporate policymaker who is age 65 or older to retire, as long as they've been in their jobs at least two years and have earned a minimum pension of $44,000 a year.

Still, there are plenty of nondiscriminatory reasons for which you can be fired. Defined by the employer's own standard, those reasons may include:

- **insubordination**
- **lying on your job application**
- **excessive absence or lateness**
- **low productivity**
- **incompetence**
- **negligence**
- **sleeping on the job**
- **violating safety rules**
- **harassing coworkers**
- **stealing, misappropriating or damaging company property**
- **fighting**
- **gambling on the job**
- **using or possessing alcohol or drugs on the job**
- **being convicted of any crime**

You can also be fired—though it might not be called that—because your job has become obsolete, because of a downturn in business, or because you are judged physically or mentally unable to perform the essential duties of the job and no reasonable accommodation can be made to make it possible for you to do so (the issue of accommodation is discussed in the box on page 162). The courts have also supported employers who fired employees found moonlighting at another job, especially those involving conflict of interest, or engaging in conduct that had a negative impact on the business. For example, a police officer might be prohibited from working as a bartender in his or her off hours. The laws governing such situations vary from state to state.

What You Can Do

It seems only fair that your employer tell you why it is firing you; some states have laws requiring employers to give you a reason (to find out if yours is one of them, contact your state's department of labor). In these states, if you are fired without a good and supportable reason, or for a reason that violates public laws (such as refusing to commit a crime or give false testimony), you can sue for wrongful discharge and seek reinstatement and recovery of lost wages and benefits.

If you live in a state where you can be fired at will without being given a reason, you could still sue for breach of implied contract, breach of good faith and fair dealing, or defamation, as the case may be. Such cases, however, can be very difficult to prove and win.

If you feel you were fired for discriminatory reasons, begin by registering your complaint with the EEOC (see page 153), which ostensibly will contact your employer and investigate your claim.

In the meantime, seek another job to show that you are willing and able to work. If you don't, you might weaken your claim that you wanted your job and were worthy of it, and possibly limit any award of back pay.

It seems only fair that your employer tell you why it is firing you; some states have laws requiring employers to give you a reason.

The Americans With Disabilities Act

The federal Americans With Disabilities Act (ADA) makes it illegal to discriminate against someone with a disability. This law affects companies with 15 or more employees.

What Qualifies as a Disability?

A disability is a substantial physical or mental impairment that limits one or more major life activities, such as walking, breathing, hearing, seeing or learning. AIDS and HIV infection are considered disabilities.

Even if you don't have a current disability, but had one in the past, you are protected by the ADA. In other words, if an employer finds out you had cancer, it can't

If you work as a volunteer with people who have AIDS, your employer cannot fire you simply for fear the insurance costs will go up, or because he fears the disease and associates you with it.

refuse to hire you simply because it is fearful its insurance costs will go up.

You are also protected if you are associated with someone who has or has had a disability or is regarded as having or having had a disability. For instance, if your spouse or housemate has been diagnosed with AIDS, or if you work as a volunteer with people who have AIDS, your employer cannot fire you simply for fear that insurance costs will go up, or because he fears the disease and associates you with it.

The ADA also covers rehabilitated drug addicts and alcoholics who remain qualified to do their jobs. In some cases obesity is covered by the ADA, but obesity claims are considered on a case-by-case basis.

The ADA does not protect pregnant women (though the Pregnancy Discrimination Act does—see page 154) or current users of illegal drugs. Short-term medical disabilities, such as a broken arm, are not covered.

How It Works

The ADA generally prohibits employers from discriminating on the basis of a disability.

EMPLOYER ACCOMMODATIONS

Employers can accommodate people with disabilities through any of the following means:

- **making existing facilities used by employees readily accessible** to and usable by persons with disabilities
- **restructuring jobs,** modifying work schedules, or reassigning vacant positions
- **acquiring or modifying equipment** or devices, adjusting or modifying examinations, training materials or policies, and providing readers or interpreters

For a more complete list of the ADA's provisions, contact the EEOC (1801 L St., N.W., Washington, DC 20507; 800-669-4000; www.eeoc.gov).

■ **An employer may not ask** job applicants about the existence, nature or severity of a disability; a job offer may be conditioned on the results of a medical exam, but only if the exam is required of all entering employees and the results of the medical exam indicate that the applicant is not qualified for the position.

■ **An employer may ask applicants** about their ability to perform specific job functions.

■ **An employer can refuse** to make an accommodation or refuse to hire a person requiring an accommodation only if the expense or difficulty of providing it would cause an undue hardship to the employer (see the box on the opposite page. The business is free to make its decision within ADA guidelines, but workers can challenge the decision.

■ **An employer can also refuse to hire** a disabled person if the employer cannot eliminate or reduce the risk of substantial harm by reasonable accommodation—for instance, if the person would be required to work with a certain piece of machinery that's unsafe for him to operate as is and can't be modified.

If you think you have been discriminated against because of a disability, you can file a complaint with the EEOC (see page 153).

The Family and Medical Leave Act

Under the Family and Medical Leave Act of 1993 (FMLA), your employer must grant you up to 12 weeks of unpaid leave annually:

■ **for the birth or adoption of a child;**
■ **for the care of a spouse, child or parent with a serious health condition;** or
■ **because you've become unable to work** due to a serious health condition.

An employer can refuse to hire a disabled person if the employer cannot eliminate or reduce the risk of substantial harm by reasonable means.

To qualify for a family or medical leave, you must have been on the job for at least 12 months and have put in at least 1,250 hours in the year.

What constitutes a serious health condition?
- **an illness, injury, or physical or mental condition** that requires an overnight stay in a hospital
- **an absence of more than three calendar days of work,** school or other regular activities
- **continuing treatment by a health care provider**

You may be required to submit medical certification of your condition.

Limits to the Law
The Family Medical and Leave Act does not apply to every worker. It applies only if you work for a company of 50 or more local employees, and you must have been on the job for at least 12 months and have put in at least 1,250 hours in the year preceding the leave.

Even within those parameters, there are further limitations:
- **The law allows companies** to exempt the highest paid 10% of employees.
- **If you and your spouse** happen to work for the same employer, you will get only one 12-week period to split between you.
- **Companies don't have to provide** leave to employees in an area where there are fewer than 50 employees in a 75-mile radius. In other words, a small regional office of a large company may be exempt.

How It Works
If your spouse, parent or child has an illness or injury that qualifies you to take leave, your employer must grant you leave. The company can't deny you leave simply because it feels someone else could take care of your family member.

For a new child, you must take the leave at once (unless your employer agrees to a different arrangement).

For medical problems, you may be able to work out a more flexible arrangement if your doctor certifies the necessity. That means you may be able to take a day or a week when needed, or reduce your work week or workday as necessary.

Your employer can, however, count your accrued paid-vacation, sick-leave and personal-leave days toward the 12 weeks of family leave. Though some employers may allow you to take your paid leave as part of your unpaid family leave, they aren't required to.

INSURANCE WHILE YOU'RE ON LEAVE. You do not qualify for unemployment insurance during your leave. However, five states (California, Hawaii, New Jersey, New York and Rhode Island) and Puerto Rico offer temporary disability insurance, which provides you with a percentage of your income during your own medical leave.

Employers covered by the law must maintain your health coverage during the leave and, once it is over, must reinstate you to the same job or an equivalent job.

If you go on leave and decide not to return to your job, your employer may ask you to reimburse the cost of health benefits paid during the leave.

STATE AND INDIVIDUAL VARIATIONS OF FAMILY LEAVE. Be aware that some companies offer family-leave policies that are more generous than those required by the FMLA. Ask your personnel department for a copy of your company's family-leave policy.

Also, many states have their own family-leave laws. If your state does (check with your state or the federal department of labor to find out), you may use whichever law—state or federal—offers you the greater benefit. State laws are generally more liberal, in some cases allowing longer leave periods or broader definitions of serious illness. However, in many

> Your employer can count your accrued paid vacation, sick leave and personal-leave days toward the 12 weeks of family leave.

FOR MORE INFORMATION

Regardless of your sex, if you have questions about the Family Medical and Leave Act (FMLA), contact the Job Problem Hotline (800-522-0925; www.feminist.com/9to5.htm), sponsored by 9 to 5, the National Association of Working Women, in Milwaukee, Wisconsin.

Just as important as getting or keeping a job is making sure you can take care of yourself when you are old enough to leave it.

states, an employer is free to deny an employee's request for leave if the time off would cause undue hardship to the employer.

WORST CASE. If, unable to deny you the leave, the company fires you instead, you can sue it to get reinstatement, lost wages, and attorney's fees. Seek the service of a lawyer experienced in employment law.

Your Benefits: Pension and Social Security

Just as important as getting or keeping a job is making sure you can take care of yourself when you are old enough to leave it. That's why you need to understand your retirement benefits and social security rules (for information about medicare benefits, see the discussion on page 198 of Chapter 8, "Your Medical Rights").

Your Pension Rights

The laws under ERISA (Employee Retirement Income Security Act of 1974) protect pension participants and their money by requiring companies that offer pensions to meet disclosure, funding and administrative standards.

There are two basic types of employer-sponsored pension plans to which these rules apply:

- **Defined-contribution plans,** in which the company—and possibly the employee—contributes a specified amount each year to the fund. When you retire, you get the money in a lump sum or via an annuity. But the amount you'll get isn't guaranteed, and it will increase only as much as the plan's investments do. These plans include 401(k) and 403(b) plans, deferred profit-sharing and stock-bonus plans.

- **Defined-benefit plans,** which use a formula that usually factors in your years of service and salary to determine the amount of your pension.

You have an advantage if your pension is part of a defined-benefit plan: Your employer is legally obligated to be sure there is enough cash on hand to pay your benefits when you retire. If your company can't pay, the government will; defined-benefit plans are insured by the federal Pension Benefit Guaranty Corp.

■ **A hybrid variation, the cash-balance plan,** is funded by the employer, as defined-benefit plans are, but the money is contributed to individual employee accounts as it is in a 401(k) defined-contribution plan. Many believe the cash-balance plan discriminates against long-time employees who would have received higher retirement benefits from their defined-benefit plan Several government agencies and Congress are investigating to determine if the plan requires modification.

BECOMING A MEMBER OF A PENSION PLAN. Federal law generally requires that if you're 21 or older you can become a member of your employer's plan and begin the process of vesting in it after one year of employment. Vesting is the process by which you build up the right to your pension benefits over time.

If you leave the company before you become fully vested, you own any money you may have contributed to the plan, plus whatever your contributions have earned. But you don't completely own the accrued benefit created by the employer's contributions until you're 100% vested. If you leave the company when you're only, say, 20% vested in the plan, then you get to take only 20% of the accrued benefit. Check your company's vesting schedule to see how much you're entitled to. Companies can use one of two schedules for vesting:

■ **vesting of 100% after five years of service** (cliff vesting); or

■ **gradual vesting that starts at 20%** after three years of service and adds 20% for each of the next four years, so that vesting is complete after seven years of employment with the company.

If your pension is part of a defined-benefit plan, your employer is legally obligated to be sure there is enough cash on hand to pay your benefits when you retire.

ERISA protects employees who might miss extended periods because of pregnancy, birth or adoption.

A multi-employer plan can use a ten-year cliff-vesting schedule. Whatever kind of plan you have, it must provide for full vesting at the plan's normal retirement age no matter how many years you've put in, or if the plan is shut down.

IF YOU STOP WORKING TEMPORARILY. Each plan lays down rules defining your pension status when you have a break in service; that is:

- **if you are unemployed** for a period of fewer than 500 hours with the company due to a layoff or extended leave; or
- **if you fail to work a full year,** which ERISA defines as 1,000 hours of service.

ERISA protects employees who might miss extended periods because of pregnancy, birth or adoption of a child, or because of the need to care for a child following birth or adoption. In such cases, up to 501 hours of the leave must be counted as service if failing to count them would create a break in service.

FOR MORE INFORMATION

To find out about your pension plan, read the summary description that must be provided by your company, as well as the plan's annual report. It will tell you how the plan works, what your rights are, and so on.

If you have questions regarding your pension rights, you may want to consult with your company's human resources or pension officer, or your labor union.

Or contact the nonprofit Pensions Rights Center in Washington, DC, 202-296-3776; (www.pensionrights.org). It offers publications on, among other things, how to tell if the people investing your pension are following federal rules, as well as fact sheets summarizing the rights of divorced spouses.

If you still aren't getting what you need from your company's pension administrator, consult an attorney who specializes in pension law.

IF YOU BECOME DISABLED. Your company's plan will define any disability benefit to which you're entitled, possibly a retirement pension if you become disabled after a certain number of years of service.

WHERE DOES A SPOUSE FIGURE IN? One thing that all defined-benefit plans have in common: Your spouse will be the automatic beneficiary of your pension via a joint-and-survivor annuity unless you and your spouse choose some other form of payout and mutually sign this right away. This is an important safeguard for spouses, guaranteeing pension payments over your lifetime and a reduced level of payments for the life of your surviving spouse or other beneficiary. But keep in mind that choosing this option will reduce your monthly benefit to offset the plan's cost of continuing benefits for your survivor.

If your deceased spouse was a federal, local or state government employee, you must be aware that you may forfeit your pension benefits if you remarry, so check with plan administrators beforehand.

Most states consider a retirement plan part of marital property—and therefore in play as part of the divorce settlement. So even though you're the one who earned the pension, your spouse may end up with part of it.

IF YOU WORK PAST AGE 65. Most plans have designed benefits for so-called normal retirement. Because you can't be forced to retire at that age, your plan must recognize service beyond that age by including the additional years of service when it computes your pension benefit.

Social Security

If you're a worker who paid into the social security system for at least ten years or 40 calendar quarters you're generally considered fully insured (your paycheck stubs will show the deductions) and you're entitled to monthly social security payments when you retire (see below) or if you become disabled. You

Your spouse will be the automatic beneficiary of your pension via a joint-and-survivor annuity unless you and your spouse choose some other form of payout and mutually sign this right away.

Normal retirement age for social security is gradually rising from the long-held age 65 to 67 for persons born after 1937. You can retire as early as age 62 with reduced benefits.

needn't be fully insured to qualify for benefits; check with your social security office.

WHEN YOU RETIRE. Normal retirement age for social security is gradually rising from the long-held age 65 to 67 for persons born after 1937. You can retire as early as age 62 with reduced benefits.

WHAT COUNTS AS DISABILITY? Disability for social security purposes is defined as an inability to work because of a physical or mental impairment that has lasted or is expected to last at least 12 months or is expected to result in death.

In the case of blindness, it means either central visual acuity of 20/200 or less in the better eye with the use of corrective lenses, or visual-field reduction to 20 degrees or less (tunnel vision.)

WHO GETS SOCIAL SECURITY IF YOU DIE? If you are an eligible worker, cash benefits may be due when you die for your family members, including:

- **a widow or widower** 60 or older (50 if disabled);
- **a widow, widower or surviving divorced mother** if caring for your child who is under 16 (or disabled) and who is receiving benefits based on your earnings;
- **unmarried children** under 18, or under 19 if full-time students at a secondary school;
- **unmarried children who were severely disabled** before 22 and who remain disabled;
- **dependent parents** 62 or older; or
- **a surviving divorced spouse age 60** or older or a disabled surviving divorced spouse age 50 or older— if the marriage lasted ten years or more.

IF YOU WORK AFTER YOU RETIRE. If you are under full retirement age when you begin receiving social security benefits, $1 in benefits will be deducted for each $2 you earn above the annual limit, which was $11,520 in 2003.

In the year you reach full retirement age, $1 in benefits will be deducted for each $3 you earn above a different limit, but only for the months before the month you reach full retirement age. For 2003, that limit was $30,720. Strating with the month you reach full retirement age, you can receive your full benefits with no limit on your earnings.

And note that the limitations are applied only to money you earn, not to income from stocks, bonds, real estate, annuities or other investments.

WHAT ABOUT NONWORKING SPOUSES AND TWO-EARNER COUPLES? Once you begin receiving social security benefits, your husband or wife can also receive benefits based on your record, even if he or she never worked in a job covered by social security. A nonworking spouse is eligible to begin receiving benefits at age 62 or at any age if he or she has a child under age 16. Benefits at full retirement age will generally be about half what you are receiving—together you can get 150% of what you'd receive on your own.

If your spouse has worked, he or she will receive a benefit based on actual earnings or 50% of your benefit, whichever is more.

WHEN SURVIVING SPOUSES REMARRY. Eligible widows or widowers age 60 or older needn't worry about losing benefits if they remarry. They will receive what-

> Once you begin receiving benefits, your spouse can also receive benefits based on your record, even if he or she never worked in a job covered by social security.

APPEALING A DISABILITY CLAIM

If you've been denied social security benefits after filing a claim for disability, you've probably already found out that the Social Security Administration is very conservative about what qualifies for coverage. Claimants may have to file multiple appeals. If worse comes to worst, you could:

■ **seek assistance and legal advice** from your local Legal Aid office, or

■ **contact the National Organization of Social Security Claimants Representatives** (6 Prospect St., Midland Park, NJ 07432; 800-431-2804; www.nosscr.org), which will provide a referral to a private attorney who specializes in social security law.

Social Security mails out benefit statements once a year to recipients. Form SSA-1099 shows the total amount of benefits received in the previous year.

ever benefit they were previously eligible for, and their eligible dependent children will retain their benefits regardless of their surviving parent's marital status. If you remarry at age 62 or older, you may receive benefits based on your new spouse's work record if they are higher.

CHECKING ON YOUR BENEFIT. Social Security mails out benefit statements once a year to recipients. Form SSA-1099 shows the total amount of benefits received in the previous year. If you lose the statement or don't receive it, call 800-772-1213 for a replacement, or request it by going online (www.ssa.gov; then click on "online direct services"). Use the same toll-free number and Web site to get a benefit-verification statement, which may be required when you apply for benefits from other government agencies.

If you're still working, Social Security will send you a report annually that shows your income for each year you have worked, an estimate of the monthly social security retirement or disability benefits you might be eligible for at age 62 or your full retirement age, and an estimate of what your family would receive if you should die.

WHAT'S THE MOST COMMON ERROR? Having zero earnings posted for a year that you were working is the most common mistake you'll find. That can happen when an employer reports your wages under an incorrect social security number.

If you think social security has your record wrong, call the toll-free number on your statement or contact your local social security office immediately to correct it (look in the blue pages of your phone book under "U.S. Government, Social Security Administration").

You'll need proof, so dig out your old pay stubs. Don't count on employers for this information; they are required by law to keep employment records for only 3 1/4 years.

If the problem is still not resolved to your satisfaction, you can file an appeal with social security.

Your Medical Rights

Chapter 8

Chances are you'll never be subject to the kind of life-threatening mistake in medical care that would merit a charge of malpractice against your physician. But short of that, you're bound to come up against the medical system sooner or later; the issue may be quality, availability, delivery or confidentiality of service. It might be a matter of exerting your wishes for your care over any default strategies the system provides or over the objections of your family. All the more reason to know your medical rights and legal options—that way you'll be sure you're getting the care you want and deserve, and you'll know what steps to take if you believe you're not.

This chapter will discuss your right to medical care and emergency treatment, and what you're entitled to even if you don't have health insurance. You'll learn under what circumstances you can expect your medical records to be private. And you'll learn what legal tools give you control in the event you become incapacitated or terminally ill—and, of course, how to recognize possible malpractice and what to do about it.

Your Rights as a Patient

With consumerism in general on the rise, the patient's-rights movement has gathered momentum in recent years, demanding better and consistent treatment for all patients. Because of those efforts, most hospitals now honor the American Hospital Association's (www.aha.org)

Continued on page 176

A PATIENT'S BILL OF RIGHTS

Reprinted with the permission of the
American Hospital Association, © 1993

1. The patient has the right to considerate and respectful care.

2. The patient has the right to and is encouraged to obtain from physicians and other direct caregivers relevant, current and understandable information concerning diagnosis, treatment, and prognosis. Except in emergencies when the patient lacks decision-making capacity and the need for treatment is urgent, the patient is entitled to the opportunity to discuss and request information related to the specific procedures and/or treatments, the risks involved, the possible length of recuperation, and the medically reasonable alternatives and their accompanying risks and benefits.

Patients have the right to know the identity of physicians, nurses, and others involved in their care, as well as when those involved are students, residents or other trainees. The patient also has the right to know the immediate and long-term financial implications of treatment choices, insofar as they are known.

3. The patient has the right to make decisions about the plan of care prior to and during the course of treatment and to refuse a recommended treatment or plan of care to the extent permitted by law and hospital policy and to be informed of the medical consequences of this action. In case of such refusal,

the patient is entitled to other appropriate care and services that the hospital provides or transfer to another hospital. The hospital should notify patients of any policy that might affect patient choice within the institution.

4. The patient has the right to have an advance directive (such as a living will, health care proxy, or durable power of attorney for health care) concerning treatment or designating a surrogate decision maker with the expectation that the hospital will honor the intent of that directive to the extent permitted by law and hospital policy.

Health care institutions must advise patients of their rights under state law and hospital policy to make informed medical choices, ask if the patient has an advance directive, and include that information in patient records. The patient has the right to timely information about hospital policy that may limit its ability to implement fully a legally valid advance directive.

5. The patient has the right to every consideration of privacy. Case discussion, consultation, examination and treatment should be conducted so as to protect each patient's privacy.

6. The patient has the right to expect that all communications and records pertaining to his/her care will be treated as confidential by the hospital, except in cases such as suspected abuse and public-health hazards when reporting is permitted or required by law. The patient has the right to expect that the hospital will emphasize the confidentiality of this information when it releases it to any other parties entitled to review information in these records.

7. The patient has the right to review the records pertaining to his/her medical care and to have the information explained or interpreted as necessary, except when restricted by law.

8. The patient has the right to expect that, within its capacity and policies, a hospital will make reasonable response to the request of a patient for appropriate and medically indicated care and services. The hospital must provide evaluation, service, and/or referral as indicated by the urgency of the case. When medically appropriate and legally permissible, or when a patient has so requested, a patient may be transferred to another facility. The institution to which the patient is to be transferred must have accepted the patient for transfer. The patient must also have the benefit of complete information and explanation concerning the need for, risks, benefits, and alternatives to such a transfer.

9. The patient has the right to ask and be informed of the existence of business relationships among the hospital, educational institutions, other health care providers or payers that may influence the patient's treatment and care.

10. The patient has the right to consent to or decline to participate in proposed research studies or human experimentation affecting care and treatment or requiring direct patient involvement, and to have those studies fully explained prior to consent. A patient who declines to participate in research or experimentation is entitled to the most effective care that the hospital can otherwise provide.

11. The patient has the right to expect reasonable continuity of care when appropriate and to be informed by physicians and other caregivers of available and realistic patient-care options when hospital care is no longer appropriate.

12. The patient has the right to be informed of available resources for resolving disputes, grievances and conflicts, such as ethics committees, patient representatives or other mechanisms available in the institution. The patient has the right to be informed of the hospital's charges for services and available payment methods.

Note: The American Hospital Association intends to produce a new version of this in May 2003. It will be called the "Patient-Care Partnership." Look for it online at www.aha.org.

Even without the force of law, the Patient's Bill of Rights defines sound professional and ethical medical practice; expect your caregivers to honor it.

Patient's Bill of Rights, which generally guarantees you the right to be treated with consideration and respect, to be informed of your prognosis and your medical alternatives, to refuse treatment, and to keep your medical treatment private (for more on each of these topics, see pages 174-175). You may receive a detailed list of your rights as a patient when you are admitted to the hospital, or it may be posted in the hallways.

Even without the force of law, however, the Patient's Bill of Rights defines sound professional and ethical medical practice; you should expect your caregivers to honor it. If you do and they do, much misunderstanding and grievance that might otherwise lead to larger legal problems can be prevented. Although the names are the same, this is different from the "Patient's Bill of Rights" legislation that deals with patient treatment by health care providers such as HMOs and managed care programs. By early 2003, Federal legislation regarding the Patient's Bill of Rights had been relegated to the back burner, but most states had passed a Patient's Bill of Rights law that contains:

- **patient "access" provisions,** such as ensuring some level of access to specialists and emergency-room care;
- **appeals procedures** designed to help patients get prompt decisions about whether they are entitled to certain services; and
- **liability provisions,** which hold insurance companies accountable for their negligent actions against patients.

TAKING ACTION. If you believe the hospital you are in has violated the provisions of the Patient's Bill of Rights, your first step should be to contact your patient representative (also known as a patient advocate). Although these people are employed by the hospital, their job is to speak to doctors and hospital administrators on your behalf, trying to make sure things go as smoothly as possible. If the hospital doesn't have a designated ombudsman (or if you prefer not to use him), you or your family can address your concerns directly to your doctor or to the hospital's chief administrator.

Your Right to Treatment— Without Discrimination

Though doctors make an ethical pledge when they take the Hippocratic oath to treat those in need, that does not mean that you generally have any inherent or implied legal right to medical treatment. And if a doctor feels she does not have the expertise to handle your case, she is entitled to refer you to another physician. However:

■ **If you enter a public hospital** that is supported by tax dollars, doctors are required to treat you even if you lack health insurance or can't pay; that's not true of private hospitals. (See the discussion of emergency care, page 178.)

■ **Doctors and hospitals are not allowed** to discriminate against prospective clients on the basis of race, religion, national origin or disability.

■ **Health insurers can't discriminate** on the basis of race, religion or national origin and can't discriminate in certain ways on the basis of disability.

On the other hand, unless there is a local law to the contrary, a doctor can refuse to treat someone because of his or her gender or sexual orientation—unless the reason is related to AIDS or some other disability.

Doctors may fear particularly infectious diseases such as AIDS, tuberculosis, hepatitis and meningitis. But because people with AIDS are covered by the Americans With Disabilities Act (ADA), if a patient is turned away because he has AIDS, the doctor is considered to be discriminating on the basis of disability rather than sexual orientation, and that is not allowed under the law. (The ADA also protects individuals with cerebral palsy, multiple sclerosis, epilepsy, muscular dystrophy, cancer, heart disease and diabetes from discrimination.)

As with all discrimination, health care discrimination can be tough to prove unless there is a pattern of behavior. For example, a doctor could legally tell you that you can't afford his services or that she's not

If a doctor feels she does not have the expertise to handle your case, she is entitled to refer you to another physician.

As with all discrimination, health care discrimination can be tough to prove unless there is a pattern of behavior.

taking new patients. Because not every doctor can treat every disorder, a physician is entitled to refer you to another doctor better trained to care for you properly. But if a doctor does this only to black people or gay people, then that could be discrimination and thus illegal.

If you think you've been discriminated against in health care, contact a civil-rights attorney. (See also the discussion of the Americans with Disabilities Act, beginning on page 161 of Chapter 7, "Your Workplace Rights and Retirement.")

Your Right to Emergency Treatment

If you arrive at a hospital that participates in the federal medicare program and are in need of its emergency care, the hospital is required under federal and most state laws to treat you—whether or not you're on medicare—until your condition is stabilized, even if you don't have health insurance.

True, there have been instances in recent years in which hospitals have refused to help patients or have transferred them elsewhere despite health risk, but this practice, known as patient dumping, is illegal.

If you believe a hospital refused to treat you because you couldn't afford to pay or don't have health insurance, you should consult a lawyer. You may be able to file a civil lawsuit against the health care provider.

IF YOU NEED AN AMBULANCE

If you call 911 for assistance, you'll be sent either a publicly owned and operated ambulance or one that is unde contract to your municipality. The federal Emergency Medical Treatment and Labor Act, passed in 1985, says that publicly employed emergency medical technicians must take you to the nearest available hospital, not necessarily the hospital of your choice. If, in a nonemergency situation, you call for a private ambulance, it must take you anywhere you ask.

Getting Health Insurance Coverage

Depending on what happens with health care reform, all of this could change, but health insurance companies currently are under no obligation to insure you if you don't meet their health criteria. If you have a preexisting condition, such as cancer, you can be turned down for health insurance altogether, charged higher-than-average premiums for coverage, or granted coverage that permanently or temporarily excludes the costs associated with your preexisting condition.

In half of all the states, otherwise uninsurable people with preexisting conditions can purchase coverage through high-risk pools. But benefits may be limited and premiums are likely to be high, possibly 25% to 200% higher than usual for the same coverage. For example, the state of Florida, which no longer accepts new enrollees in its high-risk pool, has a premium cap of 200% over the standard average health insurance premium in the state, and South Carolina won't give people with AIDS access to its high-risk pool.

If you want to find out where your state's law stands on health insurance, contact your state's insurance department. If you think you've been unfairly denied

Depending on what happens with health care reform, all of this could change, but health insurance companies currently are under no obligation to insure you if you don't meet their criteria.

PREEXISTING CONDITIONS

A prospective employer can't ask whether you have any preexisting conditions, even if it fears increased health insurance costs or time lost from the job. And under the Americans With Disabilities Act it can't require you to have a medical examination prior to being hired. If you have a preexisting condition, you don't have to volunteer anything about it. If the employer finds out about it, it can't refuse to hire you because of it. On the other hand, once you're hired, the employer's health insurer doesn't necessarily have to insure you.

In all 50 states, an adult can have an abortion without her married or unmarried partner's consent.

coverage because of a mistake, you could contact your state's insurance commissioner (see the discussion on the Medical Information Bureau, on pages 184-185). To learn whether your state sponsors a high-risk insurance pool, contact the state insurance department.

Reproductive Rights

Both the right to use contraception and the right to choose whether to have an abortion stem from the constitutional right to privacy, which has its origins in the Fourteenth Amendment's guarantee of a right to liberty. In the 1973 U.S. Supreme Court case Roe vs. Wade, this was applied to a woman's right to choose. Roe vs. Wade and the cases immediately following it established the broad right to abortion prior to the viability of the fetus. In all 50 states, an adult can have an abortion without her married or unmarried partner's consent. And she can travel to a neighboring state for the procedure if she finds her own state's law too restrictive, or for other reasons.

A number of states, including Kansas, Mississippi, Nebraska, North Dakota, Ohio, Pennsylvania and Utah, have passed legislation restricting the procedure. Their limits include:

■ **waiting periods** following the request for an abortion, of typically 24 to 48 hours. Waiting periods have been held unconstitutional in Tennessee. None of the states impose waiting periods for nonresidents only or longer waiting periods for nonresidents.

■ **mandatory information** (informed consent). The state requires physicians or other health care providers to recite specific information and offer the woman state-prepared materials.

Other limits apply to minors. Forty-three states have laws while thirty-two enforce the following:

■ **notification and consent** by one or both parents before a minor can have an abortion. If the parents are divorced, most state statutes require the custodial parent, with whom the child resides, to provide consent or be notified. Some states, however, require both parents' signatures, even if they're separated.

To find out what current abortion law is in your state, call your local chapter of Planned Parenthood (for a referral, you can call 800-230-7526 or check their Web site at www.plannedparenthood.org) or your state's department of health and human services (check the blue pages of your phone book).

Minors and Contraception

All 50 states have laws that allow kids to seek standard medical treatment, and many have statutes allowing for contraception. No state outlaws distribution of contraception to teenagers without parental consent. In fact, agencies that receive federal family-planning funds cannot require parental consent to teens' contraception. In practice, Planned Parenthood and other providers of family-planning services encourage parental involvement but will serve kids without parental consent.

Your Right to Informed Consent

Health care providers must by law give you enough information about your condition and care so that you can make an informed decision about your treatment.

How much information is enough? Each state has its own laws on the topic, defining just how much a patient is entitled to know. Generally, however, a doctor needs to tell you the risks involved in the treatment, its chance of success and what other alternatives you might pursue.

Because of the risks, informed consent is of special concern when surgery is involved, but this standard applies to any kind of treatment.

For more information on your state's informed-consent laws, contact your state's department of health and human services.

Generally, a doctor needs to tell you the risks involved in medical treatment, its chance of success and what other alternatives you might pursue.

Not only do doctors need to tell you about the risks of medical treatment, they also must use language that allows you to grasp the meaning of what you're told.

Giving Legal Consent

Not only do doctors need to tell you about the risks of medical treatment, they also must use language that allows you to grasp the meaning of what you're told in order to give an informed consent. To give valid consent to most medical treatment, a person usually must:

- **be of age,** typically 18 or 21, depending on state law. If the patient is a child, the parent or guardian must give consent for medical care (see Chapter 11, "Parenthood");
- **be of sufficient mental capacity** to understand the risks and rewards of choosing a particular treatment; and
- **make the decision without duress,** such as undue pressure from the doctor or hospital, which might arise, for example, from the doctor's strong personal or professional disagreement with the patient's choice or the patient's family's influence on the decision.

A doctor doesn't need anyone's consent to act if the patient is in an immediately life-threatening or emergency situation—say, if he has been shot in the head or gone into cardiac arrest.

If You Can't Make Your Own Decisions

What if you, as an adult, become incapacitated and can no longer make decisions about your own care? As a rule, if you cannot make decisions for yourself, doctors will generally turn to your next of kin—spouse, adult child, parent or other nearest relation.

MAKING YOUR WISHES KNOWN IN ADVANCE. If you want to be sure that someone you trust will make medical decisions for you if you are incapacitated, you can set up a *durable health care power of attorney* arrangement (see page 191) while you are still healthy.

Likewise, you could fill out a living will and give it to your doctor. This should give you the opportunity to refuse extraordinary medical measures that would otherwise be used to prolong your life. For more information, see the discussion beginning on page 194.

Medical Records: Access and Privacy

There might be several reasons why you would want to see and obtain copies of your medical records, the information kept by your doctor and hospital concerning all your conditions, diagnoses and treatments: You might be moving away and want to bring your records with you. You may just want to better understand your treatment. Or you might want to double-check the accuracy of the records themselves, perhaps to verify what you've been charged or particularly if you've been turned down for coverage by an insurance company because of information included in your records (see the discussion of health care coverage and preexisting conditions, on page 179).

Be prepared to make your request for your records in writing and even to pay for the cost of photocopying.

Although your medical records concern your medical history, it is not always easy to get access to them; while the information in them is about you, the file itself is in the possession of your health care providers, and often they are reluctant to give such technical information to laymen because of inconvenience, cost or fear of misinterpretation. This is true even though about half the states have laws explicitly granting patients or their attorneys the right to see their records in some form, whether the original, a copy or a summary of treatment.

Even in the remaining states, lacking laws to the contrary, access to your own medical records is considered an implied right, and if you pursued it, a court would be likely to take your side. The exception would

Be prepared to make your request for your records in writing and even to pay for the cost of photocopying.

FOR MORE INFORMATION

For a copy of *Medical Records: Getting Yours,* contact Public Citizen's Health Research Group (1600 20th St., N.W., Washington, DC 20009; 202-588-1000, Publications Office; www.citizen.org/hrg; $10, plus $2.50 for shipping and handling).

THE BIG BROTHER OF MEDICAL RECORDS

If you apply for health or life insurance, the insurance company will attempt to verify the information you submit and check your background. Insurance investigators can obtain information on your history from several sources, including doctors, hospitals and medical labs.

If your prospective insurer is a member of the MIB—the Medical Information Bureau, a huge computerized network created by insurance companies—and, based on its investigation, has determined that you have a condition that may affect your future health or life expectancy, it will submit a coded report of its findings to the MIB. Most of the MIB codes are medically related, but some cover such things as a poor driving record and participation in high-risk sports. These records are then available to other member insurers to whom you may later apply for coverage. The MIB says the intent in maintaining these records is to prevent fraud, but critics say there is too much room for mishandling of the data.

Though no federal laws and only scattered state laws protect the privacy of these records, the MIB has adopted many fair-information practices as recommended by the Privacy Protection Study Commission in 1977. As a result, you have a right to know who has been accessing your file and to examine it for errors, especially those that might inhibit your ability to get life or health insurance coverage. Instances of such mistakes include one man who was incorrectly labeled an alcoholic after he told an

be if a doctor could prove that gaining access would harm you.

Who Else Can Know?

Who else can have access to your medical records? Doctor-patient confidentiality is protected ethically by the Hippocratic oath, a professionally powerful but not legally binding oath that all doctors take when they enter the profession. Confidentiality is also protected legally by state privacy laws. In other words, conversations between you and your doctor are almost always strictly private. Although health care providers generally cannot discuss your medical condition with your family without your approval, they can share medical information with other doctors, nurses and health care workers with whom they need to confer or who are directly involved in your case.

WHAT DOCTORS MUST REPORT. In all states a doctor has a legal obligation to report to the public health deinsurance investigator that he attended a meeting of a 12-step recovery group because he thought it would help him quit smoking, and another who was mistakenly labeled an Alzheimer's patient due to an error in coding. The MIB says, however, that in response to the approximately138,500 requests for disclosure from consumers that it fulfills annually, 550 consumers reply to ask for a correction to their record, and of those fewer than 1% actually require a correction.

To see your records, write to the Medical Information Bureau (MIB), 160 University Ave, Westwood, MA 02090 or download a form from their Web site at www.mib.com/. There is a charge of $9 for each request for a "Record Search and Disclosure" unless you received a written notification of "adverse action" from an MIB member insurance company. In that case, MIB will waive its charge. The notification must name MIB as an information source, and the request for Record Search and Disclosure must be made within 60 days of receipt of the notification of adverse action. "Adverse action" generally means that your application for life, health, disability and long-term-care insurance has been denied, or that the premium had been increased as a result of the investigation initiated by the insurance company because of the MIB record.

If you find a discrepancy, ask your physician to check his or her records and send the correct information to the MIB.

partment any births and deaths, gunshot wounds, instances of child abuse and certain contagious diseases, such as sexually transmitted diseases, including AIDS.

There is a lack of consensus among the states on whether positive HIV status—meaning someone has been infected by the human immunodeficiency virus but hasn't yet developed full-blown AIDS—must also be reported. Even when states do require reporting, they may differ on the specifics; for example, the law may require people who test positive to be reported by name, it may allow anonymity in some cases, or it may require reporting only in special cases, such as pediatric HIV. And state laws are changing quickly. To learn what your state requires, call your local public health department or the HIV prevention coordinator in your state capitol. For other information, call the Center for Disease Control's National STD and AIDS Hotline at 800-342-2437.

On another front, if your psychiatrist thinks you pose a danger to someone other than yourself, he or she is obligated to take action to have that person noti-

The law says the next best thing to being restored to the way you were is to be compensated monetarily for your damages.

fied of the possible danger. This may involve revealing your condition or records to appropriate authorities.

THE NEED TO KNOW. There are other ways other people can get access to your medical records:

- **When you apply for health insurance or make a claim on an existing policy,** you usually must sign a consent form (generally part of the claim form) giving the insurance company and the Medical Information Bureau access to your medical records (see page 184).
- **If you sue your doctor for malpractice,** your medical records may be used as evidence.

Medical Malpractice

While a patient can't expect a doctor or other health care provider to guarantee the outcome of any operation or treatment, he can expect to be treated with a standard of care that is considered prudent and reasonable by the medical profession. For example, the patient has a right to expect the doctor not to prescribe a drug she's allergic to or to inject a drug into the wrong part of her body. After at least eight years of rigorous schooling, a doctor clearly should know better. The bottom line: If a doctor does anything that does not live up to the standards set by his education and training and confirmed by his licensing, or if the doctor fails to treat a condition in accordance with the standards of his peers (agreed upon by consensus in the profession), then the doctor may be guilty of medical malpractice, a civil offense governed by state law.

What You Can Hope to Accomplish

The law says the next best thing to being restored to the way you were is to be compensated monetarily for your damages.

Other forms of recompense are unlikely: A medical malpractice suit will probably not keep the doctor from continuing to practice, it may not punish him or her financially other than by an increase in already-

---

> ## FINDING THE RIGHT LAWYER
>
> - **Does she specialize in cases like yours?** That is, if you're suing over a heart transplant, does she specialize in cardiology cases?
> - **How many cases like yours has she tried? Won?**
> - **Will your lawyer try the case herself,** hand it over to an associate, or ultimately refer you to another lawyer (and take a cut for doing so)?
> - **Most medical malpractice trials become a battle of expert witnesses,** so ask your prospective lawyer what types of expert witnesses she thinks she can supply and who they are. Which expert witnesses has she used in the past? Are they leaders in their field? Has their testimony been effective?
> - **Make sure that you get a good feeling from the lawyer,** and that she's respectful and not trying to take advantage of you.

high malpractice insurance premiums, and you may not even have the satisfaction of meeting the doctor for a day in court. That's because 60% of all medical malpractice suits are settled by the doctors' insurance companies.

Cases are likely to go to trial only if the patient's lawyers feel that doing so will result in higher awards or if the defense thinks it's sufficiently unclear whether the patient really suffered malpractice.

You can go one step further, however, and report the physician to the appropriate medical licensing board. It can suspend or revoke a physician's license as well as impose fines in some cases.

Is It Malpractice? If Yes, Then What?

You may suspect malpractice if the outcome of your medical treatment is not within the range of what you were told it might be as part of your informed consent. An unexpected or bad result isn't necessarily malpractice, but it may be an indicator that further inquiry is appropriate. Simply discussing the situation with the

The law requires the lawyer to talk with your doctors and make a good-faith investigation into your case.

appropriate physician may allay your concerns.

But if not, you or your family should consult a reputable and ethical-medical malpractice or personal-injury lawyer immediately (for more on finding a lawyer, see Chapter 2). The law requires the lawyer to talk with your doctors and make a good-faith investigation into your case. For example, say that your spouse goes for a heart bypass operation and dies on the operating table: If your spouse fits the profile of someone who would benefit from a bypass, you were told that there was a chance of death, and the surgeon and surgical staff performed well, then a charge of malpractice probably wouldn't stand up to scrutiny.

But if it appears that you have a case, you should ask yourself:

■ **If need be, will I go the distance to trial** or do I just want to settle?

■ **Will I be okay knowing that my medical records could end up being discussed in court** and even reported in the newspapers?

If you proceed with the charge, your lawyer will probably work on a contingency fee, receiving a percentage of any monetary award won.

Don't hire the first lawyer you call; speaking with two or three wouldn't be too much. An unscrupulous lawyer may tell you that you have a case when you don't, putting you through more mental anguish.

Besides finding a lawyer, pull together any notes you've taken, papers the doctor gave you, medical forms, insurance claims, prescription forms and prescription bottles; put it all in one place and leave it intact. And, of course, if the doctor says, "Yes, I made a mistake," write down the statement and date your notes.

A Time Limit for Complaint

Each state has its own statute of limitations for bringing a malpractice suit, but generally it is one to three years from the date of the incident. Some states consider the one-to-three-year period to begin at the time the alleged malpractice occurred, others at the time the malpractice was discovered (referred to as the discovery rule). In the latter case, the laws favor the patient. For example, a patient may not discover that a surgeon left a sponge in him until several years after the surgery. If the law allows him to sue only within two years of the operation, the patient may miss the deadline. On the other hand, if the law allows him to sue within two years of the discovery of malpractice, he has a better chance of successfully pursuing legal action against the doctor or the hospital.

If you've exceeded your state's statute of limitations, don't give up hope, however. You might be able to sue—either individually or as part of a class-action suit brought by similarly afflicted patients—the manufacturer of the medical product that contributed to your injury. For example, that's now a common practice with unsatisfied breast implant patients, whose side effects may not appear until years after the implantation.

The Power of Attorney

I f you're concerned that at some point in your life you won't be able to care for yourself, you want to be sure that someone you trust will take over your affairs and can function as your legal stand-in. By conferring a durable power of attorney, you grant a person of your choice—usually a spouse, close friend, business associate or relative—the authority to make some or all legal, financial and medical decisions on your behalf.

Power-of-attorney agreements can cover a little or a lot of ground: You, as the principal, are free to set the terms and length of the agreement, defining or limiting the authority delegated to your legal stand-in, who is called the attorney-in-fact.

You could confer only a so-called simple (or common-law) power of attorney if, say, you're going to be traveling out of the country for some time and want someone to manage your affairs while you're gone. An older person might confer power of attorney after the death of a spouse if the prospect of managing his or

By conferring a durable power of attorney, you grant a person of your choice the authority to make some or all legal, financial and medical decisions on your behalf.

Hard as it is to imagine not being able to act on your own behalf, it's critical that you make contingency arrangements.

her financial affairs alone seems daunting and just not worth the worry.

But—and this is important—because a limited power of attorney is automatically voided if you (the principal) become incapacitated or incompetent, it's important for you to create either a durable or a springing durable power of attorney.

Before It's Too Late

Hard as it is to imagine not being able to act on your own behalf, it's critical that you make such contingency arrangements while you are still physically and mentally competent. You want to make sure that you will successfully confer power of attorney, without threat of challenge by your heirs, spouse or other family members who thought that the person you designated didn't have your or their best interests at heart.

There are plenty of possible reasons for incapacitation or incompetence. Perhaps you will be temporarily afflicted with clinical depression. You could suffer the gradual loss of your abilities due to the onset of mental dementia—a serious loss of intellect and memory that results, literally, in forgetting how to function and is associated with aging. Perhaps you'll be temporarily or permanently incapacitated by a stroke or fall into a coma after an automobile accident.

DURABLE OR SPRINGING DURABLE POWER OF ATTORNEY. Either—with some differences—will ensure that if you become incapacitated you won't leave your family in the lurch, uncertain how to (or legally unable to) take care of your affairs, except where a spouse is co-owner of a joint bank or brokerage account. Your family otherwise may be forced to go to court to request that the state appoint one of them as your legal guardian. If you lack immediate family, the state itself may step in and appoint a guardian for you (see the discussion of legal guardianship, on page 192) .

All states recognize a durable power of attorney, an agreement that remains valid even if you are overtaken by a devastating illness and can no longer make decisions on your own. If you want to give someone power of attorney, and want to be sure he or she can continue to make financial, legal and medical decisions on your behalf if you become totally incapacitated, then a durable power of attorney is for you.

Many states recognize a springing durable power of attorney, which is activated only when you become incapacitated or incompetent and only as long as you stay that way. This is a good safeguard to have arranged in advance. That way, if something dire happens to you, you can be sure that a person you know and trust will take over handling your affairs.

What if your state doesn't allow a springing power of attorney or you're hesitant about setting one up? You could arrange to have your attorney hold a durable power of attorney in escrow until it is needed, along with a letter of instruction stating when you want the durable power put into use. This has another advantage: Some banks or brokerages are reluctant to accept springing durable power of attorney agreements, because it's tough—even with two doctors' diagnoses—to convince them that you are incapacitated. Your attorney's judgment may make them more willing to accept the durable power.

HEALTH CARE POWER OF ATTORNEY. More limited in scope than durable or springing durable power of attorney, this form allows your agent to make only health-care decisions on your behalf when you can't. He or she could choose or dismiss a doctor, consent to surgery and represent your wishes about terminating life support (for more about the life-support issue, see the following section on living wills and health care power of attorney).

HOW TO CONFER POWER OF ATTORNEY. Power of attorney agreements can be made using prepackaged legal forms that follow the laws of your state, or they can be drawn up by a lawyer for a small fee. It's a good idea to contact your bank and brokerage to see if they require that you use their forms to grant a power of attorney.

The court will appoint you legal guardian only as a last resort, and you'll have to prove that your parents are past the point of granting you power of attorney.

Not all states require that a power of attorney agreement be witnessed and notarized, but doing so increases the chances that third parties, such as banks, creditors and hospitals, will take the document seriously and honor your wishes. If the document is not legally convincing, they may challenge your designee's authority. You should sign several powers of attorney and have them notarized because some institutions will want to keep an original.

To make sure your wishes are adhered to, it's a good idea to give copies of the power of attorney to family members, financial advisers and doctors, as appropriate. Keep an original somewhere safe, but accessible, in case it is needed. (A safe-deposit box may not be a good choice if you are the only person with access to it.)

IF YOU CHANGE YOUR MIND. Should circumstances change, you can revoke a power of attorney or a durable or springing durable power of attorney at any time, as long as you have the competency to do so. You just need to put the revocation in writing, following the same procedures as when you invoked it, and give copies to the concerned parties. If you become incompetent or incapacitated, a simple power of attorney will be automatically voided anyway.

Seeking Legal Guardianship of Your Loved One

It's great if Mom and Dad have the forethought to confer durable or springing durable power of attorney or to create a living trust while they are able (see Chapter 12, "Your Estate"). But what if they neglect or refuse to give someone else legal authority over their affairs, then begin doing irresponsible things that risk their financial or physical well-being? What can an adult child do?

You could seek legal guardianship from the court, or ask to have the court appoint you as their representative payee to handle their social security, civil service or veteran's benefits.

The court will appoint you legal guardian only as a

last resort, and you'll have to prove that your parents are past the point of granting you power of attorney. To seek guardianship, you must file a petition with the probate court. (The state can bring this petition to the court if a person is destitute or is without family.)

As legal guardian, you can make decisions for your parents in all areas of their lives, but you may be subject to your state's supervision.

Some states allow you to seek limited guardianship, whereby you are authorized to simply pay bills for your parents.

If the state grants you a conservatorship, you may manage all of your parents' financial affairs but no other aspect of their lives.

Once you assume guardianship of the estate and the person, you are responsible for managing their financial affairs and for supervising their actions; you'll be responsible for any trouble that they might get into or damage they might cause.

Legal Tools That Give You Control at the End

Many people have fears about ending up incapacitated, unconscious and sustained only by the mechanical rhythms of life-support equipment. But even then, the law lets you control your own situation, by means of advance directives. They come in two forms, and all 50 states and the District of Columbia authorize at least one of them.

Health Care Power of Attorney

Powers of attorney are described at length in the preceding section, but this particular variety is worth noting again because it lets you designate a person who shares your beliefs to be your agent and make health care decisions when you can't. Every state authorizes holders (or agents) of health care powers of attorney to withhold or withdraw life support. Appointing this person is especially important if you believe that some of your family members may be reluctant to honor

> **A health care power of attorney lets you designate a person who shares your beliefs to be your agent and make only health care decisions when you can't.**

Many experts favor executing both a living will and a health care power of attorney to ensure the best protection of your rights.

your wishes. Many states forbid naming more than one agent to share in the decision-making. But it's a good idea to choose an alternate person to make sure that someone is available when needed.

A Living Will

Your other option is to write a living will. All states and the District of Columbia have laws governing this written document in which you instruct your family and/or doctors about your wishes regarding life support.

Most living-will laws apply only if you are terminally ill or permanently unconscious, and they generally state that life-sustaining technology should not be used to prolong life. In some states, the living will of a pregnant woman will not be honored.

Many experts favor executing both a living will and a health care power of attorney to ensure the best protection of your rights.

THE SPECIFICS OF A LIVING WILL. A living will has two distinct parts:

■ **First,** it says specifically when the instructions included in it become effective, based on your medical condition and prognosis—for example, only if you are permanently unconscious or terminally ill.

■ **Second,** it names what course of life-sustaining action you want or don't want followed if you should end up in such a state, including: artificial nutrition and hydration (a feeding tube or intravenous fluids), mechanical ventilation (a respirator), resuscitation (including CPR), antibiotics, and kidney dialysis.

As crucial as a living will is, you probably won't need a lawyer to draw one up. Preprinted forms for writing a living will and for designating a health care power of attorney that are tailored to the laws of every state are available free of charge from the advocacy group Partnership for Caring Inc. (see the box on page 197).

If you live part of the year in another state, be sure to complete forms for both states.

You can generally add to the forms, adapting them to your specific needs and concerns. It's a good idea to discuss possible additions with your doctor or with Partnership for Caring Inc (see page 197). That will help you avoid writing your wishes in such a way that you accidentally preclude treatment you would want or permit treatment you don't want.

In any event, discuss your plans and options with your family physician to make sure you understand the medical ramifications of your decisions and that the doctor understands and agrees with your wishes. Make sure, too, that he or she practices at hospitals that will uphold them. If not, you might want to change doctors. While most states have their own variation of a living-will law, all states and the District of Columbia grant civil and criminal immunity to doctors who act in accordance with a living will. But they are not legally bound to.

If there's an emergency, you may be attended by an unknown doctor who won't abide by your wishes, written or otherwise. The following steps are worth trying, though they may be difficult in practice, especially in a critical-care situation: Your family could bring in your family physician as a persuasive force,

As crucial as a living will is, you probably won't need a lawyer to draw one up.

HELP FOR ELDERS

■ **National Association of Area Agencies on Aging** (927 15th St., N.W., 6th floor, Washington, DC 20005; 800-677-1116; 202-296-8130; www.n4a.org). The association's Eldercare Locator service can direct you to the closest agency on aging. It will also provide information on services ranging from legal assistance and housing options to adult day care and home health services.

■ **National Academy of Elder Law Attorneys** (1604 N. Country Club Rd., Tucson, AZ 85716; 520-881-4005; www.naela.com). The academy can provide a free copy of *Questions and Answers When Looking for an Elder Law Attorney*. The organization won't give direct referrals to attorneys, but you may search their online database.

Once you've written your living will, review it every year or so. If it no longer reflects your wishes, change it or revoke it entirely by writing a new one.

find another physician at the hospital who will agree to relieve the attending physician (the physician of record), or transfer you to another hospital.

As with conferring power of attorney (discussed beginning on page 190), you should make a living will when you're of sound mind; that is, able to make decisions on your own behalf. Most states require two adult witnesses who aren't relatives to be present at the time you sign the living will. In some states, people who stand to benefit from your death, such as heirs and insurance beneficiaries, are not allowed to be witnesses.

Once you've written your living will, it's a good idea to review it every year or so. If it no longer reflects your wishes, you should change it or revoke it entirely by writing a new one. Make sure all your family members, other appropriate people and your doctors have copies, and ask your doctor to include a copy in your medical records.

Help Your Family Help You

It's probably not enough just to prepare these legal expressions of your wishes. Take the time to personally discuss them with your family. A clear understanding of your intent will help everyone more easily honor your wishes. You can help eliminate any second-guessing and avoid the interference of an uninformed or disapproving relative who could otherwise cause conflict and delay. You could even relay your instructions in a conversational way on videotape.

If You Leave No Instructions

In some states, if there is no clear and convincing proof of your desires, you must be kept on life support. In others, if you haven't written a living will and have not given someone durable health care power of attorney, the medical decisions will fall to your next of kin. He or she will have the legal right to tell doctors whether to pursue so-called extraordinary measures to keep you alive.

Which relative has seniority? The responsibility falls

first on a guardian, if one has been appointed through the intervention of a family member or the state (see page 192); if no guardian has been appointed, then it falls to a spouse; if no spouse, then to adult children; if none, then to a parent, if one is alive.

While the decision rests with whoever ranks first in this chain of command, if someone lower down disagrees with the stand-in's health care decision, any action must be postponed if possible until he or she can go to court and contest the decision. So, for example, if a desperately ill patient's adult children don't agree with her spouse about her care, they can ask a court to block the spouse's decision for the parent's medical care.

In the other half of the states, the laws are vague regarding the next of kin's rights to make deathbed decisions. There is a presumption that they have the right, but an attending physician is not bound to abide by their decision. If the doctor does not accede to the next of kin's wishes, however, then the spouse or adult children may have to find another doctor or go to court.

For more information on your state's law, call Partnership for Caring Inc. (see the box below).

A clear understanding of your intent will help everyone more easily honor your wishes.

FOR MORE INFORMATION

■ **Partnership for Caring Inc**. (formerly Choice in Dying) (1620 Eye St., N.W., Suite 202, Washington, DC 20006; 800-989-9455; 202-296-8071; www.choices.org). This non-profit organization works for the right of patients to make their own medical decisions at the end of life and provides information on the issues surrounding terminal care. Call or check online to receive free, state-specific documents with which to write an advance directive and durable health care power of attorney.

■ **The Hemlock Society** (P.O. Box 101810, Denver, CO 80250-1810; 800-247-7421; www.hemlock.org). Provides information and support to terminally ill patients regarding voluntary euthanasia.

Can you legally ask someone to help you commit suicide? In most states, the answer is no.

The Right to Die

A living will, described beginning on page 194, is a legal way for you to tell people how you want to be treated in dire medical circumstances when you can no longer make decisions for yourself about the continuation of your care. But what if you are still competent, yet terminally ill and in great pain? Can you legally ask someone to help you commit suicide? In most states, the answer is no; it is a crime to actively assist someone in a suicide. Still, while state laws may be clear in this area, their legal interpretation is often vague and somewhat unpredictable. Violent "assistance," such as shooting someone in the head, is more likely to result in prosecution and even conviction. On the other hand, leaving a glass of water and an overdose of medication next to a terminally ill person might not be considered assistance and might be ignored by the authorities or dismissed by a jury. But because the interpretations of the law can differ greatly, any assistance puts the helper at legal risk.

So think long and hard before asking someone to help you commit suicide or helping someone you love to end his life. If you go ahead with it, make sure there is a document attesting to the terminally ill person's wishes. This won't exonerate anyone, but it may offer some small legal shelter should the case come to trial.

Medicare

Medicare is government-sponsored health insurance for people 65 or older, certain disabled people under 65 and people of any age who have permanent kidney failure. Medicare provides basic protection against the cost of health care, but it doesn't cover all your medical expenses. You can access information online at www.medicare.gov.

Enrollment in medicare depends on your circumstances. Generally, you should contact social security about three months before your normal retirement age so you can sign up for medicare benefits. This is true whether you decide to retire at that age or continue working. If you are already getting social security checks, you will be automatically enrolled in medicare.

A Summary of Coverage

Medicare is broken into two parts: hospital insurance (also called Part A medicare) and medical insurance (also called Part B medicare). Part A is financed by part of the payroll (FICA) tax that also pays for social security. Part B is financed by monthly premiums paid by people who choose to enroll. Unless otherwise instructed, the government will automatically deduct the Part B premium from your social security check.

In general, Part A medicare covers many hospital-related costs, such as inpatient hospital care, home health care and hospice care. Part B insurance helps pick up expenses not covered in Part A, such as X-rays, medical and surgical services, diagnostic tests and certain outpatient hospital care.

If Your Claim Is Denied

If you are denied medicare coverage for a Part A hospital claim, it's usually because the appropriate review committees decided that you didn't need to be an inpatient for such treatment, that your treatment wasn't medically necessary or that your stay was primarily for "custodial" care rather than for medical treatment.

When you are notified of the denial, you will receive instructions on how to appeal it. You must make your requests in writing within 60 days of being refused

Generally, you should contact social security about three months before your normal retirement age so you can sign up for medicare benefits.

ON YOUR PARENTS' BEHALF

If you want to help your elderly parents pursue a medicare claim through the level of appeals or hearings, acting as a representative on their behalf, you'll have to obtain from your parents a signed statement appointing you as their representative; you needn't have your parents' formal power of attorney. Otherwise you'll be confined to helping with paperwork and lending moral support.

If the hospital originally led you to believe your stay would be covered by medicare and, after the fact, you were told it wouldn't be, you may be able to invoke the waiver of liability claim.

coverage. Unless you can bring new and significant information to the table, you shouldn't be too hopeful.

There are several levels of appeal that you can pursue, beginning with the hospital, progressing to the Social Security Administration, and if the claim is for more than $1,000, bringing a lawsuit against medicare in federal district court.

If the hospital originally led you to believe that your stay would be covered by medicare and, after the fact, you were told that it wouldn't be, you may be able to invoke the waiver of liability claim.

If you are denied part or all of a reimbursement for a medicare Part B claim, there are again several levels of appeal. You can write a letter to your insurance carrier explaining why you think the charge should be approved and asking it to reconsider the decision. Be sure to do this within six months of being denied reimbursement.

If this is unsuccessful, depending on the amount of your claim, you may have other options. To obtain assistance with appealing payment denials or to submit a complaint about medical care or treatment, contact the Department of Senior Services toll-free at 800-243-5463.

Marriage and Other Personal Relationships

Walking down the aisle was once the only respectable choice for a couple who wanted to build a life together. And, despite a variety of other ways to form domestic partnerships, each with a corresponding degree of rights and obligations, marriage is still the preferred choice for legions of hopeful partners. It provides the benchmark by which prospective partners can judge the legal advantages and disadvantages of the other options. For example, a couple who chooses simply to live together won't need to divorce should their relationship self-destruct, but unlike married people, they won't necessarily be entitled to spousal support or a share of each other's property if they decide to go their separate ways. In this chapter, we'll take a closer look at various living arrangements, beginning with marriage, and offer some advice on how to use the law to live together happily ever after.

Marriage

Marriage is a personal and civil contract in which a man and a woman agree to become husband and wife. It's personal because it's an agreement between you and your partner; it's civil because the state must validate it, even if you choose to proclaim it in a religious ceremony. When you marry, you not only pledge to love and honor each other, but you also become legally responsible for financially supporting each other and for raising any

People on the verge of getting married need to think about more than love; they need to think about the law.

children you might have together. Because of its dual nature, this contract is different from most; you can't immediately dissolve it even if both of you agree to do so. You can end your marriage only with the state's approval in the form of a divorce.

Marriage is probably one of the biggest decisions you will ever make—and it's one that you expect will last a lifetime. People on the verge of getting married need to think about more than love; they need to think about the law. Once you say "I do," you are legally husband and wife and agree to follow your state's rules about property and support.

In a so-called community-property state, that means any earnings or assets that you acquire as a married couple will belong to both of you regardless of who earns them. Gifts and inheritances made to one spouse during the marriage, however, are generally excluded, as are awards from personal-injury suits and proceeds from a pension that was already vested before the marriage. If you live in a community-property state, check the specifics of your state's law.

Marriage also brings some new rights for each of you. You can, among other things, file a joint tax return (see the box on page 204), visit your spouse as a member of the immediate family in the hospital's intensive-care ward, and automatically inherit a portion of her

---

TIMING YOUR WEDDING

Timing is everything. If you file a joint return, the IRS doesn't care whether you marry in the merry month of May or in December; for its purposes, you were married for the whole year. That's a boon if you expect to save money by filing a joint return; a full year's worth of your joint income will be subject to a lower tax rate. It's a bane if you expect to get hit with a new and higher tax rate, because it will apply to the full year, even if you married in the last minutes of December 31. In that case, it would make sense to delay the wedding until January 1 and thereby avoid one year's worth of the marriage penalty (see box on page 204).

estate if she dies without a will (see Chapter 8, "Your Medical Rights," and Chapter 12, "Your Estate").

Who May Marry Whom

You may marry only one person at a time, no matter what your religion.

Although the age of consent varies from state to state, partners generally need to be at least 18 years old to be able to marry without having to ask permission of their parents or guardian. They also need the mental capacity to understand what marriage means. Partners who are underage in their home state could marry in another state subject to that state's requirements. No state allows marriages between two men or two women; in fact, many states have passed anti-gay marriage laws. (However, in 2000, Vermont adopted legislation that permits a "civil union" of same-sex couples that confers many of the legal benefits and responsibilities typical of marriage.) Also forbidden by law are marriages between immediate blood relations such as parent and child, aunt and nephew, uncle and niece or siblings (including half-siblings, who share a parent). Some states prohibit stepparent-stepchild marriage and parent-in-law or child-in-law marriage. And more than half of the states do not allow marriages between first cousins.

The Legal How-Tos of Marrying

THE LICENSE. Once you've decided to marry, you need to go to your county clerk's office and apply for a license. You'll also be told whether you and your partner must take a blood test for venereal disease and rubella; state laws are changing quickly on this, and your state may no longer require a test.

Although many states require that that you must be offered an HIV test or must be provided with information on AIDS and available tests, no state now requires a test for AIDS. You will probably have to pay fees for both the license and the blood tests if required.

TIME LIMITS. After you apply for your license, you

> You may marry only one person at a time, no matter what your religion.

usually must wait for a few days before it is issued, although this requirement varies by state. Don't apply for a marriage license many months before you plan to use it; it's usually valid only for a few months from the date of issue.

WHO CAN MARRY YOU? Next, you need to find someone to perform the ceremony. A justice of the peace, a judge, a clerk of the court or a clergyman licensed by the state can all perform a marriage. It's up to you to choose whomever you are comfortable with.

UNCLE SAM AND YOUR MARRIAGE

Getting married offers you and your spouse another option in the tax-compliance department by allowing you to file your taxes jointly. This can be an advantage if one of you earns significantly more than the other. Say, for example, that you have a taxable income of $50,000 a year and your fiancé earns nothing. On a single return, the breadwinner would owe a tax of $9,792 for 2003. Marrying and filing a joint return would cut that bill to $7,206—a $2,586 marriage bonus.

But for spouses whose incomes are nearly the same, filing jointly could also be a disadvantage because of the so-called marriage-tax penalty. Here's how it works: In 2003, for example, the 15% bracket covers up to $28,400 on single returns. If you and your betrothed each reported that much, you'd each owe $3,960 in tax, for a total of $7,920. On a joint return, the 15% bracket covers income up to $47,450 only—not twice as high as the limit for the single return. Combining the two $28,400 incomes gives you a total of $56,000, shoving $9,350 out of the 15% bracket and subjecting it to

the 27% rate. The tax on $56,000 on a joint 2003 return will be $9,042—$1,122 more than the two of you would have paid on single returns. The penalty can be even greater when two high-income individuals marry and their adjusted gross income pushes them into the higher tax brackets or they lose the benefit of personal exemptions or itemized deductions.

Filing separately poses its own set of problems: Both of you must either claim the standard deduction or itemize; you won't be able to claim the child-care credit; if you receive social security benefits you will have to report half of your benefits as taxable income; and you'll still be subject to the phaseout of IRA deductions. In some states, however, married-filing-separately can cut your state tax bill significantly; check the instructions on your state return carefully.

After years of debate, Congress finally did something about the marriage penalty, but the tax cut approved in the Spring of 2001 won't save you a dime until 2005 and won't be fully phased in until 2009.

The law requires witnesses to the ceremony who, along with the happy couple and the official, must sign the marriage license. The official then usually files the certificate with the county clerk. After that, you are legally married—even if you don't immediately consummate your new marriage. Once signed, the only way you can break your marriage contract is by annulment or divorce (see Chapter 10, "Ending a Marriage").

Taking Care of Business Beforehand

Before you embark on life together, each of you should take stock of what you are bringing to the marriage and consider how you want to handle such things as wills and insurance policies. Think, too, about whether you want a prenuptial agreement (see the discussion beginning on page 207).

TAKE STOCK OF YOUR PROPERTY. If you have any assets, write down exactly what they are. You want to prevent any debate in the future over what exactly you brought into the marriage.

Don't sign away part ownership of your property to your new spouse; leave it in your own name. Aside from the hassle and expense of retitling property (see the discussion of ownership in Chapter 12, "Your Estate"), if you eventually divorce, it would be clear that the property was yours prior to the marriage.

If you're marrying for the first and—you hope—only time, this advice may sound rather cold and pessimistic. But, unfortunately, no one can foretell the future—ask anyone who has been widowed or divorced. Besides, taking stock will help you prepare for other financial aspects of forming your new household, such as figuring your net worth, buying adequate insurance and developing an estate plan.

ASK ABOUT YOUR INTENDED'S DEBT. Although whatever debt a spouse brings into the marriage remains that spouse's responsibility, this extra burden could affect your lifestyle—and possibly your pocketbook, too.

For example, say that you buy a house together

> Don't sign away part ownership of your property to your new spouse; leave it in your own name.

Marriage, divorce or the birth of a child revokes an existing will, unless the will has a provision to accomodate such a change in circumstances.

using your resources but put it in both your names. If your spouse is so deep in debt that creditors put a lien on the house, you could lose your share of the equity if you chose to or were forced to sell.

What if you marry someone who owes a considerable debt to the IRS and whose wages are being garnished accordingly? Your spouse's tax debt is his own, and the IRS cannot come after you and your wages once you're married. But, again, you would need to consider the impact of the debt repayment on your household finances and also the possibility of ongoing scrutiny of your tax returns by the IRS.

It makes sense whenever possible to keep your own credit cards and lines of credit in your own name, maintain your own good credit history, and make major purchases in your name. This will help ensure that your credit history will survive unscathed if the marriage ends.

ARRANGE TO REDO YOUR WILL. Marriage, divorce or the birth of a child revokes an existing will, unless the will has a provision to accommodate such a change in circumstances. A spouse has a legal right to inherit, first and foremost, so if you want another family member to receive something, specify that when you rewrite the will (see the discussion of wills in Chapter 12, "Your Estate").

CHECK YOUR INSURANCE BENEFICIARIES. Consider whether you want to change the beneficiary of your life

---

FOR MORE INFORMATION

The American Academy of Matrimonial Lawyers (150 N. Michigan Ave., Suite 2040, Chicago, IL 60601; 312-263-6477; www.aaml.org) certifies lawyers specializing in marriage, divorce, annulment, custody, child visitation, property distribution, alimony and child support. It also publishes an annually updated list of its certified fellows and provides a searchable database of this list online.

insurance to your spouse. If this is your first marriage, you might have previously designated your parents or siblings as beneficiaries. If you're remarrying, you may have dependent children whom you must continue to provide for. If your new spouse happens to be wealthy, you might prefer to leave the proceeds to a favorite charity or institution. (For more on designating life insurance beneficiaries, see Chapter 3, "Your Finances," and Chapter 12, "Your Estate.")

PRENUPTIAL AGREEMENTS. These agreements are usually thought of as escape hatches for the super rich. But up until about 15 or 20 years ago, prenuptial contracts (also known as antenuptial agreements) were a way to provide for children from a previous marriage by limiting or abolishing a surviving spouse's claim to the couple's property. With the advent of no-fault divorces, prenuptial agreements have become popular as a means of working out equitably and in advance who gets what in case the couple chooses to divorce. (In a "fault" divorce, the partner judged at fault may receive a lesser share of the couple's wealth than the "innocent" partner. See Chapter 10, "Ending a Marriage.")

The law requires that prenuptial contracts, signed before marriage (or the alternative post-nuptial contract, executed anytime during the marriage), cannot promote divorce; in other words, you can't promise a spouse you'll give him a Jaguar if he'll agree to divorce you five years from now.

The pros and cons. A prenuptial agreement is not for everyone. If you are young and have no children from previous marriages and no property to speak of (say, you each own a car, but neither owns a home, land or other investments), there is little point in anticipating the division of what doesn't exist.

Some lawyers feel "prenups" are not always in the clients' best interest; they require making decisions that anticipate an unknown future at a time when two people are presumably still very much in love and trust each other completely. You could underestimate

Prenuptial contracts, signed before marriage, cannot promote divorce.

A prenuptial agreement usually includes a plan for division of property and assets in the event of death or divorce.

your future wealth and arbitrarily set too-low limits on its distribution or decline to discuss certain difficult issues because you can't imagine their ever being important.

On the other hand, if one or both of you have been married before, you may want to draw up a contract as an additional means of ensuring that children from your prior marriages will inherit your respective assets. You should, of course, spell this out in a will, but if children from either marriage are unhappy with the plan, they can contest it, potentially causing difficulty for the other set of children. A prenuptial agreement may help avoid this.

If you've already experienced the pain of divorce, you may want to have a prenuptial agreement to try to avoid any more bitter arguments over who owns what if this new marriage runs aground, too.

Of course, there's no airtight guarantee. In the end, a prenuptial agreement can be contested or a court can choose to disregard it if it deems that the agreement is unfair.

What does it say? A prenuptial agreement usually includes a plan for division of property and assets in the event of death or divorce. As with any contract, it's best to put a prenuptial agreement in writing. It's not a good idea to draw up a prenuptial agreement on your own—it may not hold up to a court's scrutiny. Spouses-to-be should have separate lawyers represent them; one lawyer can't ethically represent both sides.

A valid prenuptial agreement must be fair—that is, it must neither unduly penalize nor benefit either partner financially before or after the marriage and must accurately reflect each person's financial situation. It would be unfair, for example, if a wife made an agreement based on the belief that her husband's assets totaled $100,000 when, in fact, his assets were more in the neighborhood of $1 million. To that end, both must give complete disclosure of their finances, including their incomes, assets, and any debts and other financial obligations, as well as expectations for financial improvements, such as trust funds that become accessible at a certain age. It's a good idea to physically append these statements to the agreement so that there will be no confusion later about who owned what.

Not only must the prenuptial contract be fair, but also each party must have entered into it freely. For example, if a man waits until the day before the wedding—when the bride can no longer get back deposits paid on the wedding hall or caterer—to ask her to sign a prenuptial agreement, that's considered duress. If the bride signed the agreement at that point, it might not hold up if challenged at a later date.

You and your spouse can cancel a prenuptial contract at any time. Just be sure to do it officially. Put the cancellation in writing and have it witnessed and notarized. Then destroy any remaining copies of the now-outmoded prenuptial agreement.

CHANGING YOUR NAME. When a woman marries, she can choose to keep her name, take her husband's or hyphenate the two surnames. And similarly, there's

OTHER REASONS FOR A NAME CHANGE

You don't have to get married to change your name. You can change your name for any reason—if you don't like the way your old one sounds, you have painful family memories, you want to honor your grandmother's maiden name or if you want to create a new business image.

Once you reach the age of adulthood, usually 18, you are free to use any name you want, so long as it isn't for fraudulent purposes, such as to avoid paying bills.

However, many institutions will be reluctant to accept a name change without proof of an official document, such as a marriage license. So, if you're changing your name for personal reasons other than marriage, it's often a good idea—and in some states (including Alaska, Hawaii and Oklahoma) it's required by law—to have your name legally changed by applying to the appropriate court in your state. That way you avoid confusion, and it's clear to anyone you do business with that your name change has no suspicious motivations. A routine procedure, it usually takes no more than a month to get the court decree that makes it official. You can choose any name you like as long as it isn't obscene or consists merely of numerals.

For more specific information, contact your county's clerk of court.

YOUR PERSONAL PAPER TRAIL

When you marry, be prepared to change your name and status on documents including those listed in this box. Some agencies, such as the Social Security Administration, may require you to request your name change in person or in writing. Be prepared to present proof of your marriage, such as an original copy of your marriage license or certificate, or forms of identification on which you've already made the change. This is a good idea if you divorce, too.

You may need to change your:
- **birth certificate** (Just so all your legal papers are consistent, most states will let you amend your birth certificate by adding a separate piece of paper with your new name.)
- **driver's license**
- **social security card**
- **voter registration**
- **passport** (see page 299)
- **bank accounts**
- **credit cards**
- **postal information**
- **tax returns**
- **brokerage accounts**
- **insurance policies**

nothing to prevent a husband from taking his wife's name except social custom. If you do change your name, you can begin using the new one immediately following the marriage, but be sure to change it consistently on all important documents (see the box, above). In your credit record, any of your account numbers will link your married name, referred to as "also known as," to your former name. However, you'll probably hear from the IRS if the name you use on your income-tax return doesn't match the one associated with your social security number. Play it safe and avoid any record-keeping confusion down the road.

What if you eventually divorce? As with any name change, a woman needn't wait for her divorce to be final before she can begin using her maiden name again. In addition, in many states, divorce decrees specifically state that a woman may return to using her maiden name if she so desires. But to avoid confusion, it's advisable that she apply to the appropriate court and request a name change in the traditional manner, as described in the preceding section.

Remarriage

While it's a happy occasion, a remarriage brings with it concerns about property and asset distribution. For example, be aware that if you are receiving alimony, your remarriage usually means the end of such spousal maintenance, but it does not usually affect child support. (See Chapter 10, "Ending a Marriage," and Chapter 12, "Your Estate"; see also the discussion of prenuptial agreements on page 207.)

Before you remarry, when you talk seriously with your intended about financial matters, be sure you understand what obligations, if any, your fiancé has to his or her first spouse and their children.

Often with remarriage comes the question, should I adopt my stepchildren? Obviously, there is a large emotional component to this decision. There are also legal angles. Presuming that the other biological parent agrees to the adoption, an adopted child (see more in Chapter 11, "Parenthood") is your child in every legal sense of the word, so you would be responsible for the child's support, education and well-being. The child could inherit some of your estate. Conversely, if you adopt your stepchild, she may give up her legal right to possibly inherit from her other biological parent if no will exists and there are no other heirs.

Living Together

On the surface, living together—the legal term is cohabiting—seems so casual and easy. Just move in and combine your furniture. But living together can be more complicated than it seems; even the most love-struck couple may soon find themselves fighting over who owns what and who should support whom.

Because a live-in arrangement usually does not have any legal status and always remains voluntary, general contract law, not domestic law, governs relationships between unmarried couples. That means that if a couple breaks up and disagrees over the divi-

Living together can be more complicated than it seems; even the most love-struck couple may soon find themselves fighting over who owns what.

FOR MORE INFORMATION

Partners who want to live together without marriage may want to consult *Living Together: A Legal Guide for Unmarried Couples*, by lawyers Toni Ihara, Ralph Warner and Frederick Hertz (Nolo Press, $34.99; www.nolo.com). This book covers everything from sharing a home and starting a family to dividing up possessions following a break-up. It also includes an entire chapter of contract forms that you might need.

sion of property, one party could sue the other—not for divorce, but for breach of contract (see the explanation of contract law and breach of contract in Chapter 1, "Living With the Law," and the discussion of palimony in Chapter 10, "Ending a Marriage"). That's a potentially messy process and a difficult-to-prove assertion unless you share a prior written agreement stating each partner's understanding of the terms of the relationship.

State Your Terms

With all of that in mind, you might want to avoid the possibility of future disputes by making a written agreement before you move in.

If your financial situations are straightforward and neither of you has many possessions or large bank accounts, you can buy a living-together kit in a bookstore and use the forms included to draft an agreement. You'd be well-advised to also have your agreement witnessed and notarized. Or consult a lawyer, just to be sure that the contract will hold up in court if challenged.

If you want an even simpler legal approach to living together, you can draw up an agreement that says that your living together creates no legal rights. In other words, you agree that each of you will simply provide for yourself before, during and after the relationship. That way neither of you gains anything from your partner, but neither do you lose any of your property or other assets if you break up. Again, take the precaution of having the agreement witnessed and notarized.

You might want to include a clause saying that if you eventually decide to marry, any living-together contract you have will be superseded and rendered obsolete by the new legal obligations of marriage.

In a more complicated situation, or if you just want expert advice, consult separate lawyers for help; by obtaining separate counsel, you'll avoid any chance of favoritism.

OPEN FOR DISCUSSION. A living-together agreement should address the following questions:

- **Does your partner** have rights to your property and income?
- **What do you own** and what does your partner own?
- **Which debts are whose?**
- **How will you take title to property** that you buy together? (See Chapter 12, "Your Estate.")
- **Who will pay monthly bills, such as rent and utilities,** and who will manage ongoing expenses such as groceries?
- **How will you divide** your assets and property if you break up?
- **Who will do what around the house?**
- **Who will get the pets if you break up?**

> Unlike married partners, to whom the law automatically affords certain rights, unmarried partners often have no legal safeguards.

TAXES AND LIVING TOGETHER

While you may otherwise share and share alike, remember that unmarried partners can't file joint tax returns. Despite your mutual domesticity, Uncle Sam says you're still single taxpayers. Whether this is to your advantage or disadvantage depends on your respective incomes, as the examples on page 204 show.

If you're living with someone and are also caring for a dependent child or parent at home, you can file as a head of household. You'll pay somewhat less than a single taxpayer, but more than you would if you and your live-in married.

COMMON-LAW MARRIAGE

The District of Columbia and the following states allow common-law marriages:

- **Alabama**
- **Colorado**
- **Iowa**
- **Kansas**
- **Montana**
- **Oklahoma**
- **Pennsylvania**
- **Rhode Island**
- **South Carolina**
- **Texas**
- **Utah**

Benefit Rights for Unmarried and Same-Sex Partners

Unlike married partners, to whom the law automatically affords certain rights, unmarried partners often have no legal safeguards. Despite how they may view themselves, the law usually considers them separate individuals, not a unit. As a result, hospitals often won't recognize unmarried partners as next of kin for visitation in intensive-care wards or for decision-making in medical emergencies (see Chapter 8, "Your Medical Rights"). And if one partner dies without a will or a specific contract, the survivor has no right to make a claim on the estate (see Chapter 12, "Estate Planning").

There is some good news for unmarried partners, however. They can register as domestic partners in one of the many U.S. cities with domestic partner registration. Usually—but not always—unmarried couples of the same sex must be residents of the city to apply, and must apply in person at city hall.

This status may allow them visitation at the hospital, among other things. Of course, what counts as legal status in one city may not count in another city lacking similar laws. That could be an issue if domestic partners move or if one of them becomes critically ill while visiting elsewhere.

Common-Law Marriages

Eleven states and the District of Columbia allow you and your partner of the opposite sex to join in a common-law marriage, meaning that the state considers you legally married without benefit of a license and official ceremony. All you have to do is set up housekeeping as husband and wife and tell people in your community that you are married. It helps if you file a joint tax return, have joint bank accounts, decide to share a name, and introduce each other as husband and wife. As with traditional marriage, you must understand what this means and be old enough to make the decision without the consent of your parents or a court.

Even in a state that recognizes common-law marriages you can still just live together without any legal consequences, if you don't present yourselves to the community as being married in the ways described above.

For a list of states that allow common-law marriages, see the box on the opposite page. Although the majority of states do not allow couples to form common-law marriages, they do acknowledge as legal those common-law marriages made in states that do permit them. So, for example, if you and your common-law spouse move to a non-common-law state, your marriage is still valid. If one of you falls critically ill, the hospital must allow you visitation and the authority due you in medical emergencies (see Chapter 8, "Your Medical Rights").

Unlike living together, which is an informal arrangement, marrying under common law is both formal and legal. You have all the obligations of a traditionally married couple to support each other and your children (see more under "Marriage," on page 201). One partner can even automatically inherit from the other. And, although it doesn't take an official ceremony to form a common-law marriage, it takes an official divorce to end one. So while a common-law marriage might be a low-stress way to become husband and wife, it's for keeps.

Lovers and Infectious Disease

People infected with conditions such as herpes, hepatitis and AIDS have successfully sued their partners—both married and unmarried—for knowingly exposing them to these sexually transmitted diseases. All states allow someone injured by a wrongful act, known as a tort, to try to recover damages in a civil suit (see Chapter 1, "Living With the Law").

If you are named in such a suit, check the provisions of your homeowners policy; unless it specifies an exclusion (or, if improbably, you infected someone knowingly), your policy probably will cover you, up to the limits of your liability coverage for damages, and

> **Although it doesn't take an official ceremony to form a common-law marriage, it takes an official divorce to end one.**

If you've been abused by your partner, act immediately. Call the police. They may arrest the abuser, and they can help you find a shelter if you need to leave your home.

provide you with an attorney, even if the transmission took place off of your premises.

In some states, if you know you are infected with HIV (the virus that causes AIDS) and have sex with an uninformed partner, you will be open to criminal prosecution.

If you think that you have given a sexual partner a disease or that someone has infected you, consult a lawyer or a local AIDS service immediately to explore your legal options.

Domestic Violence

While all states have laws against physical assault, since the late 1970s they have begun to include domestic violence in that category. Each state creates its own definition of domestic violence through legislation and court decisions, but every state includes in the definition acts of personal violence or assaults, and many include threats or attempts at abuse and sexual assault, too.

If you've been abused by your partner, act immediately. Call the police. They may arrest the abuser, and they can help you find sources of information and advice—say, a local hotline or support group—or a shelter if you need to leave your home. If you need immediate assistance, dial 911.

Talk with someone you trust, and call a lawyer to discuss your legal options. Even if your case does not proceed criminally, you can take civil action and in most states even sue for damages. You can also ask the court for a civil-protection order requiring that your partner stay away from you; this may mean that he or she will be evicted from the home. If your partner violates the restraining order, he or she can either be fined or jailed for contempt of a court order or charged with a criminal violation of the order.

In most states and the District of Columbia, a record of domestic violence, prosecuted or unprosecuted, must be considered as a factor in child-custody decisions.

(For more information on domestic violence, contact the National Coalition Against Domestic Violence at www.ncadv.org, or call 303-839-1852, where you will find links to several other organizations concerned with domestic violence. Or call the National Domestic Violence Hotline, which is answered 24 hours a day, at: 800-799-7233. Their Web site is www.ndvh.org.)

ANTI-STALKING LAWS. In addition to laws about domestic violence, most states now have anti-stalking laws, making it a form of harassment and a crime to persistently follow someone against his or her wishes. This applies to people you know or don't know. If you believe that someone is stalking you, contact the police.

Ending a Marriage

Ending a marriage can be a grueling and confusing emotional experience in which you may suddenly find yourself on the financial and legal defensive with someone you once loved and trusted. What's more, if you're heartbroken and disappointed, it's tempting to concern yourself more with venting hurt feelings than making property settlements. This is a tendency that can get messy and result in escalating legal bills as you and your soon-to-be ex-spouse argue over who gets the wedding presents and who deserves to keep the dog. Such landmines make it all the more important to understand the law and make sure you're getting the legal advice you need. In this chapter, we'll cover the legal ins and outs of everything from annulment to child custody.

Annulment: An Easy Way Out?

While it almost always takes a divorce to end your marriage, in some cases a court will simply wipe the legal slate clean and dissolve a marriage with an annulment. In an annulment, the court decrees that you and your partner were never legally married. (A religious annulment has no legal validity.)

Once, when the only way to end a marriage was through a messy divorce based on establishing which partner was at fault, some courts liberally granted annulments to unhappy couples. Now, however, with the ease and accessibility of no-fault divorces, annulments

There is a big difference between just parting company and being legally separated.

have become anachronistic and rare. There are two general reasons for an annulment:

■ **First, you can make a claim that the basis of your marriage itself is illegal,** perhaps because your spouse was mentally ill or drunk and didn't understand the implications of marriage. Other reasons might include marrying although you are close family relations, such as first cousins, or under circumstances of bigamy, polygamy, fraud, force or duress.

■ **Second, perhaps you have discovered information** that, had you known about it earlier, would have prevented you from marrying—for example, your husband lied about wanting to consummate the marriage or have children, suffering from impotency or having a criminal record.

As in a divorce, the court will consider issues of property, support and child custody. It can grant spousal support, too. Even if it annuls a marriage, the court would consider any children born from it to be legitimate, due the same consideration as children in any divorce situation.

State laws vary, but generally, once a spouse discovers she has grounds for an annulment, she should ask the court for an annulment as soon as possible because some states have time limits that might affect the outcome of the case. If her spouse does not agree, he can try and contest the annulment.

Separation: Often a First Step

Say that you and your spouse haven't been getting along for months and, finally, you simply split up. You may say that you have separated from your spouse, but beware: There is a big difference between just parting company and being legally separated.

A Nonlegal Separation

In a non-legal separation, one of you could just hit the road, leaving the other in the lurch. You should realize, however, the serious implications if one of you deserts the other, simply running away without the other's consent. Desertion can serve as grounds for divorce and it will weaken the deserting spouse's chance for custody of the children in that event.

A better alternative, of course, is for you and your spouse to make a written or verbal agreement to lead separate lives. You, your spouse and your lawyers can make any financial arrangements you please for as long as you please without taking court action. You can use the separation agreement to settle questions of property, custody, alimony and child support.

No matter what arrangement you make for a nonlegal separation—mutually agreed upon or un-expected—you are still legally husband and wife, entitled to all the benefits and bound by all the obligations of marriage. This type of separation can be the first step toward a no-fault divorce: In many states you have grounds for divorce if you have been sepa-rated—that is, no longer living together, or living in the same house but ceasing all marital communica-tion, physical and otherwise—for a prescribed time period, ranging from six months to three years, de-pending on the state.

A Legal Separation

On the other hand, a legal separation is very similar to divorce. You go to court to have the terms of the separation agreement decided. As in a divorce, your lawyers try to reach a settlement agreement concern-ing property, child custody and the responsibilities of each spouse. The court usually goes along with the settlement you and your spouse propose, as long as it is fair to both parties. The only difference between a divorce and a legal separation, also known as a judi-cial separation, is that in a legal separation you are technically still married. If you wanted to get back together as husband and wife, you might be able to do so simply by filing with the court, before witnesses, an acknowledgment that you have resumed marital relations, or by asking a judge to rescind the binding property settlement and custody arrangements.

No matter what arrangement you make for a nonlegal separation, you are still legally husband and wife.

Legal separations aren't all that common these days; usually they are pursued only for religious reasons, including strictures against divorce or fear of excommunication, or for health insurance reasons—if one otherwise uninsurable spouse is covered under the other's health insurance and wants to maintain coverage. Before pursuing a legal separation just for health insurance reasons, though, check your policy; some health insurance will terminate upon divorce or legal separation.

Divorce

Although divorce laws vary widely from state to state, one thing is constant: When you divorce, you formally end your marriage. (For information about changing your name following a divorce, see page 210 in Chapter 9, "Marriage and Other Personal Partnerships.")

Does It Matter Whose Fault It Is?

In the past, in many states the only way to get a divorce was by proving that one partner was at fault, on such grounds as adultery, desertion, extreme intolerable cruelty or habitual intemperance. In the late 1960s, however, no-fault divorces came into existence, and couples were able to file for divorce simply because they had irreconcilable differences, they had separated or their marriage had irretrievably broken down.

DIVORCE REALITY

- **Ninety-five percent** of divorces don't go to trial.
- **Most couples have little property to divide,** but plenty of debt.
- **The biggest asset** most couples share is usually either the house or a pension.
- **Courts don't usually grant** spousal support these days, and when they do, it's for a limited period of time.

Thirty-five states still grant fault, as well as no-fault, divorces; the rest grant only some type of no-fault divorce. Usually it's much easier to show grounds for a no-fault divorce (also known as a dissolution).

The old cliché that someone's wife or husband "won't give" him or her a divorce really isn't true anymore. Under no-fault laws, one partner cannot prevent the other from obtaining a divorce—if one of you believes your marriage to be over, most courts will agree.

You might want to establish fault, however—say, if you live in a state that allows you to get a larger percentage of the property settlement by proving your spouse wronged you. Even if you decide to pursue a no-fault divorce, sometimes the property settlement or alimony decree will depend, in part, on establishing fault. Whether you pursue a fault or no-fault divorce, in more than half the states and the District of Columbia fault may be considered in the distribution of marital property; in some of those states the greater the fault, the less share that spouse receives. In about half the states, fault can limit or bar alimony awards as well. Check with your lawyer to see what your state's divorce laws are.

Do-It-Yourself Divorce?

If you have little property and no children, and you have mutually agreed on the divorce and anticipate no issues that you can't resolve yourselves, do-it-yourself legal kits are an option that will help you avoid the necessity of hiring counsel. You and your soon-to-be ex-spouse fill out the forms, enter the final judgment and have the papers filed with the court.

However, the simplicity of a do-it-yourself divorce today can cause complexities tomorrow. Your ex-spouse might claim that the agreement is unfair because he didn't really understand what he was signing away. He could sue for a greater portion of the assets and you might end up in court, spending all the money you thought you had saved by avoiding a lawyer, not to mention reopening old wounds.

Even if you decide to pursue a no-fault divorce, sometimes the property settlement or alimony decree will depend, in part, on establishing fault.

You must apply for a divorce in the state in which you live; residency requirements vary, ranging from three months to a year.

How the Process Works

Because you and your spouse ultimately have separate interests in a divorce, you should each have your own lawyer even if you think the divorce will be amicable. Despite what you see on TV, only about 5% of divorces actually go to trial; negotiation resolves all others. Usually the lawyers come to an agreement about how to divide the property, who will pay support and how much, and who will get custody of the children. If the couple can agree on the settlement (often a prenuptial agreement makes this step easier; see page 207, Chapter 9, "Marriage and Other Personal Partnerships"), then a court will almost always approve it. If the couple can't agree, the court will decide (see "Dividing the Property," on the next page). Be warned: When a divorce goes to trial, it gets more expensive. Before you know it, your lawyer's fees could eat up your settlement.

You must apply for a divorce in the state in which you live; residency requirements vary, ranging from none to a year. With the advent of relatively easy no-fault divorces, couples almost never use "quickie" divorces anymore—those sought and granted in places with liberal residency requirements, such as the Dominican Republic.

Once your state grants you a valid divorce, all other states will recognize it. Your state is not necessarily obligated to accept a divorce decree made in another country, however.

Usually you cannot remarry until your divorce is final, but in some states, including California, if the divorce is going to be lengthy and complicated and one of you wants to remarry soon, it is possible to get a judgment from the court that restores you both to single status before you have resolved the property and support issues.

Just in case you have a change of heart and fall in love all over again within six months of the divorce, some states will even allow you to ask the court to set aside the divorce decree and reinstate the marriage.

Don't Argue, Seek Mediation

You can best settle some divorce issues by seeking mediation, whereby you voluntarily agree to talk to a neutral third party to try to work out your differences and reach a viable settlement agreement. The mediator does not make a decision, but simply guides the discussion and helps the couple come to acceptable terms. Mediation works best when both parties are reasonable and eager for a fair resolution. In a few states mediation is a mandatory process before the determination of child-custody and visitation rights.

A good mediator will educate you and assist you in gathering a detailed list of all your assets, debts and liabilities to make sure that the negotiations are equitable. Most mediators will suggest that a lawyer for each of you review the draft of a mediated agreement before you sign it, in order to avoid any challenges to the agreement or other legal problems down the road.

Some states offer certification for mediators. Requirements and qualifications vary from state to state. Your state's bar association or your lawyer can help you find a reputable mediator; a neutral lawyer may be willing to act as a mediator (see the box WHERE).

> **FOR MORE INFORMATION**
>
> **The Association for Conflict Resolution** (1527 New Hampshire Avenue, N.W., Washington, DC 20036; 202-667-9700; www.acresolution.org). The Web site offers an online search for family mediators. Although the site is primarily dedicated to practitioners, some of the publications and FAQs may be of interest to prospective users of mediation.

Dividing the Property

Figuring out who gets what in a divorce can be tough—and it can also depend a lot on where you live.

A COMMUNITY-PROPERTY STATE. The nine community-property states (see the box at WHERE) consider any assets acquired during the marriage (not including inheritances and gifts made to one or the other partner) to belong to both the husband and wife. Any property brought into the marriage remains the property of that individual. Unless there is a prenuptial

COMMUNITY-PROPERTY STATES

- **Arizona**
- **California**
- **Idaho**
- **Louisiana**
- **Nevada**
- **New Mexico**
- **Texas**
- **Washington**
- **Wisconsin**

agreement to the contrary, these states try to divide the community property equally.

IN NON-COMMUNITY-PROPERTY STATES other states use an "equitable distribution" method. This takes into account many factors, such as:

- **the length of marriage;**
- **the respective age,** health and educational background of each partner;
- **their skills and employability;**
- **their style of living** and station of life;
- **the respective needs and earnings** of each party and their children;
- **the advisability** of the custodial parent's employment in light of the age of the children;
- **the contribution** (including homemaking) of both parties to the preservation and appreciation of assets;
- **their opportunity to acquire assets** down the road; and
- **in some states,** the degree of fault attributable to each partner.

In some states, only marital assets—those acquired during the marriage—can be divided; in other states, all assets—those acquired before and during the marriage—are up for grabs, although the court takes into consideration who contributed what. The custodial parent (see "Child Custody," on page 232) is often awarded possession of the house, at least until the children come of age, usually at age 18 or 21. Then the parent must sell the house and divide any resulting income with the ex-spouse according to guidelines set out in the settlement. Say a man brought $100,000 to his marriage:

- **In one state,** the court could neither distribute that money nor take its existence into account when hammering out a fair settlement.

- **In another state,** the court could not divide up the man's $100,000, but it could take it into consideration when dividing up the rest of the couple's assets, perhaps giving the wife a larger share of the couple's assets than it might otherwise have done.

■ **In yet another state,** the court could actually distribute some of the man's $100,000 to his wife if it felt that was part of a fair settlement.

WHAT ABOUT RETIREMENT BENEFITS? Pensions, deferred profit-sharing accounts and other retirement benefits are generally considered marital property in a divorce. A spouse can negotiate the rights to all or a portion of them. For example, one spouse may get the pension, the other may get the house.

A state divorce court does not need to order a husband to turn over part of these benefits to the wife; instead it can issue a qualified domestic relations order (QDRO) that requires a pension-plan administrator to pay the pension share directly to the non-employee spouse, bypassing the employee spouse altogether.

It's wise to learn before settlement whether your spouse's retirement plan will cease its payments upon the death of the recipient, your then ex-spouse. Your lawyer may be able to negotiate a share of the survivor benefit for you, resulting in a slightly reduced benefit to your spouse. If so, to ensure that you receive what's due you, ask for your share of those benefits in a lump sum at settlement.

Make sure your lawyer looks into the terms of all your spouse's benefits, including life insurance.

Although social security benefits are not considered property for purposes of a divorce settlement, if you are at least 62 years old and are divorcing after more than ten years of marriage, the law automatically entitles you to partake in your ex-spouse's social security benefits. This is true even if he hasn't begun collecting them yet but is eligible to receive them by age or disability, if you've been divorced for at least two years. And you don't need to rely on your ex-spouse to give you the money. Apply to the Social Security Administration and it will send the check directly to you. (If you are a wid-

Pensions, deferred profit-sharing accounts and other retirement benefits are generally considered marital property.

FOR MORE INFORMATION

Receiving a fair share of retirement benefits in a divorce settlement is more likely to be a woman's issue than a man's, because women are more likely to have never worked outside the home, worked at a lower-paying job, been out of the work force for extended periods of time, or worked for smaller offices or companies that provide minimal benefits.

Get a copy of *Your Pension Rights At Divorce: What Women Need to Know*, available for $24.95 from the Pension Rights Center (1140 Nineteenth St., N.W., Suite 602, Washington, DC 20036-6608; 202-296-3776; www.pensionrights.org).

owed divorcee, your benefit is payable at age 60 if you were married for ten years or more. The age requirement is lower if you're disabled or have minor children in your care.)

DIVISION OF DEBT. Just as you need to divide your property, so must you divide your debts.

Laws vary from state to state and situation to situation, but usually any money you owed before your marriage is yours alone to pay off.

If you live in a community-property state, both spouses are responsible for any debt incurred during the marriage, together or individually. In other places, any debts you incurred on your own after marrying—for example, a student loan in your own name, a car loan or charges on a credit card held in your name only—remain yours alone. Of course, if you regularly lent your spouse your credit card, you might be liable for any bills he or she ran up on it.

Regardless of who spent the money and where you live, you are both accountable for any debts incurred during the marriage for necessary family expenses such as food, clothes for the kids, shelter, and so on. The IRS would also hold you equally responsible for any delinquent tax bill until it was all paid off. The agency won't say, "You each owe half." They don't care who pays, so long as it's paid.

The Bankruptcy Reform Act of 1994 should prevent divorced people from being saddled with marital debts a former spouse agreed to pay in a divorce settlement. The new law says a divorced debtor can't discharge such debts in bankruptcy. Exceptions: If making payments would leave the debtor too little to live on or if the person's ex-spouse would suffer little hardship from having to pay the debt.

Alimony

Alimony is also known as spousal support or maintenance. It is not automatically awarded; in fact, with more and more two-career families, many court-approved settlements don't include alimony. State laws that allow alimony are gender-neutral, but still, 99% of the time when courts award alimony it is the wife who receives it and the husband who pays it. There are two types of alimony:

- **Permanent alimony** means the law entitles the recipient spouse to alimony until he or she remarries or dies or until a court adjusts the amount in light of changing circumstances. For example, the ex-wife might become employed; the ex-husband might begin a new family and take on new financial responsibilities, or suffer a disability or some other form of long-term unemployment.

- **Rehabilitative alimony** offers the spouse financial support for a limited period, often between two and five years, until she can learn to support herself. In recent years, with women increasingly expected to support themselves, a court granting any support at all tends to grant support, assuming that the spouse can and will become self-supporting.

The court determines the amount and duration of any award based on some of the same factors that influence the property settlement in a non-community-property state, such as the ages and health of the

Alimony isn't automatically awarded; in fact, with more and more two-career families, many court-approved settlements don't include alimony.

When two unmarried people who have lived together without a written contract break up, a palimony suit might follow.

parties, the length of their marriage, current employment, differences in pay, future employability and standard of living while married. Some agreements may include so-called escalator clauses that account for future increases in cost-of-living or in the paying partner's income.

In about half the states, the reason for dissolving the marriage can affect alimony, that is, the court may order the "guilty" party to pay more support to the innocent one whether or not he or she is seeking a fault divorce.

Under the Bankruptcy Act of 1994, a debtor can't include in a bankruptcy alimony (or child support) owed to an ex-spouse.

Palimony

When two unmarried people who have lived together without a written contract break up, a palimony suit might follow. One partner may sue the other for a share in the property acquired jointly during the relationship, and may seek financial support as well, arguing that there was an implied or verbal contract between the parties to live together and share their present and future income (see also the discussion of living together in Chapter 9, "Marriage and Other Personal Partnerships").

The term palimony was coined in 1976, when Michelle Triola Marvin sued actor Lee Marvin, claiming they had a verbal agreement that he would support her for life in exchange for her giving up her singing career and devoting herself to their relationship. She asked for half of what he had earned during the six years they lived together. The court set a precedent by stating that implied contracts between unmarried couples were enforceable. Even so, Michelle Marvin still didn't win; a jury ruled that she could not demonstrate that she and the actor had made any such agreement.

Protecting Your Settlement

If your ex-spouse declares bankruptcy, he won't have to pay the money he agreed to give you as part of your property settlement, unless it is alimony or child support. If your state law allows it, try to protect yourself from this possibility by getting as much of the settlement as his lawyer will agree to right after the divorce, in a "lump-sum alimony buy-out." That way, future bankruptcy or not, you will receive as much as possible of the settlement.

Also, if your ex-spouse dies before paying all that he owes you, you won't get the remainder. Insure yourself against this unfortunate fate; as part of the divorce agreement, you should require your spouse to purchase a decreasing term-insurance policy naming you as the beneficiary. The policy will insure your ex-spouse's life for a fixed period (say, five, ten, 15 or even 20 years—as long as you agree is necessary) to guarantee that you receive the full amount of your settlement. The amount of coverage will periodically drop according to a fixed schedule. If your ex-spouse won't take out a policy voluntarily, a court might order him to do so.

TAXES AND ALIMONY

Once again, Uncle Sam takes part in your private life, but here he gives you and your ex-spouse a choice: You can agree that the payer of alimony will deduct this spousal support from his taxable income and the recipient will include it as part of her taxable income. If one doesn't deduct alimony, however, the other needn't claim it as taxable income.

Why would anyone agree to taking taxable alimony? Because the spouse paying alimony will likely be willing to pay more if he knows he can deduct the payments.

For payments to qualify as deductible alimony, your written divorce agreement must require them and the payer generally must pay them in cash. Child support is not deductible.

For more details, check IRS Publication 504, *Tax Information for Divorce or Separated Individuals* (you can download it at www.irs.gov), and consult a lawyer to be sure you are making the arrangement that will best benefit you.

Usually, if parents can agree on their own custody arrangements during a divorce settlement, a judge will approve them.

Child Custody

Arranging custody of children can be an emotional and complicated process. At issue is legal custody, the parent's right to make all parental decisions regarding the child's welfare (see Chapter 11, "Parenthood"); and physical custody, the parent's right to have the child live with him or her for all or part of the year. One parent can have sole legal and physical custody of a child, or both parents can have joint custody, sharing either physical custody, legal custody or both. Usually, if parents can agree on their own custody arrangements during a divorce settlement, a judge will approve them, but the final word on custody always belongs to the court, charged with acting in the child's best interest.

Although both parents are theoretically eligible for custody—and these days more and more men are asking for custody—in practice, the court usually places the child with the mother in cases of custody disagreements. A judge considers many factors before granting custody:

- **The age and sex of the child.** For example, all other things being equal, an infant will most likely stay with his mother, while an older son might be placed with his dad.
- **The child's preference.** The older a child is, the more seriously the court considers her wishes.
- **The child's relationship with each parent.** A parent who has a history of conflict with a child is less likely to receive custody.
- **The ability of each parent** to provide for the child's needs and schooling.
- **The continuity of the environment** the parent will provide. A parent whose job requires frequent moves that would uproot the child from schools and friends might be less likely to receive custody.
- **The mental and physical health** of each parent. All other things being equal, a parent who suffers from a chronic debilitating illness or who has a physical disability or a history of mental illness, even if it is controllable, may be less likely to receive custody.

Preventing a Worst-Case Custody Situation

If there is some doubt as to a noncustodial parent's trustworthiness, a court may grant supervised visitation. This means that the parent and child will spend time together under the watchful eyes of a court or social-services officer. However, a custodial parent who fears that the other parent may injure or abduct the child, for example, cannot deny a noncustodial parent visitation without a court order.

Even after it approves a custody decision, the court can alter it if circumstances change, such as if one parent wants to move out of state and take the child with him. The Uniform Child Custody Jurisdiction Act ensures that all states will honor a child-custody decision.

If a noncustodial parent snatches his or her child, for whatever reason, the law considers it parental kidnapping. Not only do many states have laws against this, but under the Parental Kidnapping Prevention Act, it can also be a federal offense. If your ex-spouse has taken your child illegally, contact the police and then your lawyer immediately. He or she will contact the U.S. attorney in your federal district, who will begin the process of finding your child and bring charges against the offending parent.

> Even after it approves a custody decision, the court can alter it if circumstances change, such as if one parent wants to move out of state and take the child with him.

PAY UP OR PAY

To try to increase the number of parents who pay the child support they owe, Congress passed the federal Family Support Act. It requires all states to pass their own laws, so that all new or modified child-support orders would include automatic wage withholding; your employer will subtract what you owe each month from your paycheck and send it to the custodial parent. Even bankruptcy is no excuse for not paying child support. If a parent does not pay the prescribed amount of child support, a court can garnish his wages, put a lien on his property, intercept his tax refund—or even jail him for contempt of court.

> **FOR MORE INFORMATION**
>
> **The Nolo Plain-English Law Centers** (www.nolo
> .com/lawcenter). For answers to many questions related to
> child custody, select "Divorce and Cbild Custody," and
> "Child Custody and Visitation."

The Rights of Grandparents

Almost every state has laws that allow grandparents to apply for visitation rights to their grandchildren in the case of their child's death or divorce. This has become a controversial issue with parents charging that they have a legal right to determine who may be allowed to visit their children. If grandparents can demonstrate that they have an ongoing, caring relationship with their grandkids, the court may find it in the children's best interest to allow the relationship and will grant the grandparents visitation.

Child Support

Since the mid 1980s, each state has developed standardized formulas for determining fair child-support payments. The court must award at least the predetermined amount unless there are extenuating circumstances—say, if a remarried parent is already heavily burdened with child support responsibilities, or the parents agree to a different arrangement. The standard percentage varies from state to state, in Massachusetts, for example, a man with a gross income of $501 and over, supporting one child might end up paying about 27% of his gross earnings to child support.

Under federal law, states must periodically review child-support agreements to ensure, on behalf of the child, that payments keep up with any rise in the cost of living and any significant increase in the paying parent's income.

Unlike alimony, child-support payments are not

> ## FOR MORE INFORMATION
>
> ■ *Divorce and Money: How to Make the Best Financial Decisions During Divorce,* by Violet Woodhouse and Dale Fetherling (Nolo Press, $34.99). A comprehensive guide to the financial realities of divorce, including managing tax changes, discovering hidden assets and protecting property.

tax-deductible for the payer and are tax-free to the recipient. They don't cease if an ex-spouse remarries, and a parent is liable for child support until the child reaches the age of majority, usually 18. In some states, the law requires parents who are paying child support to provide for a child's higher education as well. To be sure that children will be provided for in the event of the payer's death, a court might even order that the payer name the children or the custodial parent as the beneficiaries of his life insurance policy.

The custodial parent is responsible for using child-support payments to care for and feed the child, not to cover household expenses, such as replacing the roof or getting the house painted.

Parenthood

P arenthood is probably the biggest and longest-lasting responsibility anyone ever takes on. You don't have to get a civil license for it, but depending on how you choose to become a parent, you may have to jump through some legal hoops. Once the deed is done, you can expect to encounter some legal boundaries for parenting and some legally challenging situations that never occurred to you when you dreamt of singing your baby to sleep with lullabies. In this chapter we will look at the legal rights, obligations and concerns of parenthood.

Parenthood — by Law

T he Supreme Court has ruled that parents have a fundamental right to the care, control and upbringing of their children, including the right to make primary judgments about education (within some limits, described on page 239), religion, and the values and standards of the family. As long as parents make a good-faith effort, within their means, to feed, clothe, shelter, educate and vaccinate their children, and generally do not unduly endanger them, the relationship between parent and child is private and the state has no power to tell parents how to raise their children.

It's perfectly within parents' rights to take their kids on risky adventures such as kayaking or rock climbing as long as they provide any equipment required by state or local law and follow safety regulations. But parents may

The law in all states allows parents to physically punish their children as long as the punishment does not exceed appropriate levels.

not subject kids to any daily harm or serious risk of harm, such as exposed electrical wires or lack of heat in the winter. If they do, they are liable for civil and some-times criminal lawsuits, depending on whether the state is trying to rectify the situation or punish the parent. If parents inadequately care for their children—say, if they neglect to feed and clothe them, or if a child is deathly ill and the parents refuse to allow treatment for whatever reason—authorities such as the local child-welfare agency can intervene in the name of safety. The government can also intervene if parents leave their kids home alone and unsupervised because of the risk of harm to the children. Possible actions include requiring the parents to attend remedial parenting classes or to seek family counseling. The court might decide to re-move the children from the home and place them with a relative or in foster care for some period of time.

What About Corporal Punishment?

The law in all states allows parents to physically punish their children as long as the punishment does not ex-ceed appropriate levels. For example, a parent may slap, spank or restrict a child as he or she thinks neces-sary and appropriate, but within reason as defined by any reasonable adult or by community standards. Of course, extreme punishment that injures a child—causing excessive bruising, broken skin, swelling, broken bones, damage to internal organs or burns—would be viewed as child abuse, as would unduly depriving the child of food, shelter, care or liberty. Even so, what constitutes "extreme" is usually deter-mined on a case-by-case basis. The legislatures and courts have approached child abuse much as Supreme Court Justice Potter Stewart defined obscenity: "I can't define it, but I know it when I see it."

Child Abuse

Each state defines child abuse differently, but all in-clude the infliction of intentional harm and adult-child sexual intercourse or molestation.

Although child abuse is a crime, punishable by in-

PUNISHMENT AT SCHOOL

Remember being rapped on the knuckles with a ruler? Through high school, your child doesn't have an automatic right to be free of spanking or other corporal punishment in the classroom, though state or city laws or your school district's rules may prohibit it. (More than half of the states have banned corporal punishment in their schools.) For general information, check the National Coalition to Abolish Corporal Punishment in Schools Web site (www.stophitting.com/disatschool). For information on local policies, contact your state's department of education or your local board of education or other school administrative body (check the blue pages of your phone book).

If your child has been physically punished and you think the act was illegal, excessive or unfair, begin by contacting the school principal.

---

carceration in the most extreme cases, abuse by a parent is usually dealt with in a civil court—often called juvenile court—in an effort to improve the child's welfare. In some cases, the only workable solution is to temporarily or permanently remove the child from the parent's custody.

Professionals, such as doctors, nurses, day-care providers and teachers who work with children daily, are bound by each state's mandatory reporting laws to report any suspicion of child abuse to state or local child protection authorities. Every state maintains a hotline that concerned citizens can call if they suspect a child is being abused.

Education

Based on the Jeffersonian principle that the citizenry must be enlightened, all states require that children receive compulsory education, typically from ages 7 to 16. However, under the First Amendment, no state can insist that kids go to any particular kind of school. You are within your rights to send your children to public, parochial or private school, or even to educate

Legally speaking, a parent generally isn't responsible for a child's acts unless someone can show that the parent was negligent in allowing the act to occur.

them at home. But all schools, including home schools, are subject to some state control to certify that the diplomas they grant meet the state's minimal requirements, usually a mastery of the three R's.

Only under certain circumstances can you withdraw your child from classes or school activities you find objectionable. If the local school board has deemed a class such as sex education optional, then you have the right to refuse to let your child attend. On the other hand, if the local school board requires a course, such as biology or history, you must let your child attend. If you object to the way the course is taught—to presentation of the theory of evolution, for example—you have the following alternatives:

- **You can discuss the issue** with the teacher and suggest that alternative points of view be discussed.
- **You can lobby** your local school board and try to get the course made optional or its content or approach amended.
- **You can send your child** to a different school with a different curriculum.
- **You can lobby** the textbook publishers or the board that adopts textbooks for your state to change their treatment of a particular subject.

Liability for Your Child

Some states have statutes that hold a parent legally responsible for damage cause by a child's acts—especially if someone can show that the parent was negligent in allowing the act to occur. A lot depends on what you know or don't know about your child's activities and whether you are providing adequate supervision in situations that require it or would merit it. If a child is severely out of control, the state may take custody of a child.

The Car

For example, say your child has his learner's permit and decides to take the car for a spin by himself, resulting in an accident:

■ **If you put the keys away** and Junior hot-wired the car, you would not be considered negligent or liable for the damage he caused.

■ **If you left your keys in the ignition** and Junior noticed and took the car, you might be found negligent and liable for the accident.

■ **If you gave Junior permission** to take the car out by himself, without your supervision, you would almost certainly be found negligent and liable.

Of course, you might wish to assume responsibility, paying for the damage out of your own pocket or that of your kid, or using your car insurance. But generally, you're not legally obligated to pay unless someone—the authorities or the damaged party—shows that you were negligent in allowing the act to occur. (In addition, if it appears that you were negligent, child-protection authorities may be called in to investigate.)

Otherwise, the injured party can bring suit against you. If you are proved liable, the consequences are usually financial, not criminal. And even then, parental-responsibility laws usually impose a liability limit that is often well below the cost of the actual damage. In the case of the learner's-permit violation, for example, your car insurance would probably cover your costs if you had already added your child to the policy as a driver of the family car. Or you might depend on the liability coverage of your homeowners policy, which typically applies to you and other family members living in your house. This usually pays up to $100,000 to others for injury or damage that you or a family member might have caused, at home or elsewhere, and would also cover your legal defense if you need it. (See the discussion of car insurance in Chapter 4, "Your Car," and of homeowners insurance in Chapter 6, "Your Home and the Law.")

A Gun

What happens if your child gains access to your handgun or other firearm and hurts or kills another child or himself? If you failed to take adequate precautions

> **Parental-responsibility laws usually impose a liability limit that is often well below the cost of the actual damage.**

If you own firearms, make a point of storing them unloaded in a locked and inaccessible place, installing trigger locks, and storing ammunition separately.

against your child's using the gun or failed to provide supervision when you knew he was using it, you could be held liable for the other child's injury or death and you could be charged with neglect in the case of your own child. If you are subject to criminal charges, your costs for damages and legal defense probably would not be covered under a typical homeowner's policy (see Chapter 6, "Your Home and the Law").

If you own firearms, make a point of storing them unloaded in a locked and inaccessible place, installing trigger locks, and storing ammunition separately. If you are at all unclear about your state's laws regarding gun ownership and use, contact your local police department. Florida state law says that an adult can be held responsible if a kid hurts himself or someone else with a gun; exceptions occur if the adult took reasonable precautions, such as locking the gun in a lock box, or if a minor stole the gun from a home.

Alcoholic Beverages

Another common situation in which parents run a high risk of liability is consumption of alcohol by minors in your home. For example, say that your daughter has a party at home at which alcohol is consumed by minors, one of whom later is injured while driving intoxicated. Would you be liable for the injuries suffered by your daughter's friend:

- **if you didn't know about the party, period?** Probably not. You can't foresee—much less prevent—trouble if you don't know it may exist.
- **if you knew she was having the party,** made clear that alcohol was forbidden, and left your home for the evening? Probably. Though you said no, any parent knows that his child may not listen. Therefore the danger is foreseeable and would have been preventable if you had stayed to supervise the situation.
- **if you were upstairs** while the party was going on downstairs and didn't know drinking was occurring? More probably. Again, a reasonable parent would check in on the situation once in a while and put a stop to drinking.

- **if you were in the house,** knew that drinking was going on and didn't attempt to stop it? Certainly.
- **if you discovered that alcohol was being consumed** and broke up the party, allowing some of the kids to drive themselves home? Probably, because you knew there was a danger in letting them drive after drinking.

In any of these situations, the consequences of your liability would be civil, centering on the concept of foreseeability—your responsibility and ability as a parent to peer ahead and see possible trouble. It wouldn't be a criminal issue, because there was no intent to injure anyone.

Can My Child Bring Suit Against Me?

Parents and children have traditionally not been allowed to sue each other, but that has begun to change, as the exceptions have started to overtake the rule. While a child still can't sue his parents for not raising him well, these days he can sue for intentional harm, such as sex abuse. Although there was a celebrated case in Florida in 1992 in which a young boy sued to be freed from his mother so that his foster parents could adopt him, children generally can't "divorce" their parents. Like it or not, they are stuck with them for life.

Paternity Actions

Because children are entitled to support from their parents, a father is usually liable for child support whether or not he is married to the child's mother. A father is legally required to support his child even if he did not want the mother to have the child and encouraged her to terminate the pregnancy.

If a man denies that he is the father of a woman's child, she can file a paternity action in an attempt to force him to pay support.

On the other hand, if a man wants to be legally declared the father of a child in spite of denial by the child's mother, he can also file such an action to win visitation rights or custody.

> **While a child still can't sue his parents for not raising him well, these days he can sue for intentional harm.**

If a married woman is artificially inseminated by an anonymous sperm donor, her husband will be considered the baby's legal father if he consents.

Paternity suits have been revolutionized by blood tests, the human leukocyte antigen (HLA) test and a DNA test, which are almost 100% accurate in determining whether the man is the father of the child. Most state laws require such tests as part of a paternity suit.

For some background reading of FAQs related to the question of paternity, visit www.nolo.com/lawcenter and select "Divorce and Child Custody" and "Child Support."

For more information, you should contact a lawyer specializing in family law.

Ways to Become a Parent

As technology advances and society becomes more complex, the law must keep pace. Today, the legal determination of who is a parent isn't always as simple as it used to be.

Artificial Insemination: Who Is the Parent?

There's no question that if a married woman becomes pregnant with her husband's sperm through artificial insemination, a process of delivering the sperm without sexual intercourse, then the husband is considered the legal father of the baby.

If a married woman is artificially inseminated by an anonymous sperm donor, her husband will be considered the baby's legal father if he consents (in some states he must do so in writing). An anonymous sperm donor is not considered the legal father of a child created from his sperm.

It's most common for sperm donors to donate to a sperm bank (as opposed to any private arrangements between parties who are acquainted). So far, no cases have been brought where an anonymous sperm donor has tried to gain parental rights.

PROTECT YOURSELF. A doctor may have all the necessary forms for the donor and for the recipient and her husband, but you should double-check with a lawyer to be sure that the forms comply with the donor-insemination laws of your state. Be aware that many states have no statutes at all governing artificial insemination, and some have them only in regard to married women. You don't want to find out after the fact that your rights have been compromised in any way.

IF YOU'RE UNMARRIED. For unmarried women, who lack a legal partner ready to assume the role of a father, the law is usually more ambiguous. This is particularly true of women who are artificially inseminated with the sperm of a known donor. In California, for example, if a woman is artificially inseminated under a doctor's supervision, the donor (known or anonymous) is not considered the father. However, if she performs the procedure at home with the sperm of a friend or acquaintance, the state's insemination statute would not protect a woman if the donor decided to seek parental rights. That's why it's best to check with a lawyer and take appropriate legal precautions before you proceed.

Surrogate Motherhood

Surrogate motherhood, in which another woman agrees to help conceive or carry a baby to term for a couple, is still so legally controversial that many people have given up on it as an option. A number of states consider such arrangements to be baby selling and prohibit contracts entirely. Check with your lawyer to see how your state handles surrogate issues. If you proceed without knowing the law or if the law is murky, you could end up in court fighting for the rights to your baby.

Adoption

Adoption is a legal method of making your own a child in whom you have no biological stake. There are several reasons you might want to adopt a child: You want to be a parent but you are unable to have children; you already have children but also wish to care for a child who is in need of a family; or you're a stepparent who wants to legally cement your relationship with a stepchild. Once you adopt, you become legally respon-

Adoption is a legal method of making your own a child in whom you have no biological stake.

> **In all states, to be approved by the appropriate court, an adoption must be shown to be in the "best interest of the child."**

sible for the child's care, support and education. Your new son or daughter has the same legal rights as a biological offspring, including the right to inherit a share of your estate should you die without a will.

Most adoptive parents are heterosexual, married couples, but in all states single people can adopt, too. In some states, gay and lesbian couples may adopt. In all states, to be approved by the appropriate court, an adoption must be shown to be in the "best interest of the child." The law leaves this phrase deliberately vague so that the court has leeway in each individual situation. In essence, the court seeks a permanent situation for the child in which he'll have the opportunity to grow and be loved. If the child is older, usually 12 and up, the child's wishes are considered by the court.

Adoption laws are controlled by the individual state legislatures and then interpreted by state courts. They vary so much from state to state that, before you take any other steps, you should call your local social services department, ask for its office of adoption, and learn all you can about your state's law.

Interstate adoptions are even more complicated; they usually must follow the laws of both states. If there is a conflict, usually the laws of the state in which you are filing for adoption apply.

International adoptions are yet more complicated because they involve two countries' laws, bureaucracies and cultural concerns.

In any case, it's important to work with a reputable attorney and adoption agency. For more information, see the box on page 247.

Ways to adopt

In any adoption, be prepared for at least four major steps along the way: a decision to sign placement papers for the child by the biological parent, or the termination of parental rights by a court; the filing of your adoption petition; the filing of final papers by both sides; and the final hearing to complete the process.

There are four basic types of adoptions: agency adoptions, private or independent adoptions, stepparent adoptions and international adoptions. In agency or in-dependent adoptions, state laws determine whether the birth parents may be assisted with any pregnancy-related expenses, and if so, which ones, ranging from medical and living expenses to legal costs during preg-nancy. No state allows the birth mother to receive any compensation beyond actual expenses. Paying or receiv-ing money for the adoption of a child (on the so-called black market) is considered baby selling and is illegal.

AGENCY ADOPTIONS. Agency adoptions are processed through social-service organizations licensed by the state to place children for adoption. The biological parents of the child give up all parental rights to the agency. An agency offers more legal guarantees to prospective adoptive parents: The child is clearly available to be adopted and there is less likely to be any unforeseen problem with the process. On the other hand, agencies sometimes place restrictions on applicants, requiring them to be under 40 and, though rarely, of a particular religion.

There are two main types of agency adoptions: traditional or confidential, and identified or open. In the *traditional* agency adoption, the agency locates adoptive parents for children it is placing and keeps the identity of the birth parents and the adoptive par-

No state allows the birth mother to receive any compensation beyond actual expenses.

FOR MORE INFORMATION

- **American Academy of Adoption Attorneys** (P.O. Box 33053, Washington, DC 20033-0053; 202-832-2222; www.adoptionattorneys.org)
- **National Council for Adoption** (225 N. Washington St., Alexandria, VA 22314; 703-299-6633; www.ncfa-usa.org)
- **International Concerns for Children** (911 Cypress Dr., Boulder, CO 80303; 303-494-8333; www.iccadopt.org)
- **North American Council on Adoptable Children** (those with special needs) (970 Raymond Ave., No. 106, St. Paul, MN 55114; 651-644-3036; www.nacac.org)

The risk of private adoption is that the birth parent(s) will have a change of mind and legally may be able to reclaim the child.

ents completely confidential. That doesn't mean that eventual communication between the adopted child and birth parent is impossible. Although the records are not available to the public, at least 24 states now have mutual-consent registries, which will release adoption information if both parties come forward and agree to the information exchange. These states also have a search-and-consent system in which the court contacts either the birth parent or the child and asks whether he or she would be open to meeting the other person.

In *identified* or open adoption placements, the parties have access to one another by varying degrees from the start. They usually exchange full names, meet, or exchange letters and pictures, whatever they both agree on.

PRIVATE OR INDEPENDENT ADOPTIONS. An independent adoption may be more advantageous for a nontraditional couple or for an impatient one. Usually, the adopting parents locate the birth parents; but the birth parents decide who will adopt the child based on personal knowledge or key factors of importance to them. The adoption is processed through an attorney rather than an adoption agency. Often the child is placed at birth, before parental rights are completely terminated. The risk of private adoption is that the birth parent(s) will have a change of mind and legally may be able to reclaim the child. Independent adoptions range from very open, with the parties having direct access to each other, to quite closed, with anonymity.

STEPPARENT ADOPTION. Here, the child remains related to one birth parent and is adopted by that parent's spouse. The parental rights of the other birth parent are terminated either by consent or by court proceeding, and the adoptive parent assumes the support obligations and parental responsibilities. A stepparent adoption might take place if the biological father wanted to be free of child-support obligations or if the adoptive father wanted to be sure to retain custody in the event that the child's mother dies.

INTERNATIONAL ADOPTIONS. These involve adopting a child who is a citizen of another country and who is not residing in the United States. They may be done as either agency adoptions or independent adoptions.

From a legal standpoint, international adoptions are complicated. You have to work within the laws of the child's country and the laws of the U.S. There is always the possibility that the foreign government might change its policies or even topple before your child leaves, and you'll find yourself back at square one. And just because you're prepared to welcome the child into a loving home doesn't mean the governments involved will always make the process easy for you; you may encounter immigration or visa problems—that is, difficulty in getting the necessary permissions for the child to leave one country and enter another.

Whether you work through an agency or not, it's important to retain a lawyer who has expertise in international adoption, and who can make sure that you jump through all the appropriate Immigration and Naturalization Service hoops on this end, too.

> **Just because you're prepared to welcome the child into a loving home doesn't mean the foreign governments involved will always make the process easy for you.**

Child Care

Hiring day care providers to work in the home means parents take on the role of employer, at which point Uncle Sam gets interested. We discuss some of the specific child care issues here; see the discussion beginning on page 138 of Chapter 6, "Your Home and the Law," for a broader discussion of hiring in-home help of any kind. But first, a quick look at the situation most parents encounter.

Day Care Away From Home

Day care providers who offer service in their homes or other facilities are governed by city, county and state governments that typically require them to be licensed or registered and to meet certain requirements. For

FOR MORE INFORMATION

- **The National Association for the Education of Young Children** (NAEYC; 1509 16th St., N.W., Washington, DC 20036; 800-424-2460; www.naeyc.org) provides an online search for NAEYC-accredited child-care programs, as well as numerous published resources for parents.

- **The National Association for Family Child Care** (5202 Pinemont Dr., Salt Lake City, Utah 84123; 801-269-9338; www.nafcc.org) is a membership organization of family child-care provider associations. It offers an on-line search of accredited providers.

- **Zero to Three** (2000 M St., N.W., Suite 200, Washington, DC 20036; 202-638-1144) is a national organization that promotes the healthy development of America's infants and toddlers. Its Web site offers numerous features of interest to parents and parents-to-be, including "Parenting A-Z," with a section on child care.

example, mothers may be restricted to caring for a certain number of children besides their own in their own homes. Commercial day care facilities may be required to maintain a certain caregiver-to-child ratio—for example, one caregiver per three preschool children or two infants. Licensed providers usually must meet other requirements for sanitary practices, safety, nutrition, and so on, and their facilities may be inspected. However, the degree to which local governments enforce these requirements varies.

For more information about state and local rules for day care or to request a list of licensed providers, check your local government listings in the blue pages under "Child Care," "Children's Services," or "Family or Social Services."

If you think your day care provider caused or contributed to the injury of your child, you should contact the appropriate local agency governing child care, the local law enforcement agency, and your lawyer to register your complaint or consider other legal action.

Hiring In-Home Help

If you are going to hire someone to take care of your child in your home, you have to be aware of—and comply with—the legal obligations that situation imposes.

In 2003, if you paid your household employee more than $1,400 (indexed for inflation in the future), you must pay part of his or her social security taxes and medicare taxes annually with your tax return. You needn't pay the tax as long as your employee is under 18 and doesn't list his or her principal occupation as household employment. If you're paying the employee $1,000 or more during a three-month period, you must also pay his or her federal unemployment taxes.

If you don't comply with these regulations and the IRS finds out, it can impose financial penalties and charge you interest on the tax you owe. An investigation might arise if you're audited or if your household employee of some 20 years goes to collect social security and finds there's no record of her employment.

One way to arrange for in-home help and avoid many of these taxes is to trade room and board for child care. This exception generally exempts from income tax the value of food and lodging you provide to a household employee who lives in your home.

It's also a good idea to check your state laws about insuring employees against injuries on the job. Some require you to have coverage up to certain limits. About half the states require household employers to buy worker's compensation insurance. A few states

One way to arrange for in-home help and avoid many taxes is to trade room and board for child care.

LEGAL PROTECTION

To prevent any legal confusion, make sure you have a written contract with your in-home child care provider. It should cover the worker's hours, duties and responsibilities, benefits, salary, and other arrangements. You can have a lawyer help you draw this up, or purchase a downloadable "Child Care Agreement" from the Nolo Press ($15.95; www.nolo.com/lawstore/; choose "Download Center," "WebForms" and "Employment Law").

Au pairs are considered participants in a cultural exchange program with a child-care component, not foreign workers.

require that the insurance be purchased through a state fund; the rest let you buy through private companies. Read your homeowners policy carefully to see whether it covers your liability for household help. If not, you can either buy a separate policy or perhaps buy coverage through a worker's compensation fund if your state offers one. For more information, check with your state's department of labor or employment, or with your insurance agent. Without this insurance, you could be sued by an employee who is hurt while working at your home.

For more information about tax compliance for household employers, including a list of tax forms you'll need, see page 140 of Chapter 6, "Your Home and the Law."

Hiring an Au Pair

Since 1986 the United States Information Agency has governed nonprofit organizations (see the box on the opposite page) that place young, 18- to 25-year-old, Europeans in American homes as "au pairs" for a 12-month period. These young people are considered participants in a cultural-exchange program with a child-care component, not foreign workers. In fact, they come to the U.S. on exchange-visitor visas that allow them to stay in the country for a total of only 13 months. Their stay cannot be extended, nor can they return to the U.S. to live or work within two years after that.

Strict rules regulate an au pair's duties: He or she must have a separate bedroom, work no more than 45 hours a week, and do only light housekeeping that is child-related, such as feeding, dressing or doing laundry for a child. Host families must pay au pairs a stipend of about $140 a week plus room and board. Since the au pair isn't considered an employee, the family doesn't have to pay social security or other taxes. The programs provide health insurance for their participants.

Hiring an Alien Worker

Before you can hire an alien worker, you have to meet

> **BABYSITTERS FROM ABROAD**
>
> The six groups that offer au pair programs are:
> - **goAUPAIR** (6965 Union Park Center, Suite 100, Midvale, Utah 84047; 888-287-2471; www.goaupair.com)
> - **Au Pair in America** (River Plaza, 9 West Broad St., Stamford, CT, 06902; 800-928-7247; www.aifs.com/aupair)
> - **AuPairCare** (2226 Bush St., San Francisco, CA 94115; 800-428-7247; www.aupaircare.com)
> - **eurAuPair** (Eastern office, 800-901-2002; Southern, 800-618-2002; Midwestern, 800-960-9100; Western, 800-713-2002; www.euraupair.com)
> - **EF AuPair** (Cultural Care Au Pair, One Education St., Cambridge, MA 02141; 800-333-6056; www.efaupair.org)
> - **InterExchange** (Au Pair Program, 161 Sixth Ave., New York, NY 10013; 212-924-0446; www.interexchange.org)

the following requirements of the U.S. Immigration and Naturalization Service (INS):

- **You must show** that you tried to find an American worker but that no one was available or right for the job. The Department of Labor requires that you advertise the job in your local paper and interview all applicants before hiring the alien worker.
- **You must state** that you will pay that worker the going rate in your neighborhood for comparable work.

For more information, see page 138 of Chapter 6, "Your Home and the Law," and its discussion of your legal role as an employer of household help. You can contact your local INS office to request copies of necessary forms (www.ins.gov).

Establishing Guardians for Your Kids

When your children are born, you should either write or redo your will (see the discussion of wills in Chapter 12, "Your Estate," and other aspects of guardianship in Chapter 8, "Your Medical Rights") and name a guardian who will take over all your legal responsibilities for supporting and educating the kids should you and your spouse die or become unable to care for them.

If you want to combine the financial expertise of one person and the loving nature of another, you can appoint them as separate guardians for each area of concern—one as guardian of the person and the other as guardian of the property.

You might want to leave a letter or a video stating how you would like your children reared and how you would like their finances handled. Such instructions are not legally binding, but they may be helpful to the guardian.

It's also a good idea to name an alternative guardian, in case something happens to your first choice. If you don't name a guardian, it will be up to a family court to appoint one who can act in your children's best interest; blood relatives will probably be given first preference.

Your Estate

I n life, you work hard to provide for yourself and your loved ones, and to make sure that Uncle Sam takes out the least amount legally possible in taxes. Why would you do any less in death?

Although the Tax Relief Reconciliation Act, passed by Congress in 2001, includes major changes that provide some relief from the federal estate tax, vigilance and planning are still necessary. The amount you and your spouse may jointly own without paying estate tax rises from $1 million in 2003 to $3.5 million in 2009. The estate tax will disappear altogether in 2010, but it is due to reappear in 2011 unless a future Congress votes otherwise. (See the box on page 277.)

With the right legal tools, you can leave whatever legacy you want in almost any way you want. But if you die unexpectedly without a will or with one that's outdated, you can create major legal hassles for your loved ones. That's why it's never too soon to get started on—or update—an estate plan.

In this chapter we will discuss the basics of estate planning, such as how you can create a will that will stand up to scrutiny and how to choose an executor to carry it out. You'll learn how you can provide for the care of your children and their inheritance if both you and your spouse die at the same time. We'll explain how you can create and use legal entities called trusts, and how to legally arrange your affairs so that your estate and your heirs needn't pay any more tax than necessary.

It's not pleasant to think about, but you need to—the sooner the better. When the grim reaper comes knocking, it's too late to call a lawyer.

Marriage, Joint Ownership and Estate Planning

When you marry, you and your spouse can usually choose how you want to own the property you each bring to the marriage and that which you acquire during it (except in community-property states, discussed on page 260, which impose some limits on your choices). Think carefully: The choices you make now can have repercussions further down the road, especially in the area of estate planning.

The traditional choice for most assets is joint ownership, a symbol of economic and personal togetherness. It takes two forms:

- **joint tenancy with the right of survivorship,** an arrangement that any two or more people can make (you needn't be married) and that any owner (tenant) can decide to discontinue at any time; and
- **tenancy by the entirety,** an arrangement available only to married couples, which can be ended only if both parties agree to it while they're living.

Although they differ in some respects, and about half the states don't recognize the entirety variety, both forms of ownership offer these advantages:

- **a survivorship feature** so that if one of you dies, the other automatically becomes sole owner of the property. This can ensure security for the surviving spouse;
- **the bypass of probate** (the court-directed process of validating a will, discussed below), thereby avoiding delays and trimming the costs that go along with that final accounting; and
- **in some states,** decreased inheritance taxes and protection of such property from seizure by the deceased's creditors.

The Downside of Joint Ownership

Of course, there are a few possible problems with this form of ownership:

CONTROL OF JOINTLY HELD PROPERTY IS SOMETIMES MUDDLED. Depending on the kind of property, one spouse may be able to dispose of it without the other's knowledge, as is generally the case with the entire balance of a joint checking or savings account. Or the spouses may be unable to sell the property— say a home or stocks and bonds—without each other's consent.

EVEN THOUGH IT IS BETTER THAN NOTHING, JOINT OWNERSHIP IS A POOR SUBSTITUTE FOR A WILL. For starters, if the surviving spouse eventually dies without a will (intestate) as well, the state will decide who gets what.

Joint property can dilute your will's potential power to distribute your assets as you wish. For example, if you take title of a property as joint owners, you can't will your share of the property to one or more heirs, and you can't transfer the asset to a trust for expert management. If you're not clear on this when you and your co-owner take title to the property, you might later have to make a potentially expensive fix to avoid unintentionally disinheriting someone.

Say that you and your spouse in a second marriage buy a beach house together and take title as joint owners. If you die first, your spouse will automatically become sole owner of the property. If that's what you want, fine. But if you want your son from your first marriage to someday inherit part ownership of the property, you're out of luck.

Your alternative is to buy the property with your spouse as tenants in common, an arrangement in which you each have ownership, but do not automatically inherit the other's portion of the property. This allows two or more people to co-own property without being joint owners. With tenants in common, you can will your share to your son. If the deed is already filed, you could ask your spouse if he or she would agree to retitling the property as tenants in common. Of course, this could be an expensive proposition, because you'd incur all the associated fees and transfer

Even though it is better than nothing, joint ownership is a poor substitute for a will.

Owning too much property jointly could foul efforts to hold down the tax on the estate of your surviving spouse.

taxes that would go along with changing the title.

If you're married, don't assume that jointly owned property will escape estate taxes the way it avoids probate. That's only half right. When the first spouse dies, half the value of jointly owned property will be subject to tax. The unlimited marital deduction will protect that amount from the estate tax, but only during the surviving spouse's lifetime (see the discussion of federal estate taxes beginning on page 276).

Who Should Own What?

This is a strategic decision that you should make with an eye to the future and, especially if your estate is large or complex, with the help of a lawyer who is an expert in federal estate and local property laws.

Owning too much property jointly could foul up efforts to hold down the tax on the estate of your surviving spouse. That's because jointly owned assets go automatically to the survivor; only property you own individually can go into a bypass trust designed to hold the assets out of the line of fire (described beginning on page 279).

The size of estates covered by the federal unified credit—meaning not taxed by the federal government—has been increasing incrementally since 1998; with recent changes, it reached $1 million in 2002 and will continue to rise until it reaches $3.5 million in 2009. In 2003 the tax rate begins at 41% for estates of more than $1 million and rises to 49% on taxable transfers of more than $3 million. Estate planners generally like to see at least enough separately owned property to take full advantage of the federal unified tax credit. For 2003, the federal unified tax credit is $345,800 on an applicable exclusion amount of $1 million (see the discussion of federal estate taxes beginning on page 276).

You and your spouse may want to come up with a mix of jointly and individually owned properties, depending on what's involved. For example:

YOUR HOUSE. The security of inheriting the house immediately through survivorship may be especially appealing to your spouse or other co-owner. Talk with your lawyer about other options, though, especially if your estate is large.

SAVINGS AND CHECKING ACCOUNTS. Joint accounts are convenient, but with some types of accounts in some states part or all of the balance may be frozen at the death of either owner. Because that could strap the surviving owner for cash at a difficult time, you may want to have individual accounts, too. Ask your banker about local rules and whether you can designate a so-called pay-on-death beneficiary.

LIFE INSURANCE. If you own a policy on your own life, the proceeds will be included in your estate and counted for estate-tax purposes regardless of who your beneficiary is. You own your insurance policy if you enjoy the *incident of ownership* (an aspect of legal title to property for federal estate-tax purposes), meaning you have the right to change the stated beneficiary and to borrow from the policy. If your spouse is your beneficiary, the proceeds would be shielded by the unlimited marital deduction (described on page 278).

One way to keep the proceeds of your life insurance policy out of your estate is to have someone else actually own a policy on your life. Be aware, though, that such an arrangement also means that the insured in each case gives up the right to change the beneficiary and borrow against the cash value.

For large estates, creating a life insurance trust to own the policies may be beneficial. Check with your lawyer or insurance agent for details (see page 287 for more on life insurance trusts).

STOCKS AND BONDS. Joint ownership could restrict flexibility in managing investments because both signatures are needed to buy or sell.

YOUR CAR. There's not much advantage to jointly owning a car, and traditionally experts have advised against it because of the possibility of both owners

> One way to keep the proceeds of your life insurance policy out of your estate is to have someone else actually own a policy on your life.

Community property doesn't carry the right of survivorship.

being vulnerable to a suit for damages. Although this is a possibility, it's unlikely in most cases because those kinds of serious accidents are largely settled out of court and subject to the limits of the driver's liability coverage. To protect yourself, be sure you have adequate car insurance (see Chapter 4, "Your Car").

SAFE-DEPOSIT BOX. Check local law. A jointly owned box may be sealed upon the death of either owner until authorities take inventory (see also page 269).

Ownership in Community-Property States

Community-property states add their own twist to the ownership issue. They are: Arizona, California, Idaho, Louisiana, Nevada, New Mexico, Texas, Washington and Wisconsin.

In community-property states, salaries and assets acquired during marriage—except for individual inheritances and gifts given to only one spouse—are generally considered community property. That means they're owned fifty-fifty by both spouses.

Community property doesn't carry the right of survivorship, so when one spouse dies, the other doesn't automatically assume full ownership of the deceased's possessions. The deceased partner's share of the property must be disposed of by his or her will or the state's rules for those who die without a will. Only the deceased partner's share is included in the estate for federal tax purposes, but because of the marital deduction, that's only an issue upon the death of the second spouse, and then only if the estate is worth more than the applicable exclusion amount.

Where There's a Will, There's a Way

The keystone of any estate plan is a will, a legal document that, when properly written and carried out, will ensure that your assets are divided according to your wishes after you die.

At a minimum, you can write a will to leave specific gifts (bequests), dispose of everything else you own (residuary estate) and name an executor to carry out your will's instructions. That may be all you need if you're single or married without children, or if you have adult children and no grandchildren.

If you have children or other dependent loved ones whose security you wish to ensure, you're divorced or remarried, or your estate is large, then your needs are more complex and you'll probably require more sophisticated estate-planning help and use of the legal tools and strategies described later on in this chapter.

By writing a will, you can prevent legal and financial hassles for your survivors and nip family bickering in the bud. You can honor the important people in your life with a substantial gift or a sentimental token. You can help ensure the continued good work of a church, school or other organization or program after your death.

If you already have a will, your circumstances may have changed dramatically since you first wrote it. Now may be the time to revisit it (see the box on pages 274-275).

Be aware that if you are married and wrote your will before September 12, 1981, you should know that the tax laws have changed since then and now are more favorable to surviving spouses because of the unlimited marital deduction (see page 278).

What Will Pass Along Without a Will
Regardless of whether you have a will, the law provides you with some default estate planning:

- **If you have named a beneficiary** on your IRA, pension plan or life insurance, the proceeds will pass automatically to the beneficiary.
- **Anything you own together via joint ownership with right of survivorship**—for example, a house or bank accounts—will automatically pass to your surviving co-owner. This also has the advantage of permitting the property to bypass probate, the court-directed

By writing a will, you can prevent legal and financial hassles for your survivors and nip family bickering in the bud.

If you die without a will—known as dying intestate— you can leave those you love in a real mess.

process of validating a will (discussed on page 273). In some states, it may decrease the inheritance tax on your estate and exempt the jointly owned property from seizure by creditors. (For a full discussion of the impact of joint ownership on estate planning, including disadvantages, see the discussion beginning on page 256.)

But depending on either of these exceptions doesn't substitute for a will because you give up control you otherwise would have over the total outcome.

What You Give Up Without a Will

If you die without a will—known as dying *intestate*— you can leave those you love in a real mess:

■ **No one you would have chosen will have the authority** to parcel out your non-jointly owned possessions. Instead, the state where you live will step in and divide up your assets on your behalf according to a predetermined and impersonal formula (more on this below).

■ **If you fail to set a precedent by writing a will** during your lifetime and your surviving spouse also dies without a will, the state will again step in and divvy up the remaining property as it sees fit.

■ **In either case, the probate court** will name an administrator to distribute your assets. The job may fall to a family member, who might have to post a bond, or to a court administrator, who would have to be paid out of your estate. Bonds insure against the loss of estate funds resulting from negligence or fraud by the executor (also known as a personal representative).

■ **You miss out on the option** of providing expert management of the property via a trust.

WHAT WILL HAPPEN TO YOUR CHILDREN? If minor children are involved and both you and your spouse are deceased, or if you are divorced and have custody of the children when you die, the state will decide who their legal guardian will be. If you are divorced, the court's first choice will most likely be your ex-spouse. (However, even if you write a will and choose a guardian, the state must approve your choice and reserves the right to choose someone more appropriate.)

In choosing a guardian, the court will probably give first preference to next of kin; it may or may not choose to abide by any informal understanding you had with family members or friends. It might choose your brother Harry, whereas you would have chosen your older sister Jean, whose style of parenting you prefer. Or, Harry and Jean might both seek guardianship, filing counterclaims with the court. That could result in a messy court battle, which would take a toll on your kids, family relations and your estate.

Whoever is appointed guardian would probably have to remain under the court's supervision, a cumbersome process under which the guardian has to report how he or she is managing your children's property. You can avoid court supervision by appointing a "guardian of the property" (see page 270).

HOW THE STATE WILL DIVIDE YOUR PROPERTY. In addition, if you die intestate, your assets go to your next of kin in proportions and in sequence decided by state law. Though the law varies from state to state, a surviving spouse generally gets at least a third and often as much as half of your money (other than jointly owned property and the proceeds of IRAs, pension, and life insurance policies, which the beneficiary you've named will receive). The court then divides the remainder evenly among your legal offspring. Depending on your circumstances, this default arrangement may or may not seem fair. Here are some examples:

■ **Say your spouse will be dependent** on the proceeds from the estate for his or her livelihood and your two children are already on their own. You might have wished for your spouse to receive 80% of the

> **if you die intestate, your assets go to your next of kin in proportions and in sequence decided by state law.**

If you die intestate while living with someone out of wedlock, the state will proceed as if you're single.

funds and each child to receive a gift of 10%.

■ **Or, say your spouse will be left** with your two young children. The court could still divide the estate in thirds and supervise how your husband or wife manages your children's funds. And at the age of majority (18 or 21, depending on your state's law), your children will come into their inheritance, ready or not. Your spouse will have no legal control over how they spend the money.

■ **If you're single,** the state will divide your worldly possessions among your parents and siblings, and if worse comes to worst, among your blood relatives. If the state can't find any surviving family members, the state will inherit your estate.

■ **If you're living with someone out of wedlock,** the state will proceed as if you're single and your loved one could be left out in the cold except for any property of which he or she was a beneficiary or joint owner. Because the state considered you legally single, your parents and siblings will inherit everything else, and if they disapproved of your relationship, you won't be able to count on them to bestow a gift upon your mate.

A well-written will can prevent any of these situations and give you all the control you could want.

Making a Good Will

A properly written will has the full force of the law behind it to carry out your wishes. If you're married, it's wise for you and your spouse to individually write your wills; it may otherwise be tough for the surviving spouse to get the will changed.

At a bare minimum, for a will to be valid it usually must be signed in front of two witnesses who won't benefit from the will (this varies from state to state) and notarized by a notary public. (For a description of a will's key elements, see the box on page 266.)

A good will is also carefully tailored to the individual. For example, a remarried woman who wants to provide for her kids from a prior marriage needs a different will than a married woman who doesn't want her stepchildren to inherit any of her estate.

To make sure that your will holds up after you are gone, it must be clear that:

■ **Your will conforms with federal and state requirements.**

■ **You didn't fall victim to fraud or undue influence** while making your will. For example, a "niece" you never knew existed suddenly turns up and convinces you to leave her all your money, and after you die, your own children discover that the niece was a con artist.

■ **You were mentally competent** to understand what you were doing when you made the will.

If your will is invalidated, the court would settle your estate as if you had died intestate.

Though legal challenges to a will are rare—and rarely successful—one way to avoid them is to trans-

---

WHAT DOESN'T COUNT AS A WILL

An oral will, made on your deathbed, isn't legal in a number of states, and where it is legal, it is valid only in narrow circumstances. For example, California allows an oral will only if you're in the military and are under peril of death or if you're about to die the same day you were injured. Even then, the will is valid only if two people witness you making it, and only personal property is allowed to be transferred.

A handwritten (holographic) will, written by you in your own hand (not with computer software), is legal in about half the states, subject to their rules, but it can open up a can of worms for your family in determining its validity.

Videos have no validity as wills. They won't stand up as legal documents and may invite scrutiny by persons who want to contest them—say, to determine whether you were in a reasonable state of mind.

If your will is invalidated, the court would settle your estate as if you had died intestate.

fer your assets to your heirs via a living trust (see page 283) prior to your death or any question of incompetence.

DO-IT-YOURSELF? You can make a will yourself. Books and computer software to help you do it are readily available. But most experts advise against trying to write one alone, especially if you need more than a simple will.

If you draft a will, you risk writing one that doesn't meet the letter of the law, uses imprecise language that could be misunderstood or easily challenged, or overlooks legal options advantageous to you and your family.

If you use will-writing software, you are limited to the options the software provides, which may not be what you need. For example, there are many ways to arrange a trust to hold assets until your children come of age, and an attorney could fine-tune one just

---

THE BARE BONES OF A WILL

Any will should contain the following elements:

■ **Exordium clause.** This invalidates any previous wills and lists the name, address and legal residence (domicile) of the person writing the will (the testator).

■ **Debt and taxes clause.** This provides instructions for payment of the estate's debts and taxes.

■ **Disposition of property clause.** Describes how real estate and personal property, such as furniture and jewelry, should be disposed of.

■ **Powers clause.** Details the powers the executor (also known as a personal representative) will have.

■ **Common disaster clause.** Specifies which spouse would be presumed to have survived the other if both die simultaneously; the estate will be distributed according to the "surviving" spouse's will.

■ **Testimonium and attestation clause.** Establishes that the person writing the will recognizes this as his or her will.

for you. But with most will-writing software, you're stuck with whatever kind of trust is written into the software.

With these cautions in mind, if you're still intent on doing it yourself, *Quicken Lawyer 2003 Personal* by Nolo (for Windows, $79.99; less when ordered from www.Nolo.com) is one that gets good reviews even from legal experts who otherwise oppose do-it-yourself law.

GETTING HELP. The better strategy, experts say, is to hire an attorney. For a simple estate—one that includes no business, no extensive real estate holdings, and few other assets except those that are jointly owned or those, like IRAs or life insurance policies, with stated beneficiaries—a competent generalist is probably sufficient. For a larger or more complex estate, find an attorney who specializes in estate planning.

Your local bar association, a reputable financial planner or insurance agent, a bank trust officer, or the Estate Planning Council in the city where you live (check with the trust department of your local bank or your local phone book) can provide names and suggestions. You can expect to pay as little as $200 for a simple will or $200 an hour or more for more sophisticated estate planning.

Decisions You Must Make

You have some homework to do before you go to see your lawyer. Start by sizing up your estate. Draw up a list of what you own, what you're owed, and so on. Use the worksheet on page 268 to begin the process. Then, choose people to help you carry out your wishes.

CHOOSE YOUR EXECUTOR. Also known as a personal representative, your executor will take stock of your estate, see that any debts or other obligations are paid from the proceeds of your estate, and distribute the remainder according to your instructions.

Choose someone you trust—your spouse, a relative, a friend or your lawyer—who will respect your choices, be sensitive to the concerns of your family

> **Before you go to see your lawyer, size up your estate. Draw up a list of what you own, what you're owed, and so on.**

HOW LARGE IS YOUR ESTATE?

Although you don't have to pay federal estate tax until your taxable estate exceeds $1 million (or up to $3.5 million, depending on the year; see the box on page 277), you might be surprised by all the things the government counts in getting there.

The "ownership" column is included because how you own property is pivotal to how much of its value will be included in your estate when you die. In the "value" column, include the following:

■ **the full value of property** of which you are the sole owner;

■ **half the value of property** you own jointly with your spouse with right of survivorship;

■ **your share of property owned with others;**

■ **half the value of community-property** if you live in a community property state.

Also include the value of the proceeds of an insurance policy on your life if you own the policy, your vested interest in pension and profit-sharing plans, and the value of property in revocable trusts.

Assets	Value	Ownership
Cash in checking, savings, money-market accounts		
Stocks		
Bonds		
Mutual funds		
Other investments		
Real estate		
Personal property, including furniture, cars, clothing, etc.		
Art, antiques, collectibles		
Proceeds of life insurance policies you own on your life		
Pension and profit-sharing benefits, IRAs, etc.		
Business interests: sole proprietorship, partnerships, closely held corporations		
Money owed to you, such as mortgages, rents, fees		
Other		
Total Assets		
Liabilities		
Mortgages		
Loans and notes		
Taxes		
Consumer debt		
Other		
Total Liabilities		
Net Estate (total assets minus total liabilities)		

members and play fair with everyone involved. He or she may also have to exercise good judgment when necessary because chances are you won't have thought of everything.

Watch out for any conflicts of interest, too. Say that you chose your business partner as your executor. When it came time to sell your share of the business, he would be obliged, on behalf of the estate, to ask the best (highest) price even though he would also probably want to purchase it himself for the lowest price.

For a nonprofessional, administering an estate can be time-consuming and draining, especially in a time of grief. Make sure the person you choose will be up to the task. Ask your candidate if he or she wants the job; if you don't ask and the person ultimately turns down the job, the court may have to appoint someone (see the discussion of dying without a will, beginning on page 262). It's also smart to choose a backup executor or two.

Your executor and attorney for the estate are entitled to be paid, according to state and local laws. Friends and family members generally won't take the money, receiving their inheritance instead. State laws either put a ceiling on the percentage of the estate that an estate executive and lawyer can charge or merely say that the amount should be "reasonable."

Prepare your executor. Once your executor has accepted, take time to discuss your wishes; that will help him or her explain the thinking behind your choices to your family members, if appropriate.

It's also a good idea to write a letter of instruction for your survivors, making sure to give a copy to your executor and one to your lawyer, keeping an original for yourself. You can keep yours in a safety-deposit box if you live in a state where the box won't be automatically sealed upon your death. Although this document isn't considered legally binding, you can use it to describe where your important documents are kept, provide burial instructions, make specific bequests of personal belongings that would otherwise clutter up your will, and make any other personal wishes.

Once your executor has accepted, take time to discuss your wishes; that will help him or her explain the thinking behind your choices.

Instructions you leave for your children's guardians aren't legally binding, but they will be very helpful in making your wishes clear.

CHOOSE YOUR CHILDREN'S GUARDIAN. A guardian has two major tasks: to care for your minor children and to manage the money and other property you leave to them, using it for their support and distributing it to them as you wish.

One guardian will suffice if he or she combines the nurturing and common-sense money-management skills you want. Or, you could choose a separate *guardian of the person* and a *guardian of the property*.

As with an executor, talk with your first choice of guardian and make sure that he or she is willing and able to take on the responsibility. For example, loving grandparents might be the perfect candidates except for their age, health and stage in life; they may simply not be up to the task for as long as it is necessary.

If your kids are old enough, ask them how they would like to go live with Uncle Joe or Aunt Alice.

As with an executor, pick a backup choice or two.

Feel free to leave instructions for your guardians—a letter or videotape—describing how you would like your children raised. Though such instructions aren't legally binding, they will be very helpful in making your wishes clear to the guardian.

In cases of divorce, it's likely that the court would name your ex-spouse as guardian of the children. So if you prefer that your ex-spouse not be appointed guardian or you know that he or she isn't interested, name your choice in your will. Or, you may think it's fine for the kids to live with your ex-spouse but would prefer a separate guardian of the property. In a letter or sworn statement (affidavit) that should accompany your will and be given to your choice of guardians in advance, outline your preferences and explain convincingly why your ex-spouse is unfit. You can specify that funds from your estate can be used to challenge the court's decision if it doesn't follow your wishes.

NAME YOUR BENEFICIARIES. Decide who you want to receive what, whether family, friends or charity. If you're single, you can bestow gifts upon friends and family. If a spouse and children are dependent upon you, you can provide for their future. You'll probably want to leave everything to your surviving spouse—or to your children if both of you die.

If you want to get really specific, giving away every last knickknack, leave a separate letter with instructions for your executor; writing such detailed instructions into your will could unnecessarily complicate matters and cause delay and extra expense.

Do your family one big favor: Think in advance about the possible consequences of your decisions and explore all the possibilities. For example:

- **Be realistic.** If you will your family members property that they must share, you could be setting them up for conflict. It isn't likely that five sons can realistically share in possession of Dad's antique pool table.

- **Play fair.** Provide for a younger child the advantages that you've already provided to your older one—say, a college education, a wedding or a down payment on a house.

- **Discuss your ideas and decisions** with family members, but don't make promises that you might not keep. You could solicit their ideas for divvying up your household possessions. For example, some families have held informal "penny" auctions conducted by the executor of the estate to ensure that everyone gets something to remember Grandpa or Grandma by. Or ask your family members to tell you which of your belongings would be especially meaningful to them. You might be surprised to learn that your old fedora or a pair of sewing shears would mean more than the piano or Steuben vase.

- **Be kind.** Wills aren't read aloud. Don't use a will to take a parting shot at someone you disliked in life.

- **Keep things simple.** When you want to make a change, rewrite your will instead of tacking on additions or other changes (codicils) to your original in-

Do your family one big favor: Think in advance about the possible consequences of your decisions and explore all the possibilities.

WHERE TO KEEP A WILL?

Ideally, you would leave the original copy of your will in the safekeeping of your attorney and keep one duplicate in your own safe-deposit box and another at home or work.

If you don't have a lawyer with whom you consult regularly or if you don't want your executor to be compelled to visit the lawyer and thereby feel obligated to work with him or her, keep the original in your safe-deposit box or in a fireproof, insulated safe at home.

Before you decide to store your original or only copy of your will in your safe-deposit box, call the bank and ask about the procedure for opening the box upon your death, or check your state's law: In some states, the box may be sealed upon your death. That could cause a temporary delay in carrying out your wishes. But typically, as long as there's an officer of the bank available to witness the opening of the box, your executor should be able to gain access.

Give a copy to your executor or the principal beneficiary, as well as any last instructions that you want them to have, providing them with a head start on any responsibilities.

---

structions. They can gum up the situation and are probably better left unwritten.

■ **Explain yourself in a letter or videotape** that you leave for the executor.

Changing a Will

Don't just sign your will and forget about it. As your circumstances change—say, you move to a new state, get divorced or have a baby—review and change your will to take your new situation into account.

You can change the terms of your will any time you want by executing a new one. If you have only one or two minor changes to make, you could add a *codicil* (or *amendment*) to an existing will. The codicil must be witnessed and notarized, too. Don't just pencil in something yourself; you could invalidate the entire will. And too many such changes could compromise the integrity of your will; better to write a new one altogether.

For more on why you should change your will, see the box on pages 274-275.

WHAT DOES IT MEAN TO DISINHERIT SOMEONE? With the exception of your spouse, you can exercise your own discretion in choosing whom to include or exclude from among your beneficiaries.

How much flexibility you have to disinherit a spouse depends on your state's laws. In most states, you can't disinherit a surviving spouse, even if you are separated (whether merely living apart or legally separated), without his or her permission. Usually, however, the law allows you to disinherit a child for any reason. You could leave the person a nominal amount—say, a dollar—or you could explicitly exclude him or her from your will.

What's Probate?

Probate is the procedure by which state courts validate a will's authenticity, thereby clearing the way for the executor to collect and pay debts, pay taxes, sell property, distribute funds, and carry out other necessary tasks involved with settling an estate. The process can be slow and expensive, and probate fees can absorb as much as 10% of assets.

SIMPLIFIED PROBATE. For a small and simple estate—one owning no business, no extensive real estate holdings, and few other assets except those that are jointly owned or those, like IRAs or life insurance policies, with stated beneficiaries—probate can be a quick and relatively inexpensive process (see page 284 for more on costs associated with probate).

For those cases, most states offer a streamlined probate with informal procedures requiring little court supervision. Sometimes all that's necessary is for your executor to file an affidavit—a sworn statement in writing that confirms relevant information about

Continued on page 276

With the exception of your spouse, you can exercise your own discretion in choosing whom to include or exclude from among your beneficiaries.

GOOD REASONS TO CHANGE YOUR WILL

Life's events can upset the most well-stacked apple cart. There are good reasons to review your needs, strategies and documents accordingly.

You get married

If you want to provide for your new spouse in any way other than what your state would call for if you died intestate, you need to change your will (see discussion of intestacy on page 262 and of community property on page 260).

You move in with someone

If you want your significant other to inherit any of your property, update your will accordingly.

You become a parent

The big issue here is how your children will be cared for if you and your spouse die. You'll need to:

- **name a guardian** (see page 270),
- **consider setting up trusts and naming trustees** to handle assets that your children will inherit (see page 281), and
- **give someone a durable power of attorney**—that is, appoint someone to act for you in financial matters if you can't (see page 190).

You get divorced

You need to review everything. For starters, you'll need a new will. In most states, a divorce automatically revokes those provisions that apply to your former spouse; in some states,

the whole will may be defunct.

- **Do you want to set up trusts** to control the assets you leave to your children (see page 281)?
- **Do you want to revise any existing trusts** to remove your ex-spouse as a beneficiary or trustee? Also review your power of attorney or living will. Unless your divorce decree prevents you from doing so, do you want to change the beneficiaries on your life insurance (see page 54), pension and IRAs?

You remarry

At the least, you have a new spouse to consider. But if you're combining families, you have children from your and your new spouse's previous marriages to consider, as well as children you might have together.

- **A prenuptial agreement** (see page 207), if you want one, typically keeps your assets separate and nullifies your inheritance rights to each other's estates. You can write one before or after you remarry, provided both of you agree to it.
- **If you wish to provide for your new spouse and your children from a previous marriage** if you die, consult an estate-planning lawyer about setting up a qualified terminable-interest property trust, or QTIP (see page 283).

You approach middle age

Your assets have grown, so tax planning

could save your heirs a bundle in federal estate taxes.

- **If your estate is large enough to warrant limiting jointly owned property for tax purposes,** consider a revocable living trust. It can incorporate tax-saving measures, and its assets bypass probate (see pages 258, 276, and 283).
- **Update your will** to reflect changes in your family: adoptions, births, deaths, divorces (see page 272).
- **Review your choices of guardians** for your children, trustees of any trusts, and personal representatives.
- **Reevaluate how much and what you want to give to whom,** including any charitable or other groups.
- **Recalculate how much life insurance you need** to provide for your dependents and whether an irrevocable life insurance trust would be useful to shelter the proceeds from estate taxes (see page 287).

You retire and/or move to a new state

For starters, your new state's laws may be different from those where you originally wrote your will. In addition, your needs may have changed. For instance:

- **Do your children's inheritances still need to be held in trust** (see page 281)?
- **Would this be a good time to arrange for a durable power of attorney,** in case you become incapacitated and can no longer give the required consent in your financial affairs (see page 190).
- **Do you want to drop your life insurance?** If your estate faces an estate-tax liability or if your spouse is dependent on retirement income that ends with your death, consider keeping the coverage..

Your spouse dies

Don't make any drastic changes—like selling your house—during the first several months, when you may be most emotionally vulnerable.

- **If you have sufficient assets of your own,** including some that you can easily liquidate as you need the cash, you should seek expert advice on any tax benefits you could reap from giving up (disclaiming) some of your inheritance in favor of alternate beneficiaries, such as your children. Once you accept and use the assets, it may be too late to disclaim.
- **Get a new will and, if needed, a revocable living trust** (see pages 272 and 283).
- **Execute a new durable power of attorney** for your financial affairs. You may also want to write a living will to make your wishes known in case of an illness that leaves you permanently incapacitated. Discuss these documents with those who need to know, and let them know where the documents are (see pages 190-191 and 195).

ASSETS THAT AVOID PROBATE

As discussed previously, funds from an IRA, pension or life insurance policy will pass directly to your beneficiary without getting held up in probate, as will any property that you owned jointly with right of survivorship, the form of ownership usually chosen by spouses. For more about the impact of types of ownership on estate planning, see the discussion beginning on page 256.

the estate—with the court and have relevant records, such as title to property, changed.

FOR LARGER ESTATES. In most states, formal probate is reserved for large and more complex estates. In those cases, the court will supervise all the major steps of probate. This is the kind of probate that has given the process such a bad name, and it's worth avoiding because it can take lots of time—even years—and lots of money for court costs and fees for attorneys and executors. Depending on the state, the fee for probate may be figured on a sliding scale or it may simply be a "reasonable" fee. But in the worst case, a full-blown probate can consume up to 10% of the value of the estate. Strategies for avoiding probate—particularly through living trusts—are discussed beginning on page 280.

Estate Planning: Give Uncle Sam Just His Due

When you die, Uncle Sam and your state will want their share of your life's work. Federal estate-tax rates run as high as 49% (in 2003). While the focus of this book isn't tax planning, there are tax-related issues to consider when writing your will and deciding how to dispose of your estate. And remember the earlier caution: Although Congress voted to reduce and eventually eliminate the estate tax (or as some like to call it, the death tax), it

---

HOW MUCH YOU CAN LEAVE TAX-FREE

The table below shows how the amount you can leave estate-tax free to heirs will increase over the next several years. (Note: In addition to these tax-free amounts, you can continue to leave any amount to your spouse estate-tax free.) If Congress fails to extend the elimination of the estate tax or to totally eliminate it, the estate tax will be resurrected in 2011, with a $1-million tax-free transfer limit and a top tax rate of 55%.

Year	Tax-Free Amount
2003	$1,000,000
2004	$1,500,000
2005	$1,500,000
2006	$2,000,000
2007	$2,000,000
2008	$2,000,000
2009	$3,500,000
2010	tax repealed
2011	$1,000,000

could be reinstated in 2011.

The bottom line is that most folks will naturally want to use the law to preserve as much of their estates as possible for their heirs. This section will highlight portions of the tax law related to your estate planning strategy and discuss some of the legal tools you can use to hold down your final tax bill.

The larger your estate and the more complex your planning needs, the more you'll want to seek the advice of an expert estate planner.

Federal Tax Basics

■ **Your taxable estate has to exceed** the applicable exclusion amount before any federal estate tax will kick in. That sounds like a lot, and for plenty of people it is. But don't assume anything about the size of your estate until you've filled out the worksheet on page 268. For tax purposes, your estate includes the value of your home, savings and investments, retirement plans, and life insurance policies of which you are the owner (that is, you're named as the owner, pay the premiums and have the right to change the beneficiary and to borrow against the cash value of the policy). And, of course, these amounts are likely to grow as you grow older.

■ **Married couples needn't pay a dime** of federal tax on the entire estate, however much it is, when the first spouse dies. This *marital deduction* will postpone the tax again if the surviving spouse remarries, but only until the surviving spouse of that marriage dies.

■ **Nearly everyone, even those who aren't married,** can take advantage of the unified estate and gift tax credit (or unified credit)—enough to protect an estate that is no larger than the applicable exclusion amount, after which the tax kicks in. Married couples can take advantage of the credit twice—upon each spouse's death—if they properly construct their estate (see how beginning on page 279).

■ **You can reduce the size** of your taxable estate by giving gifts of up to $11,000 a year to any number of individuals, or $22,000 a year if given by a married

YOUR STATE'S SHARE

Most states levy a death tax that will affect much smaller estates than the federal tax does. Typically it takes the form of an inheritance tax, which each of your heirs must pay from their share of the estate. (An estate tax would be taken from the estate before it is divided up.)

Most states also impose a pick-up tax—that is, they claim for themselves the amount of the credit your survivors can claim for state death taxes on the federal estate-tax return. It applies only if your estate owes a federal tax. Because the pick-up tax will be affected by changes in the federal estate tax and reduce state revenues, some states are passing legislation to enable them to tax estates in other ways.

couple, without incurring the gift tax (the recipient doesn't pay it). If Congress legislates a cost-of-living adjustment in future years, the annual exclusion may increase. So, for example, you and your spouse could give each of your three adult children and their spouses $22,000 a year tax-free. That would eliminate $132,000 from your taxable estate in one year. Things get more complicated if you exceed the $11,000 limit. For one thing, you'll be required to file a gift-tax return. If you owe any gift tax, you won't actually be required to pay it when you file the return. Instead, the gift tax you incur will typically reduce the amount of the estate-and-gift-tax credit available when you die.

For Larger Estates

Relying too much on the marital deduction upon the death of the first spouse may leave an estate valued at more than the applicable exclusion amount vulnerable to unnecessary taxes. Consider this example of the potential problem and a solution:

Say you had a taxable estate worth $1.3 million in the year 2003 and your spouse owned property worth $200,000. You died and left your $1.3 million to your surviving spouse. The marital deduction fully protected the $1.3 million from taxes. Then your spouse died; the estate, if left intact, was worth $1.5 million, of which only $1 million was protected by the unified credit. That means the rest was subject to taxes in the amount of $210,000. (Estates valued at between $1 million and $1.25 million are subject to a tax of $345,800 plus 41% of the amount between $1 million and $1.25 million and 43% of the amount between $1.25 million and $1.5 million. In this case, that works out to $555,800, minus the unified credit of $345,800, or $210,000.) A little planning could have prevented that.

USE A BYPASS TRUST TO MAKE THE MOST OF YOUR UNIFIED CREDIT. One of the most common estate plans for a couple with an estate that contains assets that are more than the applicable exclusion amount is to make sure that the first spouse to die takes advantage of not

You can reduce the size of your taxable estate by giving gifts of up to $11,000 or $22,000 a year to any number of individuals, without incurring the gift tax.

Be sure to seek the help of an experienced estate attorney who is familiar with the laws of your state.

only the marital deduction but also the unified credit. In the example above, by relying fully on the marital deduction, the first spouse basically threw away his $345,800 credit.

To avoid forfeiting the credit, you can use a *bypass* (or *exemption equivalent*) *trust*. In the example, instead of willing the full $1.3 million to your spouse, you could have split your estate, putting the annual exclusion amount ($1 million for 2003) in the trust and leaving the $500,000 outright to your spouse. (You can split your estate however you like, but the goal here is to make maximum use of the unified credit.) The outcome?

The $1 million put in the trust wouldn't qualify for the marital deduction, but it would be protected from tax by the unified credit when you die. Remember that the credit for 2003 amounted to $345,800, enough to protect a taxable estate of $1 million.

The $500,000 left outright to your spouse would be shielded by the marital deduction, which protects an unlimited amount of assets when the first spouse dies.

A key feature of the bypass trust is that income from the trust (produced as your trustee invests and manages the funds within the trust) will go to your survivor, just as if he or she had inherited the assets outright. But at his or her death, the principal would be distributed to other heirs, such as your children, without being included in your spouse's estate.

So, in the example, the estate of your surviving spouse would include the $500,000 left under the marital deduction, plus his or her original $200,000 of personal assets (described at the beginning of the example). The unified credit would shield the full amount from the estate tax. Bottom line: Your family comes out $210,000 ahead. (More on the pros and cons of trusts in the following discussion.)

With these opportunities in mind, be sure to seek the help of an experienced estate attorney who is familiar with the laws of your state. He or she can help you take advantage of every opportunity to reduce estate taxes upon your death, if you're single, or the death of the second spouse if you're married.

What Trusts Can and Can't Do for You

When you create a trust, you entrust your funds or possessions to the safekeeping of a legal entity, the trust, which is watched over by a legal caretaker, the trustee.

You can use the trust to provide in the future for any beneficiaries you choose—possibly yourself, your spouse, or your children.

You create this legal entity in a separate agreement from your will, and you choose a trustee—a person or institution, frequently a bank trust department—to administer the trust, according to your instructions if you like. For example, you can tell the trustee how you want your assets managed—say, conservatively to preserve the principal or aggressively to produce more income. You can specify when and how you want the original capital or income from the trust's investments distributed or spent for the support of your surviving spouse or children.

You can choose a bank or lawyer to act as your trustee, but because they will charge a fee (typically 1% to 2% of trust assets) that may be suitable only for larger trusts; professional trustees may charge a minimum flat fee for smaller trusts. Besides, in some cases, you may prefer to choose a family member or friend whom you trust, who knows and cares about your beneficiary, and who may do the job for free.

The Personal Side of Trusts

Trusts are frequently used to reduce taxes on an estate or for other financial reasons, or to avoid probate. Before we get to that, let's look at some examples of people who have used this legal tool for the most personal of reasons—providing for their loved ones (see also the discussion of custodial accounts on page 289).

A DEPENDENT PARENT. Amanda's father lives with her and she provides his only support. It's a certainty that if she dies before her dad, he won't be able to care for

Some people use trusts for personal reasons — to provide for their loved ones.

himself. So instead of willing her money directly to her father, Amanda sets up a testamentary trust (a testamentary document describes how you want your property disposed of after your death), naming a bank as trustee. If Amanda dies first, the bank will invest the money and use the proceeds to care for her dad. When her dad dies, any remaining funds will go to her sister, JoAnne. If Amanda outlives her dad, she can revoke the trust and return the assets to her possession.

AN INHERITANCE INSTALLMENT PLAN. Mark and Pat intend to leave quite a substantial sum to their college-age son, but they're concerned about his ability to handle that much money all at once. So they set up a trust that will pay him income from its investments annually, then half of the original capital when he turns 25 and the other half at age 30.

EASING THE BURDEN OF GUARDIANSHIP. David and Diane have two young daughters. They've asked Diane's brother, Joe, to care for the girls if they die and manage their inheritance. David and Diane are aware that if the kids inherit their money outright, the state's court will closely supervise how Joe manages the funds on their behalf until they reach the age of majority (21 in their state, but 18 in others). In their state, Joe would have to report annually how he has spent the money and ask the court's permission to spend any principal. (In some states the guardian must post a bond and, in others, invest the funds only in low-earning government-insured bank accounts.)

That's why David and Diane have chosen to set up a testamentary trust for the children with Joe as the trustee. In their will they've left Joe detailed instructions on how they want him to spend the money for their children's health, education and support; the state needn't concern itself.

PROVIDING FOR CHILDREN FROM YOUR FIRST MARRIAGE. Jeff has remarried after a divorce, but he still wants his adult children from his first marriage to share in his estate. He has chosen to set up a so-called QTIP trust, short for *qualified terminable interest property*. When Jeff dies, income from the trust and a portion of the principal will go to his second spouse for as long as she lives. Upon her death, the assets will be divided among his children according to the terms of his trust, not according to his surviving spouse's will. (Jeff could also have chosen to set up a trust as part of a prenuptial agreement with his second wife, or he could have made gifts of his assets to his children while he was alive.)

If you have no children, you can use QTIP trusts to ensure that after providing for your surviving spouse, blood relatives will inherit the assets that you specify.

QTIP trusts are similar to the bypass trusts discussed on page 279, with two major differences: QTIP trusts use the marital deduction to escape estate taxes, and assets may be taxable to the surviving spouse's estate when he or she dies.

Living Trusts and the Myths About Them

One of the most popular types of trusts is an *inter vivos*, or living trust, which operates while you are alive. There are two types of living trusts, however, and it's important to know which one is right for you. A revocable trust allows you to change its provisions, whereas an irrevocable trust can't be materially modified.

The biggest selling points of a revocable trust are that you keep control over your assets while you are alive and the assets avoid the delays and expense of probate when you die. That's because legally you don't own your property anymore, the trust does. Only those assets still in your own name at death must go through probate. Because you are the beneficiary of the trust and can also name yourself trustee, you keep control over the assets during your lifetime. But the trust is also a tool for managing your financial affairs if you become incapacitated, because a successor trustee you've already named will take over for you.

In an irrevocable living trust, you give up all ownership control of whatever property you put in the trust: Generally you can be neither the trustee nor the

> The biggest selling points of a revocable trust are that you keep control over your assets while you are alive and the assets avoid the delays and expense of probate when you die.

You still need a will to "pour over" to the trust any assets that you left out when the trust was created.

beneficiary of the trust. In return you get a big tax break on your estate's taxes after your death, but you can't receive income from the trust, nor can you change its terms or cancel it altogether if your situation changes.

Living trusts, however, aren't for everyone. Here are some of the arguments for and against them.

A LIVING TRUST IS THE BEST WAY TO PROTECT YOUR ASSETS FROM THE HASSLE OF PROBATE PROCEEDINGS. Some of your assets will skip probate even if you don't have a living trust. As discussed on page 256, any property owned jointly with right of survivorship will automatically go to your surviving co-owner. Benefits from your pension, IRA and Keogh, and your life insurance death benefits (all payable to a named beneficiary) will go directly to the beneficiary you've named. So will government bonds and bank accounts with a designated pay-on-death beneficiary. Other than these, the fewer assets you have, the less useful a living trust.

A LIVING TRUST IS LESS EXPENSIVE THAN GOING THROUGH PROBATE. A living trust could actually be more expensive. Here's how:

■ **You still need a will** to "pour over" to the trust any assets that you left out when the trust was created— ones you may have failed to transfer in the first place or acquired later. And, of course, you may want to give gifts to other loved ones and charities and appoint a guardian for your children. Lawyers may charge an extra $500 to $1,500 to draw up a living trust and pour-over will.

■ **You must officially transfer ownership** of your property from yourself to the trust. That means incurring the expense and hassle of changing titles. For example, you will have to get a new deed prepared and recorded for any real estate and possibly pay a hefty transfer tax. You'll have to fill out special forms at the bank and with your brokerage firm. And once your property is in the trust, you face potential hassles in dealing with them in your capacity as trustee.

■ **You may not save on administration fees** associated with probate. Three typical costs are:

■ **Filing and court fees.** A living trust does avoid these costs, but they're not very high to begin with. For example, the state of New York charges a maximum of $1,000 no matter how big the estate is.

■ **Executor's commission.** In most states, this is a percentage of the value of the probate estate. But most times, the executor of the estate is a family member who waives compensation anyway.

■ **Attorney's fees.** Most probates are largely paper-shuffling affairs—something your executor can probably handle with only occasional advice from a lawyer who is paid by the hour.

YOUR BENEFICIARIES WILL RECEIVE YOUR ASSETS FASTER THROUGH A LIVING TRUST THAN THROUGH PROBATE COURT. Maybe, but if your estate is simple and your will doesn't create a testamentary trust after your death, there shouldn't be much difference between proceeding through a living trust and going through probate.

If you have a complicated estate that requires federal estate-tax planning, a living trust may not save much time or money. A lawyer and accountant will probably be heavily involved, and they may have to prepare and file two death-tax returns, one for your state and one for the feds. That can take months, whether or not the plan is part of a trust.

YOU'LL SAVE ON TAXES WITH A REVOCABLE LIVING TRUST. Nope. Because you retain total control over the assets and can revoke the trust whenever you want during your lifetime, you won't enjoy any income-tax savings on the earnings of the trust. You'll be taxed on

Assets in a revocable living trust are included in your estate for federal estate-tax purposes and are generally subject to state death taxes, too.

all the income, on your personal tax return if you're the trustee.

You won't automatically save on federal estate tax, either. Assets in the trust are included in your estate for federal estate-tax purposes and are generally subject to state death taxes, too. However, a living trust can be written to include the same tax-saving provisions that can be placed in a will (see "Federal Tax Basics," beginning on page 277).

NAMING YOUR SUCCESSOR TRUSTEE IN A REVOCABLE LIVING TRUST IS THE BEST WAY to designate someone to take over the management of your assets if you become unable to do so. Revocable living trusts can be a valuable tool for folks who are, say, 55 or older and want to arrange for someone to handle their financial affairs if they can no longer do so. This arrangement keeps your family or friends from having to go to court to have a guardian appointed for you, a wrenching prospect for all of you.

But it's not the only way. You can accomplish the same thing more simply and less expensively with a durable power of attorney, through which you give someone the legal power to act on your behalf. Your state may also allow you to give "springing" durable powers of attorney, which don't take effect unless you become mentally incapacitated. Power of attorney requires no transfer of assets. (For more on durable power of attorney, see page 190.)

LIVING TRUSTS ARE MORE PRIVATE AND SAFER FROM CHALLENGE THAN WILLS. Both claims are generally true, but seldom of much importance. Wills do become public documents once they're filed with the probate court; a living trust remains private as long as it is written separately from a will. But, in all likelihood, folks who know you aren't likely to head to the courthouse to check out your arrangements. Besides, very few wills are contested. If a challenge does occur, the same rules apply to wills and trusts. In neither case are your wishes likely to be overturned.

An Irrevocable Life Insurance Trust

Proceeds of a life insurance policy could be the asset that pushes your estate into the taxable range; the federal estate tax kicks in—with a vengeance—if your estate is more than $1 million or up to $3.5 million, depending on the year. It doesn't matter who the beneficiary of the policy is; if you own the policy when you die, the money is considered part of your taxable estate.

However, if your surviving spouse is your beneficiary, the proceeds would be shielded from the estate tax by the unlimited marital deduction. Of course, even if you transfer ownership to your surviving spouse, when he or she dies the remainder of the proceeds from the policy on your life will figure into his or her estate—and that won't be protected by the unlimited marital deduction.

But there's a simple way to avoid having the money poured into your or your surviving spouse's estate: Don't own the policy yourself. How can you do that?

You could give your children money to buy and maintain a policy on your life. You can pay the premiums by means of annual cash gifts to them, within the limits of the gift tax (up to $11,000 per year tax-free to any number of individuals, and up to $22,000 if you're giving with your spouse). This informal strategy might work, but it has some risks: The policy can be treated as property if your child divorces, and his or her creditors could even claim it as an asset.

Instead, you could transfer ownership to an irrevocable life insurance trust or set up a trust to buy a policy on your life. At your death, the trust receives the insurance proceeds. According to your wishes, it can, for instance, pay income to your spouse for life and pass the principal directly to your children upon your spouse's death. That way, the proceeds escape taxation in your surviving spouse's estate as well. A safe way to fund the trust so it can pay the necessary insurance premiums is to use the annual gift exclusion. For example, you and your spouse could give the trust up to $22,000 per year tax-free for each of your children, and the trustee would pay the insurance bill. However,

If a challenge does occur, the same rules apply to wills and trusts. In neither case are your wishes likely to be overturned.

Life insurance trusts may provide additional tax benefits for families who own large illiquid assets, such as farm property or a business.

your trust must include a special provision, a so-called Crummey power, to permit this.

In either case, by giving up ownership of your policy and gaining the estate-tax advantage, you must also give up control of the policy. In either a gift or trust arrangement, you must give up the right to change your beneficiary for any reason. And, you give up the right to borrow against the policy in any situation. These features of any life insurance policy are called "incidents of ownership".

And you can't change your mind about needing the trust. If your gift arrangement permits you to change your mind and regain control of the policy, you aren't considered to have ever given up ownership and you lose the estate-tax advantage. If you change your mind, you could stop paying the premiums on the policy, but you couldn't get out the money you had already put in. With an irrevocable trust, you give up the right to change any terms of the trust.

Plus, if you die within three years of transferring ownership of the policy as a gift or to a trust, the proceeds of the policy will again count as part of your estate.

One way to avoid that is to create a life insurance trust that applies for and purchases the life insurance policy, making it the original owner. You would have to set up the trust when you first decided to buy the policy, anticipating that your estate would eventually be big enough to warrant setting up the trust in the first place.

The tax law governing life insurance trusts—especially concerning how you give money to the trust to pay the premiums—is complicated. Life insurance trusts may provide additional tax benefits for families who own large illiquid assets, such as farm property or a business that the family wants to continue to run. At any rate, you'll definitely require the advice of an estate-planning attorney. Setting up a trust will probably cost $1,500 or more, and you'll need to choose a trustee.

An Alternative to a Trust for Your Kids

Here's a low-cost and less complex alternative to setting up a trust for your children. If you wish to leave your children a relatively small estate, say $25,000 or less, you could set up a custodial account under the Uniform Transfers to Minors Act (UTMA; or in South Carolina and Vermont, the Uniform Gift to Minors Act, or UGMA). You simply arrange with a bank, broker or mutual fund to open a custodial (or gift) account. Under UTMA, you can give the account virtually any kind of property—cash, investments, real estate, and so on (UGMA generally allows only cash and securities). You name a custodian, who will control the account for the kids until they reach the age of majority. UTMA offers three tax breaks:

■ **Though this advantage isn't limited to UTMA,** you can give gifts of up to $11,000 per year ($22,000 with your spouse) without incurring the gift tax (see page 279).

■ **The first $750 of earnings in 2002 is tax-free** and the next $750 is taxed at the child's rate, presumably 10%. Thanks to the "kiddie tax" for children under age 14, investment income above $1,500 is taxed at the parent's top rate.

■ **If you name someone other than yourself as custodian** (you give up control of the funds) and you die, your gift to your children would not be considered part of your estate for federal tax purposes. (If you name yourself both donor and custodian and you die, you would lose that tax advantage.)

DISADVANTAGES. A custodial account under UTMA has a couple of major disadvantages, however:

■ **Your gift is irrevocable;** you can't take it back. Any income distributions from the account must be used for the child's benefit, but not for any purposes that are part of the support you are legally obliged to provide. Any income you do use for the child's support will be taxable to you at your rate. States define support in different ways; some include the cost of private school.

If you name someone other than yourself as custodian and you die, your gift to your children would not be considered part of your estate for federal tax purposes.

When you die, a new taxpaying entity— your estate— is born.

■ **The custodian has control over the funds** only until your child comes of age, either 18 or 21. After that, if your kid wants to buy a sports car with the money designated for college, that's his privilege. That's why custodial accounts are best suited to small estates— under $25,000 in states that require kids to inherit at age 18, or up to the estimated cost of your child's college education for states where the law allows custodianships to last until age 21 or 25.

ALTERNATIVES. If you have any doubts, it might be better to set up a trust. With a 2503(c) trust (also known as a minor's trust), you can keep control of the assets until your child reaches age 21, a better alternative if your state's age of majority is 18.

Or you could set up a trust with a so-called Crummey provision, which lets the trustee control the money as long as you want. However, the trust must give your kids the right to withdraw the amount of your gift each year, and that's the most they could get. If they acted irresponsibly, you could cut off any more gifts until they shaped up. This tighter control means the trust will cost more to set up and manage over the years.

Tax Compliance at the End

When you pass away, a new taxpaying entity— your estate—is born to make sure no taxable income falls through the cracks. Income is taxed either on the taxpayer's final return, on the return of the beneficiary who acquires the right to receive the income or, if the estate receives $750 or more of income, on the estate's income-tax return.

Filing your final return usually is the job of your executor (or administrator), but if you've named neither one in a will, a surviving member of your family must do it. The return is filed on the same form that would have been used if you were still alive, but deceased is written after your name, and the date of death entered on the name-and-address space. The filing deadline is April 15 of the year following your death.

If you were married, your widow or widower may file a joint return for the year of the death, claiming both personal exemptions and the full standard deduction and using the lower joint-return rates.

If an executor or administrator is involved, he or she must sign the return for the decedent. When a joint return is filed, the spouse must also sign. When there is no executor, whoever is responsible for filing the return should sign the return and note that he is signing on behalf of the decedent.

For more details, you can request IRS Publication 559, *Executors, Survivors and Administrators* (available from www.irs.gov).

When You're the Executor

If you're called on to be the executor of someone's will, your job is to settle the deceased's estate in a timely and efficient fashion. You'll have three chief responsibilities:

■ **to ascertain the estate's assets;**
■ **to pay the estate's creditors and taxes;** and
■ **to make distributions of assets to beneficiaries** and make sure any other provisions of the will are carried out.

Laws about probating a will vary from state to state, but generally an executor, also known as a personal representative, doesn't need to hire a lawyer for help. That's especially true if, as is typical of a small, simple estate, all or most of its assets are jointly held with the right to survivorship (as discussed on page 256) and if state law exempts such assets from taxation. (The exceptions: In Florida and Missouri, estates must hire lawyers to handle most probate proceedings.) However, you might choose to hire a lawyer to help you out if:

■ **you have any uncertainty** about the process;
■ **the estate is likely to be valued** at between $1 million and $3.5 million, depending on the year, and your estate must file a federal estate-tax return (see the preceding section, which discusses filing require-

If you were married, your widow or widower may file a joint return for the year of your death.

WHEN THE TIME COMES

As an executor, the first thing you should do upon learning of your friend or family member's death is:

- **Get a copy of the will** if you don't already have one.
- **Contact a lawyer**—the deceased's or your own.
- **File the will** with the probate court.

For more information about carrying out your duties, consult any of the following:

- *Grief & Loss: Practical Matters.* This feature of the American Association of Retired Persons Web site covers the following topics: Final Details, Funeral Arrangements, Finances, Legal Matters, and First-Year Planner (www.aarp .org/griefandloss/practical.html).
- *The Easy Way to Probate: A Step-by-Step Guide to Settling an Estate,* by Kay Ostberg (HALT: An Organization of Americans for Legal Reform, 1612 K St, N.W., Suite 510, Washington, DC 20006; 888-367-4258; www.halt.org; $10, plus shipping and handling).

ments for a deceased taxpayer);

- **there are any complicated financial circumstances**— such as an estate that includes a business, or bad blood between potential heirs—that might require the help of someone experienced in smoothing out family conflicts in order to settle the estate;
- **the deceased died in an accident;**
- **minor children will inherit property directly** rather than through a trust; or
- **there's been a second marriage.**

A lawyer's fee, usually at least 5% of the estate's value, will reduce the size of the estate. But it's good protection. As executor, you can be held personally liable if there are any problems down the line—such as an unpaid bill or a missed tax deadline—or if, knowingly or unknowingly, you misspend or mismanage funds from the estate. You won't be held responsible for any debts that the estate can't afford to pay. Generally, assets must be sold to pay creditors. If that won't work, you should obtain legal advice in the state where the deceased lived (state of domicile) to determine how to handle the problem.

Ideally, before you're named executor, your family member or friend will ask you if you want the job, and you'll have the opportunity after you've accepted it to discuss his or her financial affairs. Find out whether he or she has a will, who has a copy of it and where it's kept, whether there's a current list of assets and debts and where that's kept, and so on. Ask to receive a copy of the person's *letter of instruction,* or *memorandum* (described under "Choosing an Executor," on page 267), which can include more detailed and personal requests. This will make your job easier later on.

If you learn after someone's death that he or she has appointed you executor without your permission, you can decline the job. The court will either contact the co-executor, appoint the deceased's second choice or make its own.

Contesting a Will

The most likely reason for disliking someone's will? You think that it is unfair. Maybe you thought that you would get something that you aren't getting. Maybe the deceased orally promised you something or implied that it would be coming your way. You might have felt that you were owed in principle, or in fact, for services or support you provided. You might think that other beneficiaries are undeserving of their share or that they don't need the inheritance as much as you do, or that they won't appreciate it as much as you will. Maybe you were disinherited, and you believe it was unjust.

If you feel you must pursue the issue, start by consulting with the deceased's lawyer or executor, who may be able to explain the reasoning behind the provision you dislike.

But just because you don't like the terms of a will

Just because you don't like the terms of a will doesn't mean you can successfully contest it. The burden will be on you to prove that the will was invalid.

doesn't mean you can successfully contest it. The burden will be on you to prove that the will is invalid—that something about it was improperly handled in the first place. A will is contestable if it does not conform to state requirements, was procured by fraud or undue influence, or was authored by a mentally incompetent person (see the discussion of writing a valid will, beginning on page 264).

So if you're a family member who's been practically disinherited—for example, your sister received 75% of your father's money and you got only 25% after, you believe, she told him a horrible lie about you—then you might claim that your sibling exerted undue influence on your father. If you can prove your claim and the will is invalidated, state laws determine how the assets will be divided.

Even if you believe you can prove your point, you'll have to ask yourself whether it's worth the legal costs and court fees, not to mention the disruption of your and your family member's lives. If you still want to challenge the will, consult an estate attorney.

Requirements for Becoming a U.S. Citizen

There are two ways to become a citizen of the United States: by birth and by naturalization. If a child is born in one of the 50 states or in the District of Columbia, regardless of his parents' nationalities, he is a U.S. citizen. Children born in Guam, Puerto Rico or the U.S. Virgin Islands are generally also U.S. citizens.

To ensure citizenship to a child born to two American citizens living in a foreign country, the parents should register the birth with the U.S. consulate. If only one parent is American, not only must the child be registered but also the American parent must satisfy certain residency requirements.

To become a naturalized citizen, you must be at least 18 years old and have had a residence in the United States for at least five years consecutively. You must speak as well as read and write simple English.

No one who has been convicted and jailed for as many as 180 days during the five-year period may become a citizen, nor may anyone of questionable moral standing, such as a person connected with prostitution or drugs.

To become a U.S. citizen, you have to give up allegiance to all other countries, and swear you will support and defend the Constitution and laws of the United States. You also have to pass a citizenship test, proving that you are knowledgeable about the history and form of government in the U.S.

If you are a U.S. citizen and over 18 years old, you are eligible to serve on a jury. In fact, it's part of your duty as a citizen.

To find out how to apply for citizenship, contact any immigration counseling agency or your local office of the Immigration and Naturalization Service, or call the INS Forms Line at 800-870-3676 to request a Form N-600. More information can be found at the INS Web site—www.ins.usdoj.gov. While citizenship is usually for life, it can be revoked from anyone—whether they were born in this country or later became a citizen—under certain circumstances, such as if they have committed a treasonous act against the United States.

Serving on a Jury

If you are a U.S. citizen and over 18 years old, you are eligible to serve on a jury. In fact, it's part of your duty as a citizen. You are called for jury duty by a summons—the court's mandate that you appear—sent through the mail. State rules vary as to who can be excused from serving on a jury, but usually doctors, lawyers and government officials are exempt. Everyone else is expected to serve unless you have a recognized excuse, such as a physical disability that makes it impossible to appear, an ongoing serious illness or a business that will shut down without you there. To be excused from jury duty, you have to call the clerk of the court or go to the clerk's office at the courthouse before the date when you are supposed to appear. If you simply ignore the summons, you could be found in contempt of court and fined or even jailed.

Making the Cut
Before you will be placed on a jury, you will be interviewed by lawyers for both the plaintiff and the defendant or by the judge. You must be approved by both sides as impartial or sympathetic to their clients before you can serve on a jury. The French word by which this process is known is voir dire.

Jurors are paid a nominal fee for each day of service. Your employer may pay you your full salary while you're on jury duty, but it doesn't have to.

Under the law, an employer isn't obligated to pay you for the time you are out of the office. If your employer does pay your salary, it can also require that you turn over your jury fees. In any case, you must report jury fees as taxable income, but you can deduct any amount that you turned over to your employer. You can take this deduction even if you don't otherwise itemize on your tax return.

What If You're Arrested?

G enerally speaking, if you are arrested, a police officer is required by federal law to read you your "Miranda" rights (named for the case that established this requirement) before you can be questioned. You've probably seen it a million times on television: *"You have the right to remain silent. If you give up the right to remain silent, anything you say can and will be used against you in a court of law. You have the right to an attorney. If you desire an attorney and cannot afford one, an attorney will be obtained for you before police questioning."*

Television would have you believe that you are allowed to make only one phone call after being arrested. In fact, you will probably be allowed several calls because you need to find a lawyer and someone who will post bail for you. (Bail is set in order to guarantee that you'll appear at your trial; when you show up, you get the money back.)

The Fourth and Fifth Amendments also come into play if you are arrested:

■ **Under the Fourth Amendment,** you and your property can't be subjected to "unreasonable searches and seizures." In other words, the police are generally not allowed to search your property without a search warrant. (However, there are several exceptions. For example, in recent years, the courts have supported police decisions to enter and search private property without a warrant under emergency circumstances or if the police had convincing reason to believe that crucial evidence would otherwise be lost. (See also the

Television would have you believe that you are allowed to make only one phone call after being arrested. In fact, you will probably be allowed several calls.

The most important thing to remember if you are arrested is to consult a lawyer as soon as possible.

discussions of search and seizure in Chapter 4, "Your Car," and Chapter 6, "The Law and Your Home.")

- **The Fifth Amendment** provides that you can't be compelled to answer any questions that would force you to incriminate yourself. Remaining silent, or "taking the fifth," does not incriminate you by default. However, you can be compelled to incriminate someone else, and if you refuse, you could be charged with obstructing justice.

When you are arrested, you also have some other rights under the Constitution.

- **You have the right** to a formal hearing (an arraignment) as soon as possible.
- **You have the right** to be told the charges against you.
- **You have the right** to reasonable bail, if bail is granted. That means the amount of bail must be appropriate, given factors such as the severity of the alleged crime, your means and the likelihood that you'll flee.
- **At the arraignment,** you can enter your plea of choice, whether guilty or not guilty.
- **You can also be tried only once** for the same crime, assuming a definitive verdict has been passed down. So if a jury or judge finds you innocent of a charge, the state can't retry you before a different jury or judge in hopes that it will find you guilty.

What You Should Do Upon Your Arrest

It's good to be aware of your rights, but still the most important thing to remember if you are arrested is to consult a lawyer as soon as possible. If you already have a good lawyer, call him; if he thinks you need a specialist, he can refer you. If you don't have a lawyer, ask for a referral from friends. If you can't afford to hire a lawyer, the court must appoint one (a public defender) for you. Even if you're innocent of the charge, don't panic: Go along quietly, be respectful, and confirm any personal information such as your name and address. You can simply say that you'd like to have your lawyer present before you say anything else. This is consistent with the Miranda rule, described on page 297.

When You're the Victim

Those accused of committing crimes aren't the only ones who have rights. Victims have rights, too. The federal government has enacted a Federal Victim and Witness Protection Act, and most states have a Victim's Bill of Rights. Such laws require the government to minimize the risk that a victim will be harassed or intimidated by a defendant and to ensure that the victim be treated with respect and his claim be handled as promptly as possible.

Many states also have victim-compensation funds to help victims of violent crime cope with costs resulting from the crime, such as hospital bills or funeral costs. Check with your local district attorney's office for the laws in your area. For more background, you can also consult the American Civil Liberties Union (www.aclu.org) publication, *The Rights of Crime Victims,* by James Stark (from Amazon.com; $4.95, plus $2.35 special surcharge).

Passport Information

The Department of State requires all citizens to follow strict guidelines in obtaining or renewing a passport. Getting a passport takes approximately four weeks from the time passport agencies receive your application. The passport is valid for ten years.

Where to Apply for a Passport

To apply for a U.S. passport, you must first obtain an *Application for a United States Passport* (form DSP-11) from one of over 4,500 passport-acceptance facilities nationwide, which include many Federal, state and probate courts, many post offices, some libraries and a number of county and municipal offices. These designated acceptance facilities are usually more convenient because they are near your home or workplace. (Most

Many states have victim-compensation funds to help victims of violent crime cope with the costs that result from the crime, such as hospital bills or funeral costs.

If this is your first passport application, or if the passport is for someone age 13 to 17, you must apply in person at a clerk of court or post office authorized to accept applications.

of the 13 passport agencies are designated to serve only those departing urgently, and appointments are required.) You may also obtain this form by calling the National Passport Information Center at 900-225-5674, or you can download the form from the Center's Web site, www.travel.state.gov/get_forms.html.

If this is your first passport application (not a renewal), or if the passport is for someone age 13 to 17, you must apply in person at a clerk of court or post office authorized to accept passport applications.

All locations are open Monday through Friday, except during federal holidays. Call for office hours. During the summer, you can expect a three- to four-hour wait in line at the regional offices. Check the blue pages in the local telephone directory under "Passport Services" or "Department of State" for these locations.

Application Procedures

When you apply, you must submit a completed but unsigned form DSP-11, along with one of the following items as proof of citizenship.

■ **a previous U.S. passport;** or
■ **a birth certificate** (a certified copy issued by the official registrar of vital records in the city, county, state or territory of birth).

If you were born outside the United States and do not have a previous passport to submit, you should present a certificate of naturalization, or a certificate of citizenship issued by the Immigration and Naturalization Service, a consular report of birth abroad (form SS-240), or a Department of State certification of birth (Form DS-1350 or Form SS-545).

PHOTOGRAPH. You must submit two identical photos taken within the past six months that must meet certain specifications.

PROOF OF IDENTITY. You must submit a current, valid form of identification that contains your signature and photo or physical description. Examples of generally acceptable forms of ID are a driver's license, military ID or student ID.

FEES. The fees are $60 for persons age 16 and over, $40 for those 15 and under. The fee for a renewal is $40. You may pay by personal check or money order at all facilities. Most accept cash. Some accept credit cards.

For Children Under 16

Passports for children under age 16 are valid for only five years.If the child is under age 13, the parent or legal guardian must apply at a passport agency, authorized post office or clerk of court. The child generally need not be present.

A child age 13 to 16 must appear in person accompanied by a parent or legal guardian, who must present current, valid identification of his or her own, such as a driver's license, previous passport, government ID or military ID.

The parent or guardian will need to submit a completed but unsigned Form DSP-11, proof of citizenship for the child (same requirements as adults), two identical passport photos of the child, and the passport fee.

REGIONAL PASSPORT AGENCIES

If you need your passport urgently, generally in less than 2 weeks, you may contact one of the Passport Agencies listed below. Most Passport Agencies now accept applications only by appointment, so be sure to call in advance

Boston	**617-878-0900**
Chicago	**312-341-6020**
Honolulu	**808-522-8283**
Houston	**713-751-0294**
Los Angeles	**310-575-5700**
Miami	**305-539-3600**
New Orleans	**504-412-2600**
New York	**212-206-3500**
Philadelphia	**215-418-5937**
San Francisco	**415-538-2700**
Seattle	**206-808-5700**
Stamford, Conn.	**203-969-9000**
Washington, D.C.	**202-647-0518**

Changing Your Name on Your Passport

You must submit a completed form DSP-19, your current valid passport and documentation of your name change (such as an original or certified marriage certificate, divorce decree or court order). You can take these to any regional passport agency or authorized post office or to a local clerk of court. The documentation you submit will be returned to you with your amended passport.

Renewing Your Passport

If your most recent expired passport was issued sometime after your 16th birthday but within the past 15 years, there is no need for you to renew it in person. You can renew it by mail by providing a completed Form DSP-82, Application for Passport by Mail, your old passport, two identical passport photos taken within the past six months, and a check or money order for $40 payable to "Passport Services." Send your application to: National Passport Center, P.O. Box 371971, Pittsburgh, PA 15250-7971.

FOR MORE INFORMATION

- **Department of State Passport Information:** 900-225-5674; www.travel.state.gov
- **Canadian Embassy Department of Tourism:** 202-682-1740; www.canadian embassy.org
- **Mexican Embassy:** 202-728-1600; www.embassyofmexico.org; consulate: 202-736-1000 (tourist information)

Reporting a Lost or Stolen Passport

If your passport is lost or stolen, you should report it when you apply for your new passport. You must apply in person using Form DSP-11 and submit a detailed statement regarding the loss or theft, in addition to proof of citizenship, proof of identity, two passport photos and the passport fee.

Obtaining an Emergency Passport

If you have a life-or-death emergency and require assistance outside of normal working hours, you may contact the passport services duty officer at 900-225-5674 or 888-362-8668. Requests for assistance are handled on a case-by-case basis by the duty officer. There's a $35 surcharge per application, plus postage, for emergency assistance.

Entering Canada as a Tourist

American citizens do not need visas to enter Canada. However, one of the following documents is needed as proof of U.S. citizenship:

- **a valid U.S. passport;**
- **the original or a certified copy of your birth certificate and photo ID, such as a driver's license;**

- **voter registration card and photo ID; or**
- **selective service or draft card and photo ID.**

Young children who do not have birth certificates yet may present baptismal or hospital certificates that show the place of birth.

Persons under 16 traveling without a parent or guardian should bring a letter from the parent or guardian giving them permission to travel to Canada.

Naturalized citizens may also use their naturalization certificate as proof of citizenship.

Permanent residents must show a valid passport and their Alien Registration Card (commonly known as a "green card") when entering Canada. They do not require visas.

When re-entering the U.S., citizens and permanent residents can present the documents they used to enter Canada.

Entering Mexico as a Tourist

As with Canada, American citizens do not need visas to enter Mexico. However, one of the following sets of documents are needed as proof of U.S. citizenship:

- **a valid U.S. passport; or**
- **the original copy or certified copy of your birth certificate and a photo ID, such as a driver's license.**

Permanent residents must show their Alien Registration Card when entering Mexico.

Upon reentry to the U.S., citizens and permanent residents are required to resubmit the documents they used to enter Mexico.

Index

A